MW00810739

RUSSIAN HUSSAR

THE STANDARD

The Standard of the Sumsky Hussars while temporarily a dragoon regiment,
1890–9.

RUSSIAN HUSSAR

A Story of the Imperial Cavalry
1911 - 1920

by

VLADIMIR S. LITTAUER

formerly Captain, 1st (Sumsky) Hussars,
Russian Imperial Cavalry

Introduction by
DENNIS E. SHOWALTER

Foreword by
SIR ROBERT BRUCE LOCKHART

 WHITE MANE PUBLISHING COMPANY, INC.

The acid-free paper used in this book meets the guidelines for permanence and
durability of the Committee on Production Guidelines for Book Longevity of the
Council on Library Resources.

First Printing, 1965
Second Printing, 1993 with supplemental materials

First Printing by
J. A. Allen & Co., Ltd, 1 Lower Grosvenor Place, Buckingham
Palace Road, London, SW1W OEL, England

Second Printing by
White Mane Publishing Company, Inc., Shippensburg, PA USA

For a complete list of available publications
please write
White Mane Publishing Company, Inc.
P.O. Box 152
Shippensburg, PA 17257 USA

Library of Congress Cataloging-in-Publication Data

Littauer, Vladimir S.
      Russian Hussar : a story of the Imperial Cavalry, 1911-1920 / by
Vladimir S. Littauer ; introduction by Dennis E. Showalter ;
foreword by Sir Robert Bruce Lockhart.
         p.   cm.
      ''Second printing, 1993 with supplemental materials''--T.p. verso.
      Originally published: London : J.A. Allen & Co., 1965.
      Includes index.
      ISBN 0-942597-53-2 : $24.95 (alk. paper)
      1. Littauer, Vladimir S.   2. Soldiers--Russia--Biography.
3. Russia.   Armiia.   Kavaleriia--Biography.   4. World War,
1914-1918--Personal narratives, Russian.   5. World War, 1914-1918--
Cavalry operations.   6. World War, 1914-1918--Russia.   7. Soviet
Union--History--Revolution, 1917-1921--Personal narratives, Russian.
8. Soviet Union--History--Revolution, 1917-1921--Cavalry operations.
I. Title.
U55.L57A3   1993
355'.0092--dc20
[B]   93-2299
                                                                                CIP

ACKNOWLEDGEMENTS

In writing this book I had two editors: Nora Ledyard Knight and my wife. Theirs was the difficult task of trying to better my English yet still retain my Russian turn of thought. I wanted to present the happenings of fifty years ago as nearly as possible in the light in which I then saw them and to preserve the flavour of the place and time. My editors took much trouble over this problem, as well as over me, and I am most grateful to them for their efforts.

My brother officer, Constantine Sokolov, who on several occasions appears in this memoir, contributed a great deal towards the substance of the book by carefully checking almost every line of it. I am very much indebted to him for his meticulous work.

A number of friends read various chapters of the manuscript and made pertinent suggestions. Mrs. Nancy M. Graham read the whole of it, twice, and persuaded me both to subtract and to add a number of paragraphs. I wish to thank her and my other helpful friends, warmly.

Colonel Sergey Polkovnikoff, a Guard Cossack, kindly checked the facts of my text dealing with the Cossacks and supplied additional data. I very much appreciate his help.

I have been able to give my war stories precise chronological order only because I could refer to a history of my regiment in this century, *The Sumski Hussars*, written in Russian by my

ACKNOWLEDGEMENTS

few surviving regimental comrades and published in 1954.
I have also drawn on some of its material; for permission to
do so I wish to thank former General Boris Govorov, Colonel
George Schwed, Major Nicholas Snejkov, Colonel Constantine Sokolov and Major Theodore Vodo. It is a disappoint-
ment to us all that the book cannot be illustrated with more
and better photographs, but carrying family albums was not
the thing to do when escaping from the Bolsheviks in disguise.

V. S. LITTAUER

Long Island,
New York

In addition to the earlier acknowledgements, I would like
to express my gratitude to Bruce Ostler and Fifi Oscard of the
Fifi Oscard Agency, and to my editor, Dr. Martin K. Gordon,
for their realizing the significance of this book for understanding
post-Soviet Russia and for bringing it into print in the United
States.

MARY A. LITTAUER

Long Island,
New York
1993

iv

INTRODUCTION

by

Dennis E. Showalter

Vladimir Littauer served in the Imperial Russian cavalry before and during World War I, fought against the Reds in the Civil War, and went into exile when Admiral Alexander Kolchak's Siberian regime collapsed in 1920. He tells a story whose outlines have been made familiar in dozens of emigré accounts. Yet Littauer's unpretentious memoir acquires new significance with the disappearance of the Soviet Union. When the hammer and sickle was hauled down from the Kremlin with the new year of 1992 it was replaced not by a flag designed for the occasion, but with the historic colors of Imperial Russia. Czar Nicholas II has been unofficially celebrated in Orthodox services as Nicholas the Martyr. The Revolution itself, long perceived as the twentieth century's defining event, is in the process of reinterpretation, even being compared to Russia's seventeenth-century Time of Troubles as an interim period of tyranny and hardship.

In this context Littauer's work becomes more than an exercise in nostalgia. It takes us into the world of the Russian army whose disastrous defeats between 1914 and 1916 created the opportunity which Lenin and his cohorts seized. That army has been generally depicted as doomed from the start by a combination of its own internal weaknesses and the structural flaws of the system it served. A factionalized high command, an incompetent officer corps, a lack of weapons and supplies—all are cited and recited as causes of Imperial Russia's military debacle. Underlying those tangible shortcomings is a tendency to describe them as products of national character. "It looks," remarked a British general in the aftermath of Tannenberg, "as if the Russians were too simple and good hearted to wage modern war". Nor was he an isolated figure. The Bolsheviks had logical and pragmatic reasons to stress both the backwardness of the society they purported to destroy and the consequences of that backwardness for Russia's security. During and after World War II, Germans anxious to explain their defeat in the East insisted on having been submerged beneath brute mass unaccompanied by strategic or tactical finesse. In the years of the Cold War, western defense analysts whistled past the graveyard of Soviet numbers by insisting on the exponential superiority of Western equipment and personnel.

Norman Stone, David Jones, David Glantz—all have convincingly challenged on an academic level the myth of the Russian soldier as a military primitive and the concept of Russian armies as heavy, blunt instruments. Littauer puts flesh on that scholarly analysis. His account of his years as a teenaged officer cadet stresses the socialization of young men who came from a far broader spectrum of backgrounds than is generally understood. Although many of the officers, particularly in elite regiments such as the Sumsky Hussars, came from the nobility, military careers were not attractive to the elites or the intelligentsia of Czarist Russia. The army's officer corps reflected a broader spectrum of social and economic backgrounds than did its German, British, or even French counterparts. Their common denominator was a desire to make a career in public service. Institutions like Littauer's Nicholas Cavalry School facilitated developing both a new personal identity and a common group bonding with its own loyalties, its own rituals and its own codes of behavior.

The Russian army entered the war in 1914 with no fewer than two dozen full divisions of cavalry. By 1917, the army had so many horses that over 4,000 freight cars a day were needed to keep them supplied with forage, while healthy men went hungry and the sick and wounded languished in field hospitals. The juxtaposition of those facts would seem to make a *prima facie* case for Littauer as part of a military anachronism. But the Russian army's retention of such large cavalry forces reflected the reality that in 1914 the cavalry was the only mobile arm in existence. Like all European armies, the Russians were well aware of the stagnating effects of fire-power, and hoped to avoid them for much the same reason their Cold War successors hoped to avoid a nuclear exchange: victory in such a struggle would have no meaning to Russia.

Cavalry offered at least the opportunity for overcoming the kind of deadly stalemate that actually developed during World War I. Mounted troops were not intended to break through a fortified front, or even to exploit such a breakthrough—the infamous "G in Gap" that so mesmerized their British counterparts from 1915 to 1918. They were intended to prevent a solid front from developing in the first place. Russian planners envisioned a pattern of lightning raids against enemy supply lines and railheads—perhaps even deep-penetration strikes in the pattern of James Harrison Wilson's Selma campaign of 1865.

That concept was far beyond the actual capacities of any European army in 1914. Its implementation depended on the technical development of the internal-combustion engine, and on the economic and social development of a society motorized at least at its cutting edges. But how closely did Russia's cavalry approach the projected prewar ideal? The Sumsky Hussars were part of the Moscow garrison, and their junior officers' off-duty lives involved various combinations of slow horses and fast women. Some of Littauer's most entertaining pages describe the theaters and restaurants, the dances and the love affairs of a world that vanished forever in 1917. His text is more useful, however, in its presentation of the Russian cavalry as a military institution.

The regimental system was the core of the Tsarist army. It replicated the peasant villages from which most of the soldiers still came, with the officers as landlords and the enlisted men as workers. This was especially true for cavalry regiments, which in economic terms were labor-intensive organizations whose functioning revolved around horses. Littauer depicts the Sumsky Hussars' senior officers as men strongly committed to a patriarchal style of management, favoring personal contact over formal administration. The regiment's enlisted men, according to Littauer, lived when off duty "the normal life of Russian peasants," with limited intervention by their officers and limited differentiation from sergeants and corporals more likely to identify with their comrades in the ranks than with the formalized squirearchy created by their supervisors.

The Sumsky Hussars were not, however, merely a noble estate writ large. The regiment was a military family, with its own history, its own way of doing things, and its own distinctive place in the larger structure. That characteristic was particularly important for the Russian army which, unlike its western European counterparts, was not strictly territorially recruited. The men of the Sumsky Hussars came from several different provinces in several different parts of the empire. Their oaths of loyalty were sworn in the context of five separate religions. In such a context, patriotism or the cult of the Tsar might help provide an official sense of community. But it was the encapsulated world of the regiment which would determine whether or not the more or less bewildered recruits would indeed "find a home in the army."

The Sumsky Hussars were also not a social institution. The ambience and the *mentalité* of the regiment ultimately existed for an external purpose: to foster efficiency in war. Like European cavalrymen generally, Littauer and his comrades were emotionally influenced by romantic images of charging at the gallop with sabers drawn. Intellectually, however, they were able to accept the obsolescence, and the corresponding unlikelihood, of large-scale mounted attacks. The resulting disjunction was to some degree papered over by the comfortable routines of the regiment. The introduction of machine-guns, and of modern signal apparatus, was greeted with good-natured indifference, and the hardware placed in the hands of junior officers.

Even more important in keeping the regiment within its emotional comfort zone were its horses. Littauer's text makes the point, often overlooked in a motorized age, that teaching soldiers to ride and care for horses absorbed much of the Sumsky Hussars' collective energy. The horse is a complex, surprisingly fragile animal. An individual's experience on the farm or in a city stable was not necessarily directly transferable to the army, any more than a modern recruit with a driver's license can be put without further ado behind the steering gear of a main battle tank. The result was a self-reinforcing routine. Horses were valuable because they absorbed so much time and energy, which was legitimate because horses were valuable, and so on through eternity—or at least until the outbreak of war.

The strengths and weaknesses of the Russian army became apparent as soon as the Sumsky Hussars reached the front. The regiment was part of the great offensive into East Prussia that culminated with the Battle of Tannenberg. Eight of Russia's best cavalry divisions concentrated on the German frontier.

But they were neither trained nor organized to operate in masses. The peacetime army included no cavalry formations larger than a division: 4,000 men and 16 guns. Many of the regiments however, were led by men too old or too frail to spend days in the saddle, then make quick decisions after two or three sleepless nights. The Hussars' division commander, Major General Vasily Gourko, was a notable exception, but his next senior officer was incapacitated by hemorrhoids.

At regimental levels the cavalry suffered from peacetime perceptions compounded by mobilization jitters. Littauer describes patrols that instead of going forward boldly, dismounted to exchange shots at long range with small parties of German snipers. Such behavior is common to all armies especially in the early stages of a war. But if the Russian cavalry were to have any use at all it could not afford the luxury of that particular reaction to war. Littauer's text shows clearly that neither tactically nor operationally could the cavalry's officers exploit whatever opportunities remained to the army's mounted service. The attempt at a strategic raid into the German rear described in detail in these pages rates barely a mention in the German official history.

The rest of the Sumsky Hussars' war was an anticlimax. The regiment did a good deal of scouting and patrolling even under the relatively static conditions of 1915. The eastern "Front" was by no means a clone of the west, with its continuous lines of trenches. As would be the case in World War II, force to space ratios were so low that large sectors were thinly held. As late as 1916, when the Hussars were regularly sent dismounted into the front lines, a squadron of eighty men was expected to hold a full mile of trenches. One-quarter of the men were held in reserve, the others occupied three strong points and patrolled between them. Even under these seemingly favorable conditions, however, when one side concentrated for an attack the other was able to transfer reserves by rail quickly enough to prevent a "break in" from becoming a break through.

The front was not the only source of stagnation in the war's middle years. Littauer spent most of that period commanding the regimental signal detachment—sixty men, most of them rejects and castoffs from the line squadrons. Here the text takes a significant turn. A British, an American, even a German junior officer is likely to describe in detail his relationship with the losers and hardcases of his first independent command. Littauer's troopers take a distant second place in his memory to his comrades in the officers' mess. His detailed descriptions of everyday tensions and squabbles highlight the fact that the Russian cavalry retained a large percentage of its peacetime officers. There was less temptation than in the French, British or German armies to transfer to the infantry in hope of promotion, or to the air service in search of adventure. The result was a high level of stagnation, and an increasing isolation of cavalry officers not only from their own men, but from their commissioned comrades of the infantry and artillery as well.

The revolution took the Sumsky Hussars' officers completely by surprise. They were even more surprised when within a few days their men requested the establishment of a soldiers council. The regiment retained some semblance of order for a short time as its officers sought to reknit ties frayed by war. Their efforts were far too little, and came far too late. As chaos increased in the army's rear, the Sumsky Hussars were increasingly used for police duties. That eroded whatever cohesion remained. Whatever it might have been in 1914, the regiment was no longer a paternalistic war band. Ultimate authority had always been vested in the state, not the officers.

The collapse of the old order removed all legitimacy. Littauer deserted after striking his platoon sergeant—a potentially fatal mistake in the army's new order. Like so many of his comrades, he initially sought to return home. By midsummer of 1918, he felt at such great personal risk that he joined the White forces.

Littauer's subsequent odyssey from south Russia to Siberia, then into foreign exile, is a familiar story that highlights the Whites' crippling factionalism, their ultimate inability to rally the Russian people to their cause. As the Commonwealth of Independent states faces the political economic and social shocks of post-communism, this section of Littauer's narrative might suggest portents for the future, as well as recalling a past that may well be far less remote than it seemed when *Russian Hussar* was originally published.

CONTENTS

CONTENTS

ILLUSTRATIONS

FOREWORD

I have read Captain Littauer's book with the greatest interest. It is quite the best book on its subject that has come my way. My only regret is that I was unable to be in London during the author's recent visit to this country. We would have had much talk of old times, for I knew many of the men of the old regime in Russia and not a few of the new; I was myself a prisoner of the new men in 1918 (regardless of my being Head of a Special Mission to the Soviet government) and was only released from Moscow in exchange for Litvinoff who was in London at that time.

The Russian Imperial Army had much in common with other European armies in the first quarter of this century. It had its regimental traditions, moulded over the years and a rallying point for her soldiers, young and old. Captain Littauer's regiment, the Sumsky Hussars, had celebrated their 250th anniversary as far back as 1901, and although for a while dragoons the tradition of hussars was never broken.

As a subaltern the author and his young friends had their happy hunting grounds in the clubs and restaurants of St. Petersburg and Moscow that I too knew well. In Moscow restaurants generally the Hussars were greeted with their regimental march, and in the summer months the regimental orchestra played in the gardens of The Yar. This was the most famous and luxurious night-club in Moscow where first-class music-hall shows were given in the main hall. The Strelna was the kingdom of Maria Nikolaievna, where the Palm Court alone was like a miniature Crystal Palace. A gypsy chorus (to which whole families belonged) sang and danced in traditional costume. The photograph facing page 113 shows such a chorus in gala array, and you can imagine how very inviting they looked. The Strelna escaped the vigilance of the Bolsheviks until late in the summer of 1918, when it was closed down. I believe the redoubtable Maria died in poverty, broken hearted.

Fun and games there were, but in the army discipline was strict and training hard. Drill, guard duties, horses and equipment kept up to a high standard, the etiquette of guest nights in mess and inspections in barracks, when leave of absence was rare and money scarce, combined to induce a feeling of belonging to one big family. Observed tradition nourished this feeling and went far to promote *morale*.

I saw the patriotic enthusiasm of the people of old Russia in 1914, and I saw the gradual decline as it became clear that it was going to be a long war. Captain Littauer and his cavalrymen never lost their dash and courage in the face of overwhelming difficulties. But, although able to hold the Austrians to the end, the Russian army was no match for the Germans.

The tragedy of Russia is made plain in the pages of this book; nothing sentimental, no self-pity, little anger, but we can hardly imagine what must be the feelings of the author who lost his country, saw the disintegration and confusion, who learned of the murder of his Emperor and of the brother officers with whom he had so recently fought the German invasion.

I would like to pay my tribute to his labours, and heart-searchings, in bringing together this excellent contribution to the history of his time, and mine.

ROBERT BRUCE LOCKHART

Falmouth,
October, 1965

Peacetime

CHAPTER 1

ANOTHER WORLD

THE eastern European theatre of war during the years
between 1914 and 1917 was the last area in the world
to witness regular cavalry action of a traditional sort. The
Russian horse, in which I served as an officer, were some
200,000 strong. We operated along a front that stretched from
the open rolling country of East Prussia in the north through
marsh, forest and mountain to the plain of Rumania, 1,000
miles or so to the south. We faced varied bodies of enemy
cavalry: 'modernised' Germans, Austrians as conservative as
we, and Hungarians who, at the beginning of the war, were
even more traditional than we and who charged suicidally, in
dress uniforms and white gloves, their officers leading. And
we were engaged against other types of troops even more
than against enemy cavalry.

But the fighting I remember was rapidly becoming antiquated even then. The first months of the war gave us a dis-
couraging taste of modern fire power. Up-to-date artillery,
machine guns, or even the massed fast-shooting rifles of the
infantry when it was firing accurately, were not fun to charge
against with swords and lances. And although we had also
been taught to fight dismounted (for which we were equipped
with rifles and bayonets), we were not nearly as good at it
as those specialists, the infantry. If we had occasional successes

on the ground against an equal or even a greater number of foot soldiers, it was thanks to quicker thinking and better *morale* rather than to equipment or training.

One of our former important advantages, superior mobility, was also being threatened by the new mechanised transport. The small rattling army trucks of the time appeared wherever they could find roads good enough; and the German cavalry even stooped to attach infantry mounted on bicycles to its units.

Despite all this, on such a wide and varied front there still was a role for us. Both sides broke through from time to time; fluid warfare might last for weeks on end, and we were put to good use. We charged anything that could be taken by surprise, and we didn't count our losses. We continued to function gloriously, if not always efficiently. And, of course, when it came to scouting across country we more than held our own.

Although we were forced reluctantly to recognise that we were no longer what we had been brought up to believe ourselves to be—Queen of the Battlefields, capable of deciding with one crashing charge the outcome of an engagement—it was in this spirit that we had been trained and in this spirit that to a large extent we continued to fight. The goal set before us had been the mounted charge, whose most important element was speed, for on the latter largely depended the impact with which we could enter the enemy's formation. And since we also had been brought up to believe that no one was a match for us when it came to hand-to-hand fighting, our desire was to reach the enemy's ranks as soon as possible. Once, when we were unhappily fighting dismounted and were pinned to the ground by German fire, I remember our regimental commander rising up and shaking his fists in the direction of the enemy, exclaiming: 'If we could only get *to* you!'

In accordance with this belief, we had been trained not to use our rifles during the mounted charge. If the enemy can be killed from a distance there is not the same incentive to reach him in a hurry and, besides, firing from the saddle slows down the charge. The stress placed on hand-to-hand fighting partly explains why we in the cavalry schools took our studies so lightly and why the schools themselves were old-fashioned in comparison with those that prepared officers for other branches of the service. We believed that we would charge bravely when the time came, and that nothing else would matter very much. The sword and the lance were emphasised as the true cavalry weapons. Every man was equipped with a sword, and half of each regiment carried lances. Before we were through fighting many of these had been reddened more than once.

To anyone familiar with recent warfare we will seem unbelievably antiquated, and yet in 1914 the Russian Imperial forces were superior to many. Only Germany was really prepared militarily for the twentieth century. The Russo-Japanese War had, it is true, shocked us into many changes, and in the nine years between its ending and the beginning of World War I great strides had been made towards the modernisation of the Russian army. Cavalry, by its very nature, was the least affected. And although the Russian military might that faced the west in 1914 may have been at the time as good as any, it was not prepared for either the extent or the duration of the war. We did not have the industry to produce equipment on a proportionate scale; much of it had to come from abroad —a considerable amount from the United States.

Despite shortages of material, we put up a good fight.

Most people have heard of the Russian defeat at Tannenberg in August 1914; few know that almost immediately afterwards on the southern part of the front we started a long advance which succeeded in occupying most of Austrian Galicia, reaching the crest of the Carpathian mountains and taking 120,000 prisoners in the fortress of Przemysl alone. These were neither our only defeat nor our only victory. The war was a long and bloody one and fortune changed sides many times.

Today many people have forgotten what a gigantic conflict the First World War was, and what vast numbers of human beings either perished or were crippled in it. The total number of military casualties on both sides came, in round figures, to 33,000,000, including 8,000,000 prisoners. Our share was large: we lost 1,700,000 dead and 4,950,000 wounded. 2,500,000 Russians were taken prisoner and the Russian army captured as many of the enemy.*

The Central Powers (Germany and Austria-Hungary) often had more troops on the Russian front than they had in France. For instance, in March of 1917 they had 135 infantry divisions on the French front and 164 on the Russian. As to the cavalry, at about the same time, the Central Powers had twenty-four divisions in the east and one in the west. These figures belong to the period just before the Russian Revolution, and they do not include the Turks, whom we faced in the southern Caucasus (*vide Le Rôle de la Russie dans la Guerre Mondiale*, by General Goulevitch, France, 1934).

With these troops the Central Powers pushed us back along the whole eastern front before they were fought to a standstill, while we still held some foreign territory in the south. When the Revolution came and our soldiers refused to go forward,

* The total number of casualties will never be accurately known. *A History of The Great War*, Cruttwell, Oxford, 1934.

the long-prepared, large-scale Russian counter-attack never materialised. We found ourselves fighting our compatriots instead of our enemies.

Although there have been many serious studies of the Russian front and of the Revolution, most of these have tended to neglect the human side. Yet history is made by human beings, and to understand it we must know something of the background and mentality of the men involved. When these are as remote from today's world as we officers and our soldiers were they need quite a bit of explaining.

I served in the Russian Imperial Cavalry and later in the counter-revolutionary forces from the autumn of 1911 to the spring of 1920. As a career officer, I was part of this very different life in peacetime and throughout the First World War, the Revolution, and the subsequent Civil War. The command to charge, 'swords out, lances for the fight', will never be heard again. But because I have always enjoyed telling stories of my military days, they have stayed very fresh in my mind. Soon there will be no one who can remember what it was like, what kind of human beings we were, why we behaved as we did, the details of our daily existence.

In the first part of this book I introduce some twenty men who will continue to appear throughout most of it. My recollections concern these men as much as they do myself. To me the anecdotes of their behaviour under the widely varying circumstances of garrison life in Moscow, regular fighting at the front, or under the stress of revolution, constitute the important part of the book. Little incidents such as the one in which a spent bullet that had lodged in Lieutenant Arshaouloff's leg was pulled out by his orderly with his teeth, tell more about us than any description of the technical details of the skirmish in which this happened. In any case these anecdotes are certainly much more informative than, for instance, my descriptions of the war. The latter, as merely the eyewitness account of an unimportant officer, are bound to give only tiny details of the great strategic operations in which human beings counted for little. I remember, for instance, reading the memoirs of a low-ranking officer in Napoleon's army. At one point he describes taking part in an engagement near some hamlet. For weeks he identified this action by the name of the hamlet, until he suddenly discovered that it was in the battle of Austerlitz that he had fought.

The small episodes that are here described serve primarily as a background for the actions of individuals and, although in order to orient my readers I often give their dates and locations, these are not important. With the same intent maps have been made to situate the various little incidents rather than the large war operations.

Even in a hundred years it will still be possible to reconstruct, on the basis of existing documents, the plans and the progress of various battles, but the human stories of the period will perish with us, the survivors of those days. As the world continues to change, the value of these stories should accordingly be enhanced, although the dry record of battles won and lost may diminish in significance. Thus I do not pretend to write a formal history of war on the Russian front or of the Revolution, but rather footnotes to the social history of Russia in the early part of the twentieth century.

Many of the stories I tell are typical of the Russian cavalry in general, but others could happen only in the regiment in which I served. There was an army saying, 'All Russian cavalry regiments are equally good'—but this does not mean they were all alike. The character of garrison life, for instance, depended on where it was. In Moscow, where my regiment was stationed,

city life offered a variety of entertainment; worldly pleasures
attracted many officers, and their regimental work suffered
accordingly. Those young lieutenants and captains who could
afford a good time were particularly susceptible, and most
officers in the Sumsky Hussars had the means for it. Moreover,
as in any group, a few individuals usually influence the rest
and set certain standards which eventually may become a
tradition. The conspicuous characteristics of my regiment
were simplicity in our daily life, gaiety around a bottle of
wine, and a spirit of independence; we respected some generals,
had no very high opinion of some others, and kow-towed to
none. Naturally, the stories that I remember are mostly
about men who exemplified these qualities flamboyantly.
Many others, who were less of individuals, lived quietly,
worked hard, and were undoubtedly better peacetime officers,
but there is little to tell about them. Some of these perfect
peacetime officers did not do too well in war, while others
who had not been very serious in Moscow led the regiment
in many of its creditable battles.

I have tried as far as I have been able to present the events
in this memoir in the light in which I saw them as they happened. My attitude then was that of a professional soldier of the
period, who was brought up to make light of what was either
boredom, danger, or tragedy, to speak freely of one's failures,
barely to mention one's acts of bravery, and to joke about
both. I have consciously attempted to preserve the matter-of-
fact and casual tone in which the officers of my regiment talked
of each other and of the war in those days. To heighten the
drama of many of my stories would be to alter and destroy
the very atmosphere that I am trying to re-create. The simple
and realistic attitude that prevailed in our regiment was a
reaction to the 'Light Brigade' school of thought of the

nineteenth century that still set the tone in much of the army.

Having a realistic turn of mind, I believe I have also been able to avoid presenting life fifty years ago in the consistently favourable light in which old men usually regard their past. Purely fond recollections may have value for oneself or one's contemporaries; they have none for anyone else.

In spite of its realism, much in this book is bound to appear peculiar and even exotic, looked at today from a different world. And that other world of which I now write was a very special one even in its own time—the world of the Russian cavalry. Our troopers came from the country, not the city; they were the product of backward life in remote peasant villages, where the population was only fifty years away from serfdom. Our officers' cadre had its own code, its special ideals and taboos. These were ingrained in many officers from childhood, for the majority came from military families; but all were indoctrinated consciously and consistently during their military education. Without some familiarity with this and with our peculiar *mœurs* in peacetime it would be difficult to understand why we behaved as we did in the War and the Revolution. Hence these reminiscences begin with cavalry school.

CHAPTER 2

THE NICHOLAS CAVALRY SCHOOL

ONLY one military school in the Russia of Imperial days, the *Corps des Pages*, prepared future officers for service in all branches of the army. The rest of the schools were specialised ones: infantry, cavalry, artillery, sappers. There were three schools of the regular cavalry, of which the Nicholas Cavalry School, quartered in St. Petersburg, was the oldest and the smartest. In the Russian cavalry it was called 'The Glorious School' or simply 'The School', and was referred to as the Nicholas Cavalry School only in official papers. It was founded in 1823.

In my day there were two divisions, one for the Cossack 'younkers' (who had schools of their own as well) and the other for the 'younkers' of the regular cavalry. The term 'cadets' applied only to the pupils of military secondary schools; the pupils of the more advanced specialised army schools were called 'younkers'. One normally entered cadet school at the age of ten or eleven and the course lasted seven years. So the majority of boys began younker school when they were seventeen or eighteen years old. One could also enter the school from a civilian gymnasium (the equivalent of a secondary school, plus two years of college in the U.S.A.). To be accepted, one had to pass a stiff physical examination. The novice who had graduated from a gymnasium was called, in school slang, 'a youngster from the railroad station'—in other words, with-

11

out a military past. I was one of these, and there were not many of us.

In my time the Cossack troop had about 150 younkers, but only 105 of us were in our so-called 'squadron'. Because the Cossacks' way of riding, their saddles, bridles, uniforms, swords and some of their commands and formations were traditionally different from ours, the two divisions of the school practised their military exercises separately. Since the academic work was the same, we sat together in classes. Our dormitories were on the second floor, theirs on the third. In mess we ate on one side of the main aisle of the hall, they on the other. In spite of such close living there was little friendship between the two branches of the Russian cavalry and each side believed itself to be superior.

The large, cheerless main building of the school had been erected at the beginning of the nineteenth century, and life within its walls was spartan. Our small squadron was divided into three platoons, each platoon having its own dormitory. The thirty-odd beds stood in two rows, a low chest by each cot. To the head of every bed was attached a tall iron rod on which hung one's sword and military cap; at its foot was a stool on which one's clothes were placed, carefully folded, every night. There was no other furniture. The room was lofty and in one corner stood a ladder which climbed to the ceiling at an angle of forty-five degrees. On it we were expected to do our morning exercises before breakfast by scaling it hand over hand; I hated the sight of it. Our rifles were stacked on a long rack. In the washrooms there were hand basins, but no tubs or showers. Cleanliness was restored once a week by a Russian bath, which was in a separate building in the courtyard. Our only luxury was having valets to look after our things—one to every eight younkers.

The course lasted two years. In school parlance the seniors were called 'cornets', which was to be their first officers' rank (equal to a second lieutenant's), and the juniors were called 'beasts'. Hazing (for which bullying is not an adequate translation) was based on this distinction. The 'beasts' took the oath a month after their arrival. After this they could not be thrown out of the school into civilian life for misdemeanours; instead they were sent as ordinary soldiers to a cavalry regiment for one year. This was called 'to command a regiment'. Upon returning to school the younker was addressed as 'Major' or 'Colonel' by other younkers, depending upon whether he was in the first or second year. I knew a couple of 'generals of the Glorious School'—that is, those who had 'commanded' a regiment twice; they were much respected.

The first month of school, before the oath was administered, was made particularly tough for the 'beasts' by both the instructors and the 'cornets'. The purpose of such ill-treatment was obvious: to get rid of anyone with the slightest weakness of character. Large numbers of juniors left yearly during this month. I stuck to it, but I wept once when I was home for a week-end.

Each 'beast' was assigned a 'cornet', and they became 'nephew' and 'uncle' to each other for the year. The duty of the 'uncle' was to indoctrinate his 'beast' in the traditions of the 'Glorious School' and the equally glorious Russian Cavalry. Mine was a very suitable fellow for the purpose; even today, a retired old man, he spends much of his time writing verse glorifying the military past. His attitude was typical: a good cavalry officer should be a good rider and swordsman, be smartly turned out and be able, above all, to lead a charge and die for 'Faith, Tsar and Country' if necessary.

As to studies, they were regarded as beneath the concern of

13

the noble younker. One of the subjects was a short artillery course intended to give us enough knowledge so that in a pinch we could turn a captured gun round and fire it—if only to make a noise. This course was particularly looked down on by the younkers, as was scientific artillery in general. In my first test on the subject I received the highest marks, twelve. That evening, while my 'uncle' and I were sitting on neighbouring cots undressing, he said: 'Now, cheer your uncle up; tell me what your marks were today in artillery.' Rather proudly I replied: 'Twelve.' He dropped an item of his underwear which was in his hands, and said: 'Do you understand what you have done? You have put our "Glorious School" to shame! Next time get zero.' Incomprehensible as this then was to me, next time I did as I was ordered, and my pleased 'uncle' remarked: 'There is hope for you.'

A few years before my time a subject rather peculiar for a cavalry school, chemistry, was discontinued. During these lessons the younkers had sat in white gloves, so that their noble hands should not be soiled by the contaminating powders and liquids. With such an attitude, studies in the school could not be very efficient. Most of the younkers' energies went into physical exercises, which were considered ennobling. During these, the instructors did not concern themselves with our health, nor did we spare ourselves; many of us had major accidents during the two years.

On the subject of artillery I remember the following incident. Once, during a lesson, the commander of the school, General Miller, dropped in. At that moment a younker was at the blackboard unable to answer a single question. As the general entered, the artillery colonel became distressed. Obviously, it would look suspicious if he were to send the younker back to his seat immediately; what was he to do?

Quickly he found a solution and said to the general: 'I am already through with this younker but, before dismissing him, I would like to ask him a general question.' Miller nodded approval, and the teacher racked his brains to find a question that the younker could answer. Finally he asked him: 'Can a gun be shot at a target that is not seen directly?' Although everyone knows that this is precisely how artillery usually fires, the question posed quite a problem to the younker. And so, after a few pensive moments, he straightened himself and smartly answered: 'If the order is given, it can.' General Miller, formerly a younker of the school himself, was very pleased, and in a loud whisper said to the now pale-with-rage colonel: 'A very well-disciplined younker.'

All our classroom teachers, except the veterinarian and those who taught the German language and Russian literature, were officers. With the Russian literature teacher one could bargain; not for the sake of the marks really, but just for fun. 'All right,' he would say, 'I shall mark you eight.' 'Only eight?' the younker would ask, as if surprised. 'I think I deserve eleven, or at least ten.' By now the whole class was pleading: 'Give him ten, Agapid Timofeovich.' Agapid Timofeovich would think for a moment, and then say: 'All right, I shall mark you ten; sit down.'

Once, the Emperor, while visiting the school, came to this class, asked questions, and recited passages from the Russian classics by heart for a good half-hour. Agapid Timofeovich was so impressed and bewildered that instead of calling the Emperor 'Your Majesty', he repeatedly addressed him as a general, by calling him 'Your Excellency', a title that fitted neither his Imperial nor his military status, for he was a colonel. The Emperor just kept on smiling.

A subject that interested all of us was hippology, which

included shoeing. The final examination in the latter consisted in preparing and then shoeing two feet of a horse, one fore and one hind.

With less enthusiasm we studied another useful subject, the army's mechanical communications, which were field telephones, telegraph and heliograph; the latter two were based on the Morse code. The course also included the use of explosives for damaging enemy railways and bridges. Later, on at least one occasion during the war, I was to be sorry that I had not studied this subject more conscientiously.

The classroom work that was really taken seriously was the study of army regulations. These were printed in several small books, each of between 150 and 300 pages. They were: (1) Interior Service—in barracks, stables, etc.; (2) Garrison Service; (3) Disciplinary—establishment of the relationship between inferiors and superiors; (4) Formation Drills; (5) Field Service—scouting, fighting; (6) Shooting; (7) Schooling Horses for the Ranks. All these publications were how-to-do-it books, and knowing them practically by heart was indispensable for a line officer.

Attempts were also made to teach us military history, tactics, fortification, map-making, and administration; the last one was the least popular of these. Once a week our priest gave us lessons in religion (a subject taught in all Russian schools of the time), and a German professor by the name of Brandt taught us the German language.

Brandt was then very ancient; he was already teaching in the school when our commander was a younker, and even earlier than that. By 1911, when I entered the school, Brandt was pretty dotty and could no longer distinguish between a Cossack and a younker of the 'squadron', although we wore different uniforms. When picking someone at random from the class to answer a question without checking his list of names, he would peer at him intently and finally ask in despair: 'Are you from the squadron, my angel, or are you a Cossack?'

Another old man, a general, taught army administration. His own summing up of the situation was as follows: 'I've been teaching here for a long, long time and I've seen all sorts of sights. Nothing you may do will surprise me.' He did not bother to lecture, but merely read aloud from the textbook and, if someone became too annoying, would ask the culprit: 'What was the last word I read?' When the younker admitted that he didn't know, the general would say: 'It was "*staff*". Now, open at page forty-five, find the word "*staff*" in the fifth line, put your finger on it, and repeat it twenty times.'

Although some of our classroom teachers were old and many had long given up hope of teaching us anything, our formation instructors were martinets: with them there was no nonsense.

The squadron was commanded by Colonel Yarminsky, whom the younkers, among themselves, affectionately called Papa Sasha. His weak point was his love of speech-making to the squadron in formation, but for this he had little talent. Listening to the beginning of any of his talks one knew that before long he would make a *faux pas*.

Papa Sasha and his family lived in an apartment in one of the officers' buildings where, if one had something urgent to communicate to him in the evening, one could drop in. The Yarminskys had a very good-looking chambermaid, and one of the younkers developed the habit of conferring with his commander in the evenings. One unlucky day Papa Sasha caught him kissing the maid in the hall. The younker was immediately arrested, and the next day brought up from the jail to stand in front of the formation and listen to the commander's preaching. After talking about the generally prevalent immorality, and the immorality of this younker in particular, Papa Sasha, striking the upturned palm of one hand with the back of the other (his usual gesture), said: 'After all, younker Yurlov, for whom do I keep the maid—for you or for myself?'

A month or so after I became a hussar, Papa Sasha received the 3rd Hussar regiment in command, and both of us, as hussars, happened to meet in a restaurant. To an outsider it probably looked like a meeting of bosom friends. The ties of the school were extraordinarily strong. On occasion, in the theatre or at the race-track, for instance, old generals would approach me, merely a younker, and introduce themselves saying: 'I am so-and-so, and I am of such-and-such a year of the "Glorious School".'

These close bonds were commemorated on the school ring worn by all cornets. It was of silver and in the form of a horseshoe nail, flattened and curved to encircle the finger, with the star of the Guards on its head (we also wore this star on our shakos). It was lined with gold, emblematic of concealed nobility. The lining bore the inscription, 'Soldier, cornet, and general were eternal friends'. This phrase was from the school song and if the word 'soldier' were deleted the sentiment would have been true, as the Revolution was to make very plain.

The most important person in a younker's life was the special officer who commanded his class (there were eighteen boys in mine) throughout his two years. The immediate commander of my class was Captain Ziakin, who taught us military regulations and all physical exercises, except fencing and gymnastics. He was the officer particularly responsible for our upbringing. I have little good to say of him; I do not think he was a good teacher, and his methods were more than strict, at times they were sadistic, or so it seems to me today.

He taught us to ride with the help of a long driving whip and, upon slashing one on the back, he would say in the studied accent of a fop: 'I beg your pardon, I meant the horse.' On the second or third slash in a lesson one began to wonder whom he really meant to hit. If Ziakin was in a bad mood one could be put under arrest, left without leave the following week-end, or ordered to stand at attention for an hour in full equipment, for nothing more serious than jerking a horse on a fence. Because one stood at attention with drawn sword, this punishment was called 'under the sword'. On many occasions when Captain Ziakin became really angry at the class as a whole, he would first throw his hat on the ground and stamp on it, then he would take his overcoat off, throw it on the ground, too, and stamp on it, and finally he would shout: 'All of you, without leave until Christmas', or 'until Easter', depending upon the time of year. With his method of teaching, accidents were frequent, and a younker lying on the ground unable to move was a common sight. When this happened he would approach the body on the ground mincingly and in his foppish voice ask: 'Does it hurt?' 'Not at all,' would come the standard answer from below. Then, seemingly losing all interest in the case, he would make a lordly gesture with his hand and, addressing nobody in particular, order 'Take him away.' Within seconds, soldiers would appear from nowhere and carry off the younker.

I also heard 'Take him away' when I badly damaged the tendons in my knee. I lay flat on my back for about two weeks, and then was on crutches for a month or so. At first I was in great pain, so much so that even pulling the blanket over my toes was agony. At that time the Emperor visited the school.

I was told that if he came to the hospital I was to remain lying flat on my back. He did come to the hospital and he came to my room. All that I can remember was the Emperor in the uniform of a colonel of His Majesty's Own Hussars entering the door; after that I went blank. I was told later that I smartly sat up and, sitting stiffly in bed, in the firm voice of a good soldier answered the few questions that the Emperor asked me; there was no pain. This is what indoctrination can do for you when you are nineteen.

Although today I think that Ziakin was a bad teacher, he had a knack for drill; consequently our class was once chosen to perform a riding demonstration for the Emperor. It was a drill similar to that performed today by the Royal Canadian Mounties. The crowning number of this particular programme was the unbuckling of the girth and pulling the saddle forward from under you, finally resting it on the left arm, controlling the horse at the same time with the right hand, and then taking a few low fences. The class performed this as one man. Precision was obtained by memorising at exactly which point of the ring one did this or that, the ring's huge windows being the main points of orientation. What went on before we were perfectly oriented I should hate to tell you; in the course of the preparatory drills we were punished by being left without leave until graduation, some of us had another look at our jail, and we all spent many hours 'under the sword'. When the Emperor said that he was pleased, the 'no leave' order was cancelled. During the preparatory drills we had become so angry at Ziakin that there was a plot afoot to make a mess out of the ride for the Emperor. But we did not dare do it, and when Ziakin cancelled his 'no leave' order, everyone forgot the hours spent 'under the sword' or in jail, and we all thought that, after all, he was not so bad.

Plate 1   The author as a younker of the Nicholas Cavalry School in summer uniform, khaki blouse and scarlet cap.

Plate 2 Cadets of a military secondary school.

The school jail consisted of several tiny cells, each containing a bed, a chair and a table; a single electric bulb hung over the latter. The bed was a wooden shelf let down from the wall. It had no mattress, springs, or coverings. One's folded jacket served as a pillow and one's overcoat as a blanket. The walls had gradually been covered with the names and sentiments of former inmates. One of these simply read, 'Here *lived* Cornet Koslov'. Usually a younker would be under arrest for only one or two days. During this time he attended all classes but did his homework, ate, and slept in jail. He was escorted to and from his cell by a younker on duty.

I should, however, be grateful to Ziakin for one thing: he promoted me to the rank of corporal in my second year, which was important when selecting regiments. A list of vacancies in all cavalry regiments was available long before graduation. Each younker had the right to choose in the order of his marks, but sergeants and corporals were privileged to choose first.

My promotion to the rank of corporal took place in a spectacular setting. The Emperor's Winter Palace was permanently guarded by a large force of special police, both uniformed and in plain clothes. In addition, every regiment and military school of the St. Petersburg garrison took its turn guarding the palace. The Nicholas Cavalry School squadron did this one day a year. We had inside and outside posts. You stood at attention at these posts for two-hour periods four times in the twenty-four hours. For four periods you sat in the guard room ready to jump to your feet in case of an alarm; the remaining four periods you slept, fully clad. On the day that I took part in this guard duty, as we were leaving the gate of the palace, our school commander drove up, and right there on the beautiful Palace square, near the column of Alexander I, he made me a corporal of the 'Glorious School'.

My post in the palace guard was in the gallery of the heroes of the Napoleonic wars. It contained perhaps as many as a hundred portraits of military leaders, mostly painted by the English artist, George Dawe.* A cluster of banners stood in one corner, and the sentinel's post was there. At night, this huge hall, lit by a single small bulb near the banners, was eerie. One's remoteness was emphasised by the length of time it took the marching change of guard to reach you; their footsteps could be heard for two or three minutes as they echoed in the enfilade of halls and corridors.

Once, our school had an unpleasant incident at the palace. The 6th of January, according to the Russian calendar, was the day of the Feast of the Baptism of Christ. Every year on this day there was a big parade, which started inside the Winter Palace and proceeded outside to the Neva river, where a pavilion had been erected above a hole cut in the ice. On this particular occasion we stood dismounted in an enormous hall, together with the individual squadrons of the guard cavalry regiments. The Emperor passed through this hall on his way from his apartments to the square outside. As he entered the hall, all the 'eagles' were dipped, but our standard had somehow been retarded in its motion and its tip hit the floor a few seconds after the rest of the banners did. Our poor Papa Sasha was arrested for this. He tried to hide his embarassment by telling us that he was going on a hunting trip.

This hunting trip of Papa Sasha's was depicted in a caricature, where he was represented in hunting attire sitting in a cage. The colonel was delighted with it, and this is how he came to see it. The Nicholas Cavalry School had on its premises a

* George Dawe, R.A. (1781–1829), portrait painter. One of a number of distinguished London artists in mezzotint, which included his father and his brother. Dawe was also the biographer of George Morland, 1807.

grammar school, supported by the younkers. Besides private donations, there was also a yearly benefit show, during which any joke about our superiors was permissible—this was charity. At this show Papa Sasha's caricature sold for a very high price. A high price was also given every year for a picture drawn by the sergeant-major, who was traditionally called the 'God of the Earth'. The picture was also traditional; it consisted of one horizontal line dividing the paper in two. This was entitled either 'The Ocean' or 'The Desert'. The important thing was not this line, but the signature, 'The God of the Earth of the Glorious School of such-and-such a year'.

Although spurs were a part of our uniform, the 'beasts' did not wear them inside the walls of the school until they had earned them. They were given for progress in riding, and it was a great honour to be among the first ten to receive them; I was lucky enough to be one of these. On 10, May when we annually left for camp, all the 'beasts' were finally allowed to wear spurs. The first ten pairs of spurs were awarded with a traditional ceremony: the sergeant-major invited the ten 'beasts' to a sumptuous dinner in the school recreation room, and all that night they slept with eight-inch-long heavy iron spurs on their bare heels. Every cornet who woke up in the course of the night would shout, 'I don't hear any spurs jingling', and the hopelessly sleepy 'beasts' of the platoon had to jingle their spurs. By morning, you knew you would never forget the occasion.

This was a part of the hazing that dominated school life. It was not as crude as in English schools where, I understand, the older boys could put the younger ones to menial tasks. Ours consisted in showing respect to the cornets by standing at attention when talking to them and by rising when a cornet entered the room; 'beasts' also had to memorise certain facts about the Russian cavalry that were not part of our formal education. For instance, they had to learn the names of the commanders of all the cavalry regiments, their stations, minute details of their uniforms, and more of the like. To this was added memorising the names of the best girls of all the cornets. These names changed frequently, and there was no end to learning them. For dull looks or answers, or for simple lack of knowledge, cornets punished the 'beasts'—mostly by making them do a specified number of knee-bends. The normal sentence was one hundred of these exercises, but it might be as many as five hundred. Since this exercise developed the muscles of the legs, it could be regarded as helpful to riding.

These gymnastics, and standing at attention practically every minute of the day, except during working hours, were the hardest part of hazing. Its beneficial result for the army was the development of respect for any superior—even for one only a year above you. Consequently, although hazing was illegal, the officers of the school, all of whom had experienced it in their own days, closed their eyes to it. Only the cruel or ridiculous forms that it occasionally took were quickly suppressed.

Once a year the school held a horse show. The cornets demonstrated a drill, jumping, and even some Roman riding, and the Cossacks gave a display of *djigitovka* (acrobatics at a gallop), while the 'beasts' presented so-called Scythian riding. For the latter purpose three low fences were placed across the main ring from wall to wall. There was a small mounting ring at either end of the big ring. The horses were to race from one small ring to the other. All the juniors, on bridleless horses, riding bareback, were assembled in one of the mounting rings. Its gate was opened and grooms with whips chased the horses out in quick succession.

The entire performance lasted no more than three or four

minutes. At one jump my horse swerved to the side and I fell near the wall. Above me were boxes filled with people. Fifty excited horses were crossing the ring at a wild gallop, and as I picked myself up, quite bewildered, the first thing that I saw was a general in a box. Not knowing what I was doing for a moment, I stood at attention from sheer force of habit. For such stupid behaviour I was put 'under the sword'.

We were also supposed to regard a couple of yearly balls in exclusive girls' boarding schools as entertainment, which they certainly were not. You were allowed to dance only twice around the ballroom with the same girl and to talk to her for just a few minutes when not dancing, while innumerable business-like chaperons were there to see that segregation was maintained. And, anyway, according to school tradition, dancing was not regarded as a suitable pastime for a noble cornet. So, about twice a year, during the evening roll-call, Papa Sasha would announce: 'I have twelve invitations to a ball. Who would like to go?' He knew beforehand that he would meet with stony silence, and therefore would quickly add: 'I shall nominate twelve.' After this was done, every one of the twelve in his turn would ask: 'May I report?' 'Do so.' 'I don't know how to dance.' Yarminsky had heard the same story for many years and was prepared for it also, and he would reply: 'You have two weeks to learn to dance. An hour before you are to leave for the ball, come to my apartment in your dress uniform and show me how well you have learned.' On that evening the twelve poor younkers danced with each other in Colonel Yarminsky's drawing room to music played on the piano, but everyone went to the ball no matter how he danced.

Naturally we were a desirable addition to any ball: our uniform was striking: a black jacket with two rows of brass buttons, wide apart near the epaulets and close together at the red-and-black striped belt. For parade occasions a red plastron was buttoned on. Our breeches were dark blue with red piping, and our boots black. On special occasions, among them balls, we wore tight black trousers with two wide red stripes down the outside of each leg; they were held taut by straps passing under the instep. With these went low elastic-sided shoes on to which spurs were screwed. In school and during the summer we always wore red caps without visors, but in the winter, when out of school, we wore large black leather-and-metal shakos, with tall plumes added for parades.

Although so beautifully dressed, there were not many places where we could go to show ourselves in the city. Walking in the street was taboo by school tradition, and I preferred to wait in the entrance whenever a doorman was trying to fetch a cab for me. Probably during my two years in school I did not walk half a block on the streets of St. Petersburg.

Because ostentation was frowned upon both in the school and in the cavalry, and because cabs were open, younkers could not hire the particularly chic cabs with balloon tyres, nickel-plated trim, and extra-smart coachmen. On the other hand, the ordinary cabbies were apt to have inferior horses, whose pace made the passenger look foolish. On Saturdays at the school's gate there were to be found attractive cabs in good taste—plain, but with good fast horses. They were expensive, but they struck the approved note and some of us hired them for the whole week-end. One annoyance we ran into with these was in passing an officer whose cab might be going more slowly than ours. Drawing abreast of him, one was required to ask permission to pass.

Younkers were not allowed to attend operetta or farce or to go to hotels or restaurants. Just prior to my graduation I came to the city from camp to do some last-minute shopping with my mother's help. At one point she said: 'I'm tired, let's go and have lunch at the "Bear".' 'They won't let me in,' I said. 'What nonsense,' retorted my mother, who did not like any restrictions. 'You will be an officer in a few days and, after all, I am your mother.' Of course they would not let us in; and when my very young-looking mother tried to hire a private room they even became suspicious.

The school took great care of our morals. Whenever we received visitors during our free hour, Papa Sasha would peep into the minute sitting room several times to see who was calling. Once he asked me: 'Who was that girl who came to see you this afternoon?' 'My cousin,' I answered. For a second, Papa Sasha was taken aback, but he quickly regained his wits and said: 'Well, I don't want to see *that* cousin any more.'

The school's anniversary was celebrated on 9 May, by the Russian (Julian) calendar, and all *alumni* were welcome. There was a big dinner, and the school was filled with the various uniforms of the Russian cavalry. Next day we left for camp.

The immense summer camp for all regiments and military schools of the St. Petersburg garrison was situated about seventeen miles from the city, just outside Krasnoe Selo (Red Village), which name it bore. Our school had its barracks in the vanguard section. On one side of our camp ran the so-called front line, a wide well-groomed sandy road, which kept on past the barracks of the other units. The regiments would line up on it. On the other side of the road stretched a great flat field, in the middle of which was a man-made mound called Tsarsky Valik; from this, on occasion, the Tsar observed troop exercises. On the other side of the camp lay the shores of the Duderhoff lake.

Krasnoe Selo and the surrounding countryside were full of small summer houses. Undoubtedly many nice people lived there, but I, as well as most of my friends I am sure, remember only the female camp-followers. Their number was regimental. For us younkers there were two ways of getting in touch with them. The first was map-making. In practising this the class dispersed over a wide area, and thus for an hour or two we were without supervision. The alternative was to take a boat on the lake, where one could meet other boats full of girls. The latter, however, was somewhat risky, for the officer on duty had a telescope through which from time to time he scanned the water. For any contact with the girls on the lake one would be ordered to stay in camp over the week-end.

Most of the activities in the camp consisted of formation drills and field work. For two weeks or so we had to clean and feed our horses ourselves. The ceaseless drills on the field culminated in a parade of the whole camp before the Emperor. The rehearsal for this review was conducted by the Grand Duke Nicholas, Commander of the Guards. The Grand Duke, an extremely tall and handsome man, was apt to use very strong language—a habit that endeared him to the soldiers, who could easily understand what he was saying. One summer our squadron had a hard time during this rehearsal. As we passed in review, the Grand Duke shouted: 'What is this? A boarding school for noble girls?' We passed again, only to hear that we looked like 'rows of pregnant women!'.

During my second year the commander of the school was promoted. His replacement, General Marchenko, was not a graduate of the school, so our traditions did not mean much to him. Furthermore, he had spent part of his life as a military attaché at Russian embassies in western Europe and had returned home very much of an Anglophile. Traditionally, younkers never indulged in any sport that was not of a purely military nature. The first English sport that General Marchenko tried to introduce was soccer. There were no volunteers; both teams had to be assigned. A meeting of the cornets decided that playing soccer would dishonour our traditions, and the players who had been chosen were ordered to strike and take the consequences. And so it happened: upon arriving at the field we took up our respective positions and stood at attention. No persuasion by the general could budge us and, surprisingly, we were not punished for such behaviour.

The next sport that the general tried to introduce was swimming. One afternoon the officer on duty walked around the camp with a long sheet of paper and a pencil, compiling a list of those who knew how to swim. Such an unusual occurrence naturally gave rise to all sorts of rumours, one of them being that those who could not swim were to stay in camp over the week-end and learn. This particular rumour struck home: I had an important rendezvous in the city the next week-end and so, although I could not swim, I put my name on the list of swimmers.

Events then developed with disconcerting rapidity. Within half an hour all the swimmers, I among them, were marching towards the shore of the lake. Another couple of minutes and we all were naked and, in lines of six, being marched to the edge of a wide pier. We were to jump into the water as the general said 'Go'. In no time, I found myself standing on the edge of the pier looking at the water far below. I heard 'go', and jumped, but even before hitting the water, I yelled: 'Help!' I was dragged out and brought before the general, who said: 'So, you lied?' I confessed, and even gave my reasons. Probably this honesty was disarming, for the general permitted me to go to St. Petersburg the next week-end.

Graduation was early in August. All of the army schools of St. Petersburg were assembled in one part of the large field.

Before the ceremony, Papa Sasha told us that one of the finest traditions of the school was always returning in disciplined formation from the graduation. Both he and we knew that this was not true. The Emperor rode up to us and talked for a few minutes about our duties as officers. I do not remember the speech; I was too excited to listen properly, and the Emperor's presence was overwhelming. Then, after a pause, the Emperor added the really significant words: 'Gentlemen, I congratulate you with the first officer's rank.' When it was all over and Papa Sasha resumed command, he changed his stern look to a gentle smile and, instead of ordering: 'Squadron, walk, march', charmingly said: 'Sirs, officers, please walk.' At that moment graduation became a reality.

CHAPTER 3

THE FIRST MONTH IN THE REGIMENT

ON 6 August 1913 I became a cornet (2nd lieutenant) in The 1st Sumsky Hussar Regiment of General Seslavin, which was a part of the 1st Cavalry Division. The other three regiments of the unit were Uhlans, Dragoons and Don Cossacks. Each of these regiments bore the number '1', indicating the division to which it belonged.

Besides a number, every line regiment in the Russian cavalry had a name denoting the locality of its origin. To this, in most cases, was added the name of that member of the Russian or other European royal family who was its honorary colonel, or of an important Russian general of the past whose name was thus commemorated.

The formation of the name of my regiment was typical: the number indicated the division to which it belonged; the name, Sumsky, was derived from the place of the regiment's origin, while General Seslavin was a hero of the Napoleonic wars and had commanded the regiment at that time.

The regiment had its beginnings in 1651, as one of the Cossack regiments organised by the Moscow government in the southern Russian plains.

No definite data exists on the origin of the Russian Cossacks, but from the fifteenth century they are mentioned with increasing frequency in Russian chronicles and official documents.

Russia's territory was then small and did not extend very far south of Moscow. Between the Russian frontier and those Tartars who lived on the shores of the Caspian and the Black Seas lay large, almost uninhabited steppes (in what is now southern Russia); this was no-man's land. Exiles and outlaws from Muscovy came to this free territory, gradually establishing little colonies; they were called Cossacks. The name Cossack is of Turko-Tartaric origin, from Qussaq meaning adventurer, vagabond, or predatory horseman. In popular Russian it acquired the meaning of free man, and later specifically of a warrior or a soldier.

Occasionally, Cossack bands attacked and plundered Russian towns, but most of the time they fought Russia's enemies, the Tartars, Turks, and Poles. Because of this the Moscow government considered them outposts of the Russian realm even before they formally entered the Russian service.

In the middle of the seventeenth century a large group of Cossacks in difficulties with Poland left their homes on the lower Dnieper and moved north-east towards the Russian border. They founded many settlements and took service under the Russian crown as border guards. Several settlements joined forces to furnish a cavalry regiment. The district of the town of Sumy furnished the Sumsky Cossack regiment. When this territory was incorporated into Russia some of the irregular Cossack regiments were turned into regular cavalry.

The gradual growth of Russia eventually overstepped all Cossack regions, and in my day the majority of Cossacks were farmers far inside Russia, with an upper and middle class of their own. But they still preserved some of their ancient privileges, one of which was the right to form their own regiments (mostly mounted) with their own officers.

The first major groups of Cossacks inhabited the regions of the Don and Dnieper rivers; later, other Cossack districts were founded in the Caucasus, south of the Ural mountains, and in Siberia; these, although outposts at one time or another, had different histories.

Besides ours there were three other cavalry regiments that also began in the same year and in the same way. The difference in age was only a matter of months or weeks. This was difficult to establish, and it opened the door to endless arguments. We, of course, believed that we were the oldest, but so did each of the other three. Being first in this case also meant being the oldest in the Russian cavalry; so a lot was at stake.

We became Hussars in 1756, only to be changed to Light Horse eight years later. But in 1796 we became Hussars again. In 1882 we were made Dragoons, and in 1907 returned to being Hussars once more. These changes were the result of the fact that in former days the different categories of cavalry were differently armed and served different purposes. The Cuirassiers were the heavy tanks of the time. The Uhlans were lancers, the Hussars were light cavalry used particularly for reconnaissance and skirmishes, and the Dragoons were mounted infantry. Depending upon the latest development in the art of war, the army needed more of one kind of regiment and fewer of another.

In the second half of the nineteenth century it could be foreseen that the future development of intensive infantry and artillery fire would eventually make cavalry charges obsolete. Therefore, in 1882, the Russian army converted all its cavalry regiments, excepting a few of the Guards, to Dragoons—that is, mounted infantry, dressed very simply and practically for the time. In this respect we were ahead of other European cavalries. The unsuccessful Russo-Japanese War, and the abortive revolution of 1905, brought up the question of the *morale* of the army. An attempt to raise it by restoring the colourful uniforms and the old nomenclature was made in 1907; but the equipment and function of the regiments were now the same and they differed in name and uniform only.

In the course of its existence my regiment took part in many wars. It fought in Poland, Austria, Germany, Switzerland, France, the Balkans, and in Russia itself during Napoleon's invasion. Among its decorations were the St. George standard, twenty-two silver trumpets with the St. George insignia, and the inscription 'For Distinction' on its shakos. All these decorations were reminders of the regiment's glorious past; we cherished them and they inspired us.

Ordinarily, the new cornets had a month-long vacation after graduation before joining their regiments. It was not so, however, in the case of myself and my class-mate, Yazvin, who had also chosen the Sumsky Hussars. We were asked to proceed directly to the regiment, which was on manœuvres at some distance from Moscow. We were promised a vacation later.

We found the regiment resting for a couple of days in a small provincial town where we presented ourselves. Those were dreadful days. Nobody particularly wanted to see us, except the commander of the regiment who was short of officers. Nobody said 'How nice of you to come', or 'Glad to meet you'. Instead, everyone tried to find something wrong with us, everyone looked askance at us, and we were kept standing at attention, like 'beasts' in the 'school'. This kind of hazing persisted until the regimental anniversary late in November. If everyone was convinced by then that you suited the regiment, you became a part of the family.

But even after this, a junior cornet continued to maintain a respectful attitude when addressing a senior cornet and was, of course, careful never to do so with a cigarette in his mouth. This stiff politeness, which I still partly retain for better or for worse, prevailed on all occasions and in all ranks, even among close friends.

Both Yazvin and I were assigned to the first squadron, and were put to work immediately. The following day was spent on manœuvres and the following night in a village on the way. That evening, the senior cornet of the first squadron, Nicholas Snejkov, having had one drink too many, leaned against a village fence while we stood at attention, and delivered us a sermon. It was on the subject of how we should behave from now on. From it I remember the key phrase: 'By virtue of being Sumsky Hussars you can do no wrong, but *if* you do anything wrong we'll kick you out.' This illogical statement meant that henceforth only our brother officers could judge us. For all this we had been well prepared by the 'Glorious School'.

At that time the regiment was commanded by Colonel Pavel Groten, formerly of a guard regiment, His Majesty's Own Hussars. He was a bachelor of about forty, a well-made handsome man, with a small black beard; he was a martinet of the first order, not too bright, but basically a good man. Well known to, and well liked by, the Imperial family, Groten behaved very independently and, in his limited vocabulary, said what he thought. He seldom missed a church service, did not drink, and lived very simply. In the large house in Moscow which was assigned to him as commander of the regiment, he occupied only one room, where he slept on a camp cot.

Only later on, during the war, was a friendly relationship

established between the officers and Groten. At the time I met him, Groten, who believed that many officers of the regiment lacked discipline and took a frivolous attitude towards their duties, was aloof and strict. He arrested us as readily for small as for large misdemeanours. These arrests were particularly unpleasant because they were inscribed in a document which was the record of an officer's service. It was called The Service List, and it followed you through the whole of your army life.

Although an exemplary formation officer, Groten had never completely outlived the impressions of his childhood on his family estate. Once during a battle he watched a messenger galloping towards him across a field of rye, while bullets whistled overhead, and exclaimed: 'And why is that son of a bitch ruining the crop!'

It was only during the war that his good heart became apparent. He genuinely felt the death of every man and even of every horse. When, for instance, an officer who had returned from scouting would begin his report, Groten would always interrupt him, asking: 'Wait a minute; did you bring all your men and horses back undamaged?' His personal bravery was another factor that also endeared him to us, while the courage displayed by many formerly light-hearted officers changed his feelings towards us.

A conspicuous representative of that particular spirit in the regiment that Groten believed should be discouraged was the Commander of the 1st squadron, my immediate superior, Prince Menschikov. Of middle stature, about thirty-eight years old, Captain Menschikov looked well fed. During a review in 1912, the Emperor noticed him, and the next day at lunch he asked Groten: 'Who is that fat squadron commander in your regiment?' Although, like all of us, he was a career officer and

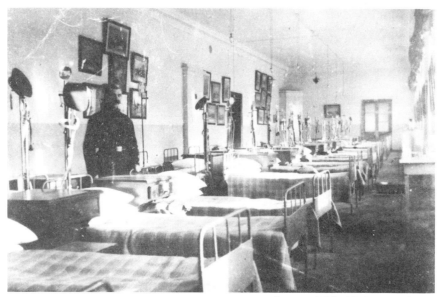

Plate 3   A platoon dormitory (about 35 younkers) of the Nicholas Cavalry
School. The man is one of the valets.

Plate 4   The mounted formation of the Nicholas Cavalry School in camp.

Plate 5   The ballroom, Smolny Institute: the school Balls were not popular
with us younkers.

Plate 6   A typical St. Petersburg cab. Younkers always had to hire one as
walking in the streets or taking a trolley-car was prohibited.

had served in the ranks for eighteen years, he looked like a squire in uniform.

Menschikov lived at least a hundred years too late. He regarded the men in his squadron as his personal property, in the way a conscientious squire would have regarded his serfs before the emancipation. He was good to them, never abused them, looked after them as one looks after one's possessions, and no one, not even a superior officer, could touch them: they were his men. So, when we once performed quite badly during an inspection conducted by the Commander of the Corps, and were given hell by him, we had barely left the reviewing ground before Menschikov stopped the squadron and said: 'And I am very pleased with you.' He was arrested for such things a couple of times.

Defending his men, Menschikov could become pig-headed. On Easter morning 1914, before starting our social calls (a Russian custom at Easter), all of us officers assembled in our club to have the day's first glass of wine together. The senior colonel, Rachmaninov, entering the club, approached Menschikov, who had been his close friend for many years, and said in a casual manner, 'Your man, Prochorov, is walking around drunk and didn't even salute me. Perhaps you should arrest him.'

Unquestionably, that was precisely what Menschikov would have done if he himself had discovered his drunken soldier. But the same thing coming from someone else was a different matter, and Menschikov answered: 'I shall arrest him to-morrow, but not on Easter day.' Rachmaninov could also be stubborn, and they continued to argue while drinking at the bar. Finally Rachmaninov who was, after all, the senior colonel, lost his temper and said quite officially: 'Captain Menschikov, I order you to arrest hussar Prochorov.' To this Menschikov replied: 'I would like to have this order in writing.' 'All right,' said Rachmaninov, and asked one of the waiters to call a clerk from the office. A clerk soon appeared, and a completely idiotic performance took place. In the midst of the officers milling round the bar, Rachmaninov dictated his order, signed it, and said to the clerk: 'Now, deliver this to Captain Prince Menschikov.' The clerk took two steps and extended his arm with the order towards Menschikov. The latter, without touching the paper, said to the clerk: 'Take it to my squadron office,' and then, turning to Rachmaninov, he added: 'And to you, Colonel, I wish to say that my squadron office is closed today.'

Menschikov was easy-going and often said that he wished he could command a squadron which had neither men nor horses and where there was no work to be done. In spite of his irregular attitude towards work and towards military life, his squadron was as good as any. He was able to make it so because of intelligence combined with exceptional organising ability. With jokes and smiles, his young officers were made to work; his sergeants and corporals worked. Some dull commanders worked harder and achieved less. But there are few stories worth remembering about them.

Menschikov liked his horses fat and his men smart-looking and cheerful, answering him in loud snappy tones. He enjoyed this picture of well-being around him, and did not like anything that might disrupt it. Manœuvres were one threat to it, war was another. So completely had his sergeant-major assimilated Menschikov's point of view that, later, when asked what he thought of the war, he used to say: 'It's all right—except for the horses being thin and the soldiers dirty most of the time.'

I became acquainted with Menschikov's attitude towards manœuvres during my first week in the regiment. These particular manœuvres were big ones, with large masses of infantry, and they took the regiment as much as 150 miles away from Moscow.

Every evening we would receive the problem for the morrow, and by morning Menschikov would have figured out how to have his squadron eliminated early in the day, so that we could proceed directly to the village assigned for the night. For a couple of days his schemes worked well, but not on the third day. On that morning we began by sending our scouts forward to determine along which route the enemy's column was advancing. This known, we dismounted in a prominent location straddling the road, in view of everyone for some distance around. Menschikov ordered the soldiers to be at ease, to make tea, and not to notice the enemy when he attacked us. He himself, surrounded by his four officers, sat on the ground and served tea with a variety of home-made jams from his estate, which were kept in a handsome little wooden chest made especially for the purpose. Like every good squire, he was proud of the products of his land.

Girths had been loosened and the horses were happily grazing. The camp fires were flaming and smoking and the hussars were drinking tea, while some sang and others napped. This peaceful scene lasted perhaps as long as an hour and a half. By then the enemy, quite visible from our vantage point, had surrounded us completely. But Menschikov's orders were always scrupulously obeyed, and no one paid any attention to the crawling infantry. They advanced carefully and slowly to the point from which they intended to make their final charge.

Suddenly hundreds of yelling men with fixed bayonets ran towards us from all directions. We still remained on the ground. The first to reach our officers' group was a young infantry lieutenant who, with drawn sword, shouted: 'You are destroyed! You are destroyed!' Menschikov sat beneath the officer's sword with a tea cup in his hands. He looked up at the breathless lieutenant and quietly asked: 'And what are you so excited about?'

By now our sergeant-major was already at Menschikov's side to receive orders. 'Tighten girths, we have been annihilated and are about to start for night quarters,' said Menschikov. So far so good. But in a matter of minutes an umpire, a colonel of the staff, appeared on the scene and, after weighing all the circumstances to which he had been a witness, decided that we had not been destroyed but, because of our total lack of resistance, had been captured. Now, as prisoners, we should trail our captors. To this, of course, Menschikov could not agree. He repeated over and over again: 'But we have all been killed.' By then our still dismounted, but already lined-up, squadron had been surrounded by jubilant infantry soldiers. Meanwhile, Menschikov, still arguing, was moving gradually towards his horse and, once there, suddenly shouted the informal order of a squire in distress: 'Squadron, mount and break through!' Some infantry soldiers jumped at our horses, grabbing their bridles: the hussars hit them with feet and fists and we broke through. For this, Menschikov was arrested.

In a few days our squadron was surrounded again, but this time we were attached to the infantry. We were surrounded through the shrewdness of our enemy and there was no nonsense; our infantry kept on fighting, trying to extricate itself from the unfortunate situation. The commander of the unit asked us to send several messengers to advise his superiors of what was happening. Later we learned that all but one were taken prisoner. This one was also caught by the Cossacks, but won his freedom and delivered his message by being a good liar. He pleaded, as he afterwards told us: 'Let me go, Cossacks;

I've lost my way; I'm hungry.' And the usually foxy Cossacks were outwitted.

Between periods of mock fighting, when we were simply marching along roads towards Moscow, the men sang and the band played as we passed through towns and villages. I do not remember whether this was an official or an unwritten regulation, but it certainly produced the impression that life was gay in the army. So, when nearing a village, the order would be given in each squadron: 'Singers ahead.' About twelve men would ride forward and place themselves immediately behind the squadron commander, in lines of six, the rest of the squadron continuing to march in a column of three. The trumpeters played ahead of the regiment. The column was long and the different choruses and trumpets interfered little with each other. The practice and tradition of choral singing was so strong in Russia that it was recognised even by the army. Both military and village songs were sung, a few with dirty words. 'Now, cut this one out, we're almost in the village and there will be girls', Menschikov would say. When the village had been passed the order would be given: 'Singers take your places.'

On manœuvres and on marches we were always preceded by an officer and perhaps a dozen men who would arrive at our next lodgings a few hours ahead of us. These men would assign hussars and horses to houses—as a rule three or four to a house and its barn. The officers were naturally billeted in the better houses, often one to a house. Sometimes the entire regiment could be put up in a large village or a small town. Sometimes we had to occupy two or three villages. As we arrived, our quartermasters would lead the squadrons and platoons to their lodgings.

Occasionally there were arguments: some people did not

want us and, strictly speaking, we did not have the right to impose ourselves upon them. When Menschikov's attention would be called to a noisy group in which our soldiers and the village women were shouting at each other, he would trot to the group, listen for a moment and then say: 'Very well, if you don't want us, we won't stay in your house. But just give me proof that you don't want us. Write on a piece of paper that you object to us being quartered in your house. You have the right to refuse us and I have no objection. Here, I'll write the paper for you and all you have to do is sign it. If you're illiterate, just make a cross.' The Russian peasant was instinctively afraid of signing a paper; cutting someone's throat would have been easier. The noise would stop and our hussars would lead their horses through the courtyard gate.

I remember spending a night in the house of a small merchant in a tiny provincial town. The merchant himself was away on business and was to return that evening. My folding cot was put in the parlour. Some odours linger in one's memory more persistently than other recollections, and this parlour had a peculiar fragrance of its own. In this case the aroma was produced by the innumerable potted plants, both large and small, that crammed every window. One of the corners was equally crammed with icons, in front of which a little red oil lamp was burning. When the merchant returned, and before greeting me, he went straight to the corner where the icons hung. There he knelt and prayed silently for a few minutes, then rose, came to me, and presented himself, saying: 'Popov, the owner of this house.'

During the same manœuvres I came across a rather irregular interpretation of the army rule that the superior in command is responsible for the behaviour of his inferiors. One night the officers' mess was quartered in the single classroom of a village schoolhouse. We invited the schoolmistress, a sweet-looking girl, to dine with us. She sat next to Cornet Snejkov. Afterwards she retired to her room behind a thin partition while some of us stayed late with a bottle of good wine. At one point Snejkov left us and knocked on her door. In a short while we could hear him trying to seduce the girl. It seemed to us that he was on the verge of succeeding when she, evidently remembering that we were in transit, asked: 'Who will be responsible if anything happens?' 'Prince Menschikov,' answered Snejkov perfectly seriously. 'Who? Why him?' 'He is my squadron commander,' came the reply.

Once during these manœuvres, we were warned that there would be a reception awaiting us in a little town where we were to spend the night. So, a couple of miles outside it, we stopped long enough to spruce ourselves up and to polish our boots. The schools had been closed and groups of organised children, as well as of disorganised adults, walked gaily out of town to meet us. An hour or so after our entry our trumpeters were playing in the square. They did so late into the night. People danced, and even I tried my hand at it.

About the first of September the regiment returned to Moscow. We entered from the opposite side to that where the regiment was quartered, and so had to cross a good part of the city to reach our barracks. As we proceeded with music along the streets, more and more boys kept running along, before, beside, and behind the regiment, and girls smiled at us. In this manner, in the saddle, rather than by carriage or train, I came to the city that was to be my home.

CHAPTER 4

MOSCOW—LIFE IN THE BARRACKS

THE Sumsky Hussars were quartered on the outskirts of the city in the district then called Hamovniky (now Frunze). Beyond it, cabbage fields extended to the Moscow river and just across were the hills from which Napoleon first saw Moscow. '*La célèbre ville Asiatique.*'

I remember those cabbage fields and even the name of their owner, Pishkin, for the regiment had made some sort of an arrangement with this market gardener to get cabbage from him at a low price, at times providing him with labour. To me, an ambitious young officer, this was often annoying. On occasion I had to cancel the exercises on the day's programme because the sergeant reported that the hussars were cutting cabbage in Pishkin's fields. Considering that cabbage soup was the daily diet of the Russian soldier, the deal was probably profitable, but whether it was entirely legal I have my doubts. Through this transaction, plus our cheap horse manure (a separate deal made with the sergeants), we helped Pishkin become rich.

Our three-storey regimental barracks stood behind the enormous barracks of a grenadiers' brigade; together they formed a quadrangle. The grenadiers' caserns had been built around 1809, in the classical style, by an outstanding architect, Kazakov, and were an example of the best Russian military architecture of the first half of the nineteenth century. By contrast, ours, erected at the end of the century, were merely red-brick boxes. Those who felt bound to find something good to say about them usually pointed out that they were light and, having electricity, permitted the use of fans. Although the latter may sound like a luxury for those mechanically primitive days, they were really a necessity of the first order. The soldiers, who were involved in one kind of physical activity or another from morning until night, went to the Russian bath only once a week, and there were no showers in the barracks. Without these fans the air would have been so thick that, as the Russian saying goes, an axe could hang on it.

The bad air which one sometimes encountered in the barracks reminds me of a story by an artillery officer who wrote under the *nom de plume* of Egor Egoroff. It concerned an army fad of the moment: a nap after dinner. The soldiers were supposed to lie down for an hour, taking their boots off. One day the commanding general decided to make an unannounced inspection of this nap. But the moment he left his office, the telephone began to ring in the barracks, advising the battery of his coming. When the general entered, all the soldiers were lying stiffly on their backs, their eyes closed, their arms straight alongside their bodies, their belts forming a straight line, their boots standing at the side of their cots, heels together and toes apart. And when the pleased general said loudly: 'Well done!' the unexpected happened: the whole battery jumped up and, standing at attention, shouted in unison: 'Glad to do it, your Excellency!' the way Russian soldiers always answered any commendation of their superiors. The general then proceeded to the next battery, but the telephone had been ringing again and when he arrived he found the same picture. Again, all the belts were lined up and the boots neatly arranged, with heels together, etc. There, even the air was typical of sleeping barracks. But when the general again repeated loudly several times: 'Well done!' no one dared to budge, as the sergeant behind him raised a silencing fist.

Some of our stables and our two riding halls were outside the quadrangle and across an exercise field. There also was the small church frequented every Sunday by those who wished to go to church.

Our barracks had neither mess halls nor study halls. The soldiers ate and studied military rules and regulations sitting on their beds, and practised some of the dismounted exercises in the wide central aisle between the latter. The wash basins were inconveniently situated in a wide passage between the stairs and the sleeping quarters. On inspection days hand brushes were placed on these basins. Once, an inspecting general picked up one of these brand-new brushes that had never been in water and asked the squadron commander, Prince Menschikov: 'Do your men ever use these brushes?' 'No, Your Excellency,' he answered. 'Then why do you have them?' 'Only for occasions such as today,' he said with a twinkle in his eye. The general, who knew such things from his younger days, rather appreciated Menschikov's sincerity and effrontery.

Tooth brushes were unknown in the Russian army. I suspect that they are a rather recent addition to the world in general. In spite of their absence, a large percentage of our soldiers had excellent teeth. This was usually explained by the fact that they ate simple coarse food and that black bread had some kind of cleansing properties.

On the barracks walls, besides the corner icon, there hung portraits of the Emperor, of the commanders of the Corps and the Division, and a number of framed pictures depicting the heroic deeds of Russian soldiers. There was Major Gortalov dying on Turkish bayonets; Private Riaboff in the process of being executed by the Japanese for refusing to divulge information; Private Osipov blowing up a powder magazine and himself with it. All of these bore legends more or less like the one below Osipov's picture: 'Perished for the glory of Russian arms, defending the Michailovsky fortification.' There were also pictures with a moral message. One of a pair of prints, each containing a series of small scenes, depicted the dreary existence of a drunken factory worker, and the other the happy life of a sober, hard-working peasant. The peasant is finally elected deputy to the Duma, while the drunken worker is shown embracing a fallen girl. Naturally, it was with this last picture that the soldiers were particularly intrigued.

On these walls also hung shelves divided into open cubicles. Each soldier was supposed to keep his bread in one of these cubicles during the day; for the $2\frac{3}{4}$ pounds of black bread allotted daily obviously could not be eaten all at once. The soldiers, however, preferred to keep their bread under lock and key in their wooden chests, together with an extra pair of boots and, often, dirty linen. Somehow, in my squadron this issue was not pursued, and it was only during inspections that the bread appeared on the shelves. The commander of the division, General Gourko, a cavalryman himself, was naturally familiar with all this. Once, during an inspection of the barracks, when each soldier was standing by his bed with all his belongings out of his chest and displayed on the cot, General Gourko, tongue in cheek, deliberately chose a stupid-looking fellow and asked: 'Where do you keep your bread?' The soldier pointed to the shelf and said: 'Up there, Your Excellency.' The officers and the non-coms. sighed with relief. But then came a completely unexpected question: 'Do you always keep your bread there?' Before he knew what he was saying the soldier answered:

'No, Your Excellency.' With the fatal word 'no' out of his mouth, he remembered that that morning the sergeant had strictly forbidden¹ them to admit that they kept the bread in their personal chests. 'Then where do you usually keep it?' asked the general. There was a long silence. Finally the flash of an idea brightened the soldier's face and, pointing to his neighbour, he cheerfully said: 'In his chest, Your Excellency.' General Gourko was very pleased with himself.

The regiment consisted of six squadrons, each composed of 150-odd men, a machine-gun unit, trumpeters, a small wagon transport, etc. Thus the regiment had about 1,200 horses. These were kept in standing stalls in interminably long stables —three squadrons under one roof. Their size was particularly impressive to me when, as the officer on duty, I walked their length at night. In each squadron the soldier on stable duty sat at a little table with a light over it. Seeing me, he would jump up and approaching stiffly report: 'In the stables of the 3rd squadron all is well.' After pausing for a moment to receive the report, I would resume my walk between the seemingly endless rows of horses, until the soldier in the next squadron would halt me for a moment again.

The duty officer was assigned for twenty-four hours. At night he had the right to lie down on a sofa in our small regimental museum, but he was not supposed to undress or to remove his boots. On one such assignment, I had dared to take off my boots for just half an hour, to rest my legs. As luck would have it, the commander of the regiment returning home late that night from a party dropped in on me. Not noticing that I was unshod, he took me for a walk through the stables and the snow-covered courtyards. I walked behind him almost noiselessly, and he never discovered what I was missing, but my feet had turned blue.

The ranks of the regiment were filled on the basis of the so-called territorial system, that is, each regiment got its recruits from a certain few provinces. One of the provinces on which my regiment drew was in what had been Poland, and thirty per cent of our hussars were Poles. Since they came from Polish villages, not cities, they rarely spoke Russian, and every autumn we had difficulty in talking to the newly arrived men. The Russian and the Polish languages, although quite similar, are still sufficiently different to prevent easy conversation between a Russian and a Pole. When my squadron commander, Prince Menschikov, would address a recently arrived Pole and get no answer from the soldier, the sergeant who accompanied the commander would explain: 'He is a Pole, Your Highness.' To which Menschikov often replied: 'There is a bird, the parrot, and *it* speaks Russian.' This statement was final and there was no answer to it.

The men, when drafted, were twenty-one years old, and they served in the cavalry almost four years (three years in the infantry). While the artillery or the military engineers received a certain percentage of drafts from industrial regions who had had some practice in the handling of machines, ours were predominantly peasants who knew how to handle horses. Coming from rural areas, many of our young men saw the inside of a railroad train for the first time in their lives when it brought them to us. As two thirds of them were illiterate and unable to read a map, they had no idea where they were in relation to their homes. If one were asked where he came from, he would scratch his head and say: 'We? Oh, we're from far away.'

The commander of the regiment distributed the recruits throughout the squadrons. Walking along the line of future soldiers, he chalked the number of the appropriate squadron on each recruit's chest. The tallest and best-looking were assigned to the flank squadrons. Before this, however, each top sergeant had talked with the men privately and had chosen several he particularly wished to have. All the sergeants wanted either the smart men or those who possessed certain skills. Bootmakers, carpenters, and tailors were especially desirable as repair men. The sergeants settled the matter amicably among themselves and advised the recruits how to ask the commander to be assigned to a certain squadron. The commonest plea was to have a friend from one's own village in such-and-such squadron. Each year there were a couple of squadron commanders who felt that they had not had a fair deal, and Captain Lazarev, the commander of the 4th, felt this way every year. 'All the worthless men were given to me, as usual,' he complained annually.

The distribution of recruits among the various guard regiments was based not only on height, but on other physical characteristics as well. Very big blond men were enrolled in one of the infantry regiments; small dark men were assigned to His Majesty's Own Hussars; tall dark men went to the Blue Cuirassiers; snub-nosed men were sent to the Pavlovski foot guards.

In 1913, illiteracy in Russia amounted to seventy-three per cent, but varied from province to province. In my regiment it was sixty-five per cent. The regiment provided no lessons in reading and writing, and often illiterate soldiers were even preferred: no reading, no ideas. The non-commissioned officer candidates were chosen from among those who were literate. These were trained in a special regimental School Command, which was the pride of the regiment. To this special unit were also assigned the few young men who had finished a university or merely a secondary school. They served only one year, but as ordinary soldiers. Upon completing their service they had the right to take examinations at one of the military schools for an officer's rank. A few did.

Most of the officer candidates in my regiment were of wealthy Moscow families, and thus constituted a private income to the sergeants. But this did not make life much easier for them and it was common to hear one of the sergeants shouting: 'Mister, you have two diplomas and you cannot mount a horse properly.' Or: 'Left, right, snappier; this is not the university.'

From the second line of the literates were chosen the regimental scouts. In my day every squadron had twelve scouts; a young officer in each squadron worked with them. This was my first job in the 1st squadron. Besides being literate, those chosen to be scouts were, as a rule, smart, quick-thinking men. But my enthusiasm for teaching them was eventually dampened. The regiment supplied batmen to a number of generals and senior officers on the staff of the Moscow garrison. By tradition these men came from the 1st squadron, and Prince Menschikov sent my best scouts away. His reasoning ran thus: 'They are good men. Here in the regiment nobody sees them, while in the city they will be seen and admired and everyone will speak favourably of our squadron.'

Each spring the commander of the brigade, General Nilov, examined the scouts. The approximately seventy-two scouts sat erect on benches, while their six commanding officers, the general, the commander of the regiment, and the other examining officers sat behind a long table covered with green baize. In this scholastic atmosphere each soldier in his turn would step forward to the table to be questioned. Map reading was one of the important items of the examination. And in the course of this long day, year after year, Nilov would ask the same question. Pointing to a river and a lake on the map he would ask: 'Does the river flow into the lake or the lake into the river?' Without pausing, the quick scout would smartly answer: 'The river into the lake, Your Excellency.' Then Nilov would query: 'And so, the lake gets fuller and fuller, and then what?' 'I beg your pardon, Your Excellency, the lake into the river,' the scout would quickly correct himself. 'And so, the lake gets emptier and emptier, and then what?' None of the teachers knew the answer to this question either. Later, during supper, they would discuss the necessity of finding the correct solution; but then it would be forgotten, and the next year the same question would again take everyone by surprise.

The new recruits arrived each year early in October. In peasant clothes, with long hair, awkward manners, they were shy and sad, some of them in tears. They struck a discordant note in the otherwise uniform picture of the regiment. Most of them were unhappy about being assigned to the cavalry. Service in the infantry was both shorter and easier; in it one did not have to feed a horse three times a day, clean it twice a day, and learn to ride. This gave the old soldiers an opportunity to have an evening's fun once a year at the expense of the new arrivals. One of the lively sergeants in each squadron would get the new soldiers together and announce: 'Whoever wishes to be transferred to the infantry, pack up.' In no time, nearly all the youngsters would be standing in line with their belongings hanging on straps over their shoulders. 'Ah, so you wish to be transferred?' the sergeant would ask and would make them trot and canter on foot with their wooden chests banging on their backs, while the whole squadron roared with laughter.

About a month after their arrival the new conscripts took the oath. During this ceremony the young soldiers stood

Plate 7   After a musical ride in the late 1880's. In the background, the barracks of
our neighbours, the Grenadiers.

Plate 8 The badge of the 1st. Sumsky Hussars, issued to commemorate the 250th anniversary of the Regiment in 1901.

Plate 9 Coloured regimental postcard used by soldiers to send greetings home.

apart from the rest of the regiment while the adjutant read excerpts from the military laws. First, he would read about the qualifications for receiving decorations for distinguished service. The original text, prepared under Peter the Great, had been altered little in two hundred years, and was couched in archaic language. Many of its conditions had been formulated to suit the wars of an earlier period; for instance, the reward for capturing a Turkish pasha was precisely stipulated.

Finishing with the decorations, the adjutant read the punishments for crimes committed primarily in wartime, such as desertion or treason. The reading of each of these items concluded with the words 'punishable by death', which the adjutant pronounced particularly distinctly.

After these promises and warnings the process of taking the oath began. The Orthodox, Roman Catholics, Lutherans, Jews, and Moslems stood in separate groups, each facing its own spiritual leader, who read an oath appropriate to his faith.

The largest group was made up of soldiers belonging to the Orthodox Church. The Russian priest slowly read the text of the oath to them: 'I promise and swear in the name of Almighty God and in the presence of the Holy Evangel that I wish to and must serve His Imperial Majesty the Autocrat of all the Russias, and His Imperial Highness the Heir to the Russian throne, loyally and truthfully without sparing my life, to the last drop of my blood', etc. The young soldiers in unison, with right hands raised, repeated the oath, word for word, after the priest. Then each in his turn approached the priest, kissed the cross and the regimental standard, and said: 'I swear.' The soldiers had been coached earlier in the morning as to what to expect and what to say.

The soldiers in the ranks had no regular leaves, and even

a permit to go to the city was not very easy to obtain. For the first few months, at least until the new recruits possessed the desirable snappy appearance, they were not allowed to leave the barracks. Only for special occasions were they permitted to go home for a few days, the most obvious reason being illness in the family. Menschikov was quite liberal in letting his men go, but before giving his permission he could not restrain himself from exercising a sense of humour quite incomprehensible to the soldiers. So, when a hussar would ask to be allowed to go home because his mother was very ill, Menschikov would first ask: 'And what are you, a doctor?'

Considering that the average peasant family had little cash and that a soldier received only token pay, vacations, even if they had existed, could have been enjoyed by very few. All that a soldier earned in money was fifty kopecs (about one shilling) a month, plus a few more kopecs for needles and thread. I remember an incident concerning the latter in our squadron, again during an inspection by General Gourko. A month or so before this inspection an important old general had died. The number of troops escorting a funeral cortège depended upon the rank of the deceased. In this case a sizable part of the Moscow garrison followed the coffin. It was very cold weather and I nearly froze sitting for hours on my horse walking at a solemn pace. In his will the general left one rouble to every soldier who took part in his funeral.

During an inspection a few weeks later Gourko, again picking out a stupid face, asked: 'Do you get any money besides your salary?' 'Yes, Your Excellency,' automatically answered the soldier. 'What is it?' the general asked, thinking of the four or five kopecs for needles and thread. These the soldier could not remember, despite the fact that everyone behind the general's back was pretending to sew on buttons. The soldier did not grasp the hint and finally said: 'For burying old generals.' Obviously, a rouble was easier to remember than five kopecs.

Besides the $2\frac{3}{4}$ pounds of black bread already mentioned, a soldier received three quarters of a pound of meat and a ration of tea and sugar daily. Breakfast consisted of bread and tea; dinner at noon was sauerkraut-and-potato soup and meat (dessert was unheard of in the Russian army). The evening meal was buckwheat gruel. The menu seldom varied.

Every soldier was provided with his own metal plate for meat and a canteen for soup. This individual mode of eating was strange to many of our lads. In Russian villages the family usually ate from a single large wooden bowl with everyone sitting around it. Perhaps once a week, when meat was available, this was cut into small pieces and thrown into the soup. Following this tradition, the soldiers liked to form 'companies' of three or four and, procuring a large vessel of their own, throw their individual portions into it and eat together sociably. Dietitians had not yet come into their own, but even without them, official efforts were made to fight this custom, which proved to be stronger than the army.

The soldiers were well dressed; every man had three sets of dress uniform. The best set was kept in reserve; the second best was worn in the city and on parades, and the third was used in the barracks whenever occasion required. After 1905 bed sheets and blankets were issued; prior to this the overcoat had served as both. In the matter of footwear the soldiers followed the peasant custom of wrapping their feet in long narrow strips of cloth under their boots. They claimed they were softer and warmer than socks. These were a part of the regular army issue. A few things like buttons were issued 'timelessly'—that is once and for all; if you lost one you had to find the replacement yourself.

One winter day in 1914, new overcoats were to be fitted to the 1st squadron. The coats were laid out in a row on the floor in the main aisle of the barracks, a corresponding number of soldiers facing them. The senior colonel, Rachmaninov, commanded the procedure, while we officers of the squadron, with the sergeants, stood respectfully behind him. The sight was impressive in its regularity, stiffness and silence, and the civilian tailors were obviously overawed by it. But there was a dreadful flaw in this smart picture: the left flank of the soldiers (the smallest men) was facing the right flank of the row of coats. The first coat to be tried on was a good four inches too long. Rachmaninov, who had a short temper, yelled at the tailors: 'Idiots, cut it, shorten it!' One of the completely stupefied tailors pulled out his long scissors and cut the garment down. The next coat—the same thing. By then Rachmaninov was roaring with rage, and three or four more coats were drastically shortened before it was possible to point out to him what had happened.

The colour of our horses was black. This was the colour of all odd-numbered Hussar regiments, while those with even numbers were mounted on greys. The Dragoons had chestnuts and the Uhlans bays. Our black horses were further subdivided thus: in the first squadron—pure black; in the second—with white stars or blazes; in the third and fourth—dark brown; in the fifth—with socks, and in the sixth—with socks and stars. In my first squadron, however, there were a few horses with white markings. They were there because they were good horses and, having had the chance to get them, the commander had not the heart to stick to the rule. These white markings were painted black for parades. Black horses with hussars in blue dolmans, with yellow braid (gold for officers only), brick-red breeches, and little red-blue-and-yellow flags on the tips of their lances formed, *en masse*, a striking picture.

Menschikov, as every good squire, liked to see both men and horses well fed, and the horses in the 1st Squadron were actually fat; they were known in the regiment as whales. This was achieved not only by good feeding but also by minimising the work. The moment a young cornet would start his platoon galloping, the sergeant would come running to him to report that for some reason (usually obscure) the horses should not go faster than a trot that day. Later, at the beginning of the war, their lack of fitness gave us a lot of trouble; but on parade we looked very smart. Besides their usual ration of nine pounds of oats and nine pounds of hay per day, our horses received the soldiers' surplus bread. Soon after their arrival, the young soldiers, previously unaccustomed to a daily portion of meat, would begin to cut down on their consumption of bread; what was left over was fed to the horses. Our men even went, armed with gunny sacks, to the grenadiers' barracks to collect their left-overs too.

The army horses were bought all over Russia, but many of our dark brown ones came from the Cossack region of the Don, where government-owned thoroughbred stallions stood, whose services cost, if I am not mistaken, only three roubles. The army bought their progeny as four-year-olds for as high as 400 roubles, which was good business for the local farmers. These half-breds, standing fifteen hands two inches to fifteen hands three inches, were then shipped to one of the so-called reserve regiments, which were nothing more than huge training depots, each supplying horses to several regiments. There, they were schooled for a whole year. The best horses bought by the army were offered to officers for about

450 roubles. From this special pool of horses I bought my favourite horse of those days, 'Moscal'. He served me well all through the war, and jumped five feet to boot. I finally parted with him half a year after the Revolution, leaving him behind when I deserted the regiment after it had joined the Bolsheviks. My other horses were government issue (each officer had to have a minimum of two horses). During my service I changed this second horse a few times upon new assignments. Of these others I remember kindly a dark brown gelding, 'Bug', who was traditionally the government horse of the commander of the 1st squadron. I inherited him when I received command of the squadron in which I had started as a cornet.

All the horses bought by the army during a certain year were given names beginning with the same letter. These letters followed each other in alphabetical order and thus, knowing the name of a horse, one knew his age. The horses were supposed to serve only eight years and to be sold at public auction at the age of twelve. But because many horses were not suitable for the service even at an early age, while others, although old, were still desirable in the ranks, a change of names took place yearly before the auction. The 1st squadron started the war with three or four horses aged twenty; one of these, 'Whist', was a really strong old man.

Many peasants from the villages around the city, as well as cabbies in Moscow, had horses that had formerly been in our regiment. Whenever one saw a black horse one suspected that he had once been ridden by a hussar.

The fire department of our district also had black horses; but these were big powerful animals of a draft type, unlikely to be confused with ours. Once, however, they were confused. It happened before my time. According to the story, our small wagon transport had been working hard for a month or so bringing in hay, which the regiment bought in the villages around Moscow. The horses had lost weight and they did not look very presentable, when suddenly an unscheduled inspection was announced. Then the enterprising transport commander decided to borrow the local fire department horses for the occasion and, to the astonishment of everyone during the review, the wagons went by at full gallop. 'I've never seen such a wagon transport!' exclaimed the general.

A soldier, called an orderly, took care of the officer's horses as well as performing his usual duties in the ranks. The officer paid him for this extra work. I had the same man, Kaurkhin, throughout my service. He took good care of my horses, and was remarkable for his total absence of imagination, which led to unusual and quite foolish bravery. Once during the war, when our squadron had dismounted and moved ahead, leaving its horses behind to be held, three to a man, the Germans noticed them in the rear and fired shrapnel at them. Hearing this and visualising what was happening to our mounts, we hurried back to them. Loose horses and running men were tearing around the field. But my Kaurkhin was unaffected by it all. He stood holding our horses on the very spot where I had left him. He was laughing himself sick. He thought it great fun to see a non-com. running, stumbling and falling, while some soldiers lost all three horses at once or were panic-stricken. No fear for himself ever entered his mahogany head.

The other man assigned to an officer was his batman. His was a full-time job taking care of his master: mine, by the name of Kourovski, lived with me in the apartment. He was a Pole—a good-looking shy, polite man, to whom I became very attached. Whenever the door bell rang, he would put on white gloves before opening the door; this little touch describes him very well, I think.

A soldier's life in the Moscow barracks was monotonous, to say the least: daily feeding and cleaning of horses and equipment; exercises mounted and afoot; practice with the sword and the lance; shooting; learning army regulations; no entertainment of any kind, but somewhat better food and beer on the regimental anniversary, on the special yearly holiday of the squadron, on Christmas Day and at Easter.

The army felt, however, that some sort of evening recreation, such as singing, should be organised. Of all these projects I remember only a joke current at the time. It was about a sergeant-major who, after the evening roll-call, ordered: 'Ivanov, step forward; now dance, sing, enjoy yourself, you son of a bitch!'

A break in the routine of barracks life came in the summer when, for about four months, the regiment was in the country, in camp and on manœuvres. The cavalry had no tents, so it was quartered in villages, three or four soldiers to a house. Then the soldiers were able to live the way they were used to at home and had some freedom. More about this later.

Every autumn, shortly before the arrival of the new conscripts, the old soldiers who had finished their time in the army went home. Depending upon the direction in which they were going, they were taken in groups to one or another railroad station. Discharged infantrymen sometimes travelled on the same train. I once escorted a group of our hussars, gay and somewhat drunk. As we marched on to the station platform, a small column of our grenadiers appeared at the other end. 'Infantry, stop making dust,' yelled my soldiers (this was what the infantry constantly accused the cavalry of doing). In a second there was a general fight. But equally swiftly, the many doors leading from the main station building on to the platform burst open and from each rushed *gendarmes* who were evidently prepared for such incidents. They quickly laid the brawlers flat, and as rapidly packed the stunned soldiers into the train. From now on these men were 'in reserve'.

A soldier who had not served his full term because of one kind of disability or another did not enter the reserve when discharged, but was officially considered by the army as 're-turned to his primordial state', a term which always caused us much amusement.

CHAPTER 5

LIFE IN THE OFFICERS' CLUB

THE officers' mess of a regiment, or the 'Officers' Assembly', as it was called in the Russian army, was a private club to which only the officers of the regiment could belong. Army doctors, veterinarians, accountants, masters-at-arms, etc. could not be members of the Officers' Assembly and might enter it only if invited or on business. They did not belong to the officers' corps proper, but had civil service rankings and wore the special uniform of the army clerks, which did not vary throughout the army.

The army usually built the Officers' Assembly at the same time as the barracks. Our barracks and our Assembly, however, were the property of the city of Moscow. Built for a four-squadron regiment, they had not been enlarged in 1883 when the regiment became a six-squadron one. They did not provide sufficient accommodation and, although there was a project afoot to build us new barracks, in the meantime we were very cramped. I have already mentioned that our men had neither study halls nor dining rooms (with the exception of those in the school for non-commissioned officers). About a year before I joined the regiment a part of our Assembly building was surrendered to other regimental needs. The officers then lost their library, billiard room, and the room for the duty officer. All this was to be temporary until new barracks were built;

and we, of course, were promised a much better club. As a matter of fact, some of the Moscow grenadier regiments possessed very beautiful ones, as did many cavalry regiments in other places.

In my time our Assembly consisted of an entrance hall, a large, long drawing room which also served as a banqueting hall, another small drawing room, a good-sized dining room, and a small one-room museum which also was the bureau of the officer on duty—and that was all.

These rooms were very indifferently furnished. We could be proud of our silverware only. For many generations a set of flat silver had been ordered for each new officer as he joined the regiment; his name was inscribed on it. We had several cases of this regimental history in knives and forks. Then there were presents. Upon our 250th anniversary our paternal town, Sumy, had given an enormous silver punch bowl, which was decorated with enamelled medallions depicting mounted soldiers in different historical uniforms of our regiment. The silver tray and cups that went with it showed our various shakos of the past. There was also a yard-high, seven-light candelabrum with the inscription: 'Let the light shine on the glorious regiment'; this was a present from two brothers who had served in the regiment. Another punch bowl was a steeplechase trophy won by one of our officers and donated to the Assembly. Many other trophies and gifts filled the cabinets which lined the walls of the banquet hall.

Some historically interesting paintings, prints, and photographs hung on the walls. The largest of these was a painting, six feet by ten feet, representing an attack by the regiment during the Napoleonic wars. The artist, Jaba, inspired by Tolstoy's novel *War and Peace*, wanted to paint a charge in which one of the principal figures of the novel, Rostov, participated. In the novel Rostov was an officer of the 2nd Hussars, but Jaba, searching in the library for exact data on this attack, found that in reality it had been made by our regiment. So he painted the picture accordingly with our uniforms, and a group of our retired officers presented it to the regiment.

The dining room was large enough to seat about twenty people at one long table. At a comfortable distance from the table and along the length of the room ran the bar, laden with a variety of hors d'œuvres, starting with a whole ham and continuing with pirozhkies, different kinds of smoked fish, and other cold and hot meat dishes suitable to go with vodka. There were no seats at this bar; one ate and drank standing, which was, in fact, the general Russian custom.

One of the officers was elected to take charge of the dining room; he was called the 'Host of the Assembly', and his was a time-consuming extra duty. The cook and the two waiters were hired civilians. One of these, Lvov, had been serving our officers since the days of the Turkish campaign of 1877. Some of the regular soldiers helped out when we had guests.

The quality of the food depended largely on the gastronomic flair of the host. Several years before my time the quality of food and drink in the Assembly had hit bottom. In order to improve it, Starenkevitch, who was a bon vivant and otherwise rather useless in the squadron, was elected host. Almost overnight everything changed: first-class hors d'œuvres appeared on the bar, top wines on the table. The officers were delighted and remarked: 'Everyone has his own talent.' But when at the end of the month the bills were distributed, the commander of the regiment, Nilov, who liked to eat and drink and did not mind the cost, dropped his spectacles as he perused his bill.

Starenkevich was fired, and the officers were thus saved from bankruptcy, but no one could save the former from this fate. Shortly thereafter, the ruined state of his finances forced him to leave the regiment. I remember him as a civilian, lunching in the club as our guest when he had no money to buy a lunch elsewhere. He was a big, tall handsome man, dressed in the style of the mid-nineteenth century; he wore side-whiskers, a top hat and a black cape. Twice a year, I believe, he received income from his estate. Then he would arrive at the regiment in a carriage and, letting his cape fall into the hands of the waiter, he would order in his deep voice: 'Lunch and vodka for my coachman.' He would treat everyone present to wine, and invite some of us to go to the races. There, he would study the programme seriously and, calling one of the boys who took bets, would announce in a loud voice: 'Here, two hundred roubles on number seven.' His figure and his assurance were so impressive that people around him would rush to bid on number seven also. He would then follow the race through his binoculars and, when number seven would come in somewhere at the end of the field, would calmly remark in his usual authoritative tone: 'Strange.' In a few days there would be no money left and he would begin once more coming to the regiment by trolley car for a free lunch. He never re-entered the regiment, but served during the war with Russian troops in Persia. He perished there. Rumour has it that he was crucified by the Kurds.

Nearly all the officers lunched at the Assembly. At the head of the table sat the commander of the regiment, to his right and left the three colonels; then came the commanders of the squadrons, and so on down the ranks, with the youngest cornets at the foot of the table. I was happy to sit there during my first year in the regiment, far away from the seniors. At the head of the table the conversation was serious and mostly about the business of the regiment, while at my end we gaily discussed girls and horses. Few people smoked at table in those days, but although hussars did, it was not before the commander gave his permission by saying: 'Gentlemen, please smoke.'

Ordinarily only vodka and champagne were drunk in the regiment; the latter was called simply 'wine'. The privilege of ordering various red or white wines belonged to senior officers; cornets did not dare to be so choosy and drank champagne from lunch onwards.

Because it was Moscow, very few officers dined in the Assembly. I did so on those occasions when I had neither invitations nor cash. Sometimes in the evenings a few of us would get together, order a supper, call the trumpeters or singers, and make a night of it. They did not mind this extra work because they were well paid for it. For every specially requested piece they received three roubles. As the evening wore on, emotions rose with the help of wine, and as more and more favourite tunes were requested, more and more green three-rouble notes were pocketed by them.

The regimental museum in the Assembly was a single small room. The outstanding items of the collection were the staff, sword and pouch of the first commander of the regiment, Colonel Gerasim Kondratiev (1651). We also had manuscripts dating as far back as the seventeenth century signed by the Tsars and thanking the regiment for its services. One of these gave the regiment the right to sell, among other things, alcohol and beer tax-free. The Cossack region of Sumy produced these. This privilege, given for distinction on the battlefield, was perhaps more realistic than the crosses and ribbons of a later period.

In a special glass case was kept the dolman of our regiment

that had originally belonged to the King of Denmark, Frederick VIII. He was the brother of our dowager Empress, Maria Feodorovna, and had become our honorary commander in 1863, while he was the heir to the throne. He remained our honorary colonel until his death in 1912. The ambition of every young cornet was to try this dolman on. It could be done only at night, when no seniors were around. I tried it on once and, although it differed from any other dolman in the regiment only because it bore a general's insignia, having it on my shoulders gave me a feeling far exceeding the difference in rank.

Uniforms, swords and guns of different eras constituted the bulk of the museum's exhibits. In charge of it was the senior colonel, Alexander Rachmaninov, a handsome man of about forty-five, somewhat too big for a cavalryman. Short-tempered and hard-working, Rachmaninov was constantly motivated by one noble sentiment or another. During the war in East Prussia, for instance, when he saw food and forage taken from an abandoned German farm he would say: '*Mon cher*, if nobody is home, leave the money on the table.' He had a nasty horse who often kicked and bit the orderlies. Eventually, the regiment's commander forbade orderlies to be assigned to Rachmaninov, and he had to hire volunteers. Groten called all horses nags and once remarked to Rachmaninov: 'Your nag has crippled the orderly again.' Red in the face, Rachmaninov demanded: 'Why do you call my horse a nag?' It was very easy to hurt his feelings.

In his spare time he was an amateur sculptor. Although the cornets liked to make fun of him as an artist, asserting that his outstanding achievement was the tip of the tail of a lion that stood at the entrance to a Moscow house, he was actually not a bad sculptor and even had one of his statues erected. It was a monument to a hero of the Napoleonic wars, Dorohov, who had also been a hussar.

We had in the regiment a cornet by the name of Baron Kister who, with his black side-whiskers and certain little archaic stylisations in his uniform, looked like a hussar of a hundred years before. Rachmaninov chose him as a model for one of his period figures. When taking a life-mask of his face, Rachmaninov, in a hurry as always, did not put enough grease on his moustache and side-whiskers, so the dried plaster stuck to them. The nervous Rachmaninov began to pull the mask and Kister began to yell. The mask had to be broken with a hammer. When Kister appeared in the regiment several days later, he was lacking both side-whiskers and moustache.

The spring of 1914 was the centenary of the campaign in which the Sumsky Hussars commanded by General Seslavin had crossed Europe and entered Paris in the vanguard of the Russian army. The regiment celebrated this event at Seslavin's grave on his former estate, some hundred miles from Moscow. Colonel Rachmaninov headed a delegation of about five officers, of which I was one. As Keeper of the Museum he was particularly excited about this trip, hoping to find something of historical value.

Seslavin, when he retired from the army, had lived on this estate until his death in 1858 at the age of seventy-eight. Besides us, there were present a few officers from other regiments of our division, a crowd of local squires with their blushing daughters dressed in pale pink and baby blue, and the orchestra of our Uhlans who were stationed not too far away.

While there we found out, among other things, that Seslavin had lived with a girl from his village, his serf. When the girl died, Seslavin, although he felt that he should not follow the

Plate 10   Constantine Sokolov, in 1913, with the trophy he had just won at the Moscow Horse Show. The dolman is light blue with gold braid and the breeches brick red. This was our winter uniform. Note how the sabre was worn.

Plate 11   Left to right: Vladimir Sokolov, Nicholas Snejkov, an officer of the 1st Uhlans and Theodore Petrjkevich.

Plate 12 *Back row*, first on left, Evgeny Adamovich, second from right, Vladimir Rot. *Middle row*, last on right, Prince Ivan Menschikov.

Plate 13   From a group taken in 1901, on the occasion of the 250th anniversary of the Regiment, while Dragoons. *Left to right:* Prince Sergei Troubetzkoi, Alexander Rachmaninov, another officer, and Ivan Nilov.

coffin, still wished to witness the funeral. The village church was close by and he could have easily observed the ceremony from his second-storey balcony had it not been for an avenue of birch trees which led from the house to the church, obscuring the view. So he ordered the trees to be cut down. We were shown the place where this avenue once stood.

Eventually the stiff official dinner with speeches began; Rachmaninov was not present. We guessed that he must be in the village trying to find something for the museum. Then, in the midst of the formalities, he entered, followed by a very old peasant. He was excited and evidently wanted to say something immediately. A speech was interrupted, and Rachmaninov dramatically declared: 'Ladies and gentlemen, I have the honour of presenting to you the natural son of Seslavin.' He had found his historic piece. The old man was seated at the table (after all, he was the son of the general whose name we bore), the provincial girls blushed, and for a while all speeches stopped; silence reigned. Fortunately there was the orchestra.

Two other colonels in the regiment, Vladimir Rot and Prince Sergei Trubetzkoy, had served in the regiment for over twenty years. As the junior Lieutenant-Colonel of the regiment, Rot did not have exacting duties. He was in charge of the shooting grounds when the regiment was shooting; he led the scouts on their occasional trips to the country; he conducted some tactical lessons for young officers; he was a member of the Court of Honour—and nothing was more time-consuming than these. There was plenty of leisure to drink vodka, of which he was particularly fond, to tell stories *apropos*, as he used to say, and to enjoy himself criticising all our generals.

Once, late in the winter of 1914, Rot commanded the scouts on a six-day journey in the province of Moscow. I took part in it with the scouts of the 1st Squadron. During those six days we were to conduct certain field exercises and make maps. Rot prepared very seriously for this trip, spending many hours at the dining-room table, surrounded by maps and bottles of wine. It was an important matter to him to organise this excursion in such a manner that we could move from the estate of one friend to that of another without losing time in between. He achieved this brilliantly, and the trip was a gay party—not only for us seven officers but for some eighty of our soldiers as well: while we were being fêted in the manor houses, our hussars were regaling themselves in the villages. There was no time for making maps, of course, and upon our return to Moscow, Rot reported that all our paper work had perished when he, crossing a narrow bridge ahead of his troops, had accidentally dropped his brief case containing all the maps into the swift-running water.

We young officers were supposed to hold tactical discussions about twice a month under the direction of Colonel Rot. Nobody was particularly interested in them: when the time came we would charge and, if necessary, die with glory. Therefore, the so-called discussions consisted in sitting round the dining table in the Assembly drinking champagne, and listening to Rot's stories *apropos*. Only a pile of rolled maps at the end of the table indicated that we had gotten together for anything else. Once, towards the end of a discussion period, a breathless soldier ran into the room and reported: 'The commander of the corps is getting out of his carriage.' With great commotion the glasses and bottles were removed and, by the time the commander entered the room, the table was clear and Rot even had one of the rolled maps in his hands. 'We were just starting to sort the maps, Your Excellency,' he said. Fortunately the commander chose not to question what we had been doing all this time.

After Rachmaninov was wounded in the war, Rot became the senior colonel. As such, he commanded the regiment whenever the commander, Colonel Groten, was away, and also for quite a while in 1915, after Groten was wounded and evacuated.

The senior Lieutenant-Colonel, Prince Troubetzkoy, was in charge of supplies; these non-fighting duties suited his timid temperament very well. During the war he commanded the combined wagon transport of all four regiments of the division. We never saw these wagons; they were always quartered far behind us in the rear. But even in such a safe location his carts were usually arranged in a circle like a wagon fortress of early wars. And if he had to stop overnight on the road, the wagons would be placed headed east, although the enemy was in the west. Troubetzkoy was cautious! He usually read military business papers aloud without ever halting for commas or periods, but continued in a monotone as long as he had wind. Then he would drop the paper and say: 'Can't understand a damned thing'—nor could the listeners.

His method of running his supply office was based on bullying a very able accountant, Jmaev, who did the work. Once, one of the cornets passing the office saw Jmaev sitting on the steps in tears. Jmaev explained that the colonel, as he entered the office every morning and while still at the door, would shout: 'Jmaev, is everything ready?' 'I answer honestly that all is ready except perhaps one paper. Then the colonel yells with rage: "Why isn't this paper ready?" And this is how it goes day after day.' The cornet gave him some sound advice: 'Next time, Jmaev, when Troubetzkoy asks you whether everything is ready, ask him, in your turn, precisely which papers he means.' This did the trick: Troubetzkoy could not answer the question.

I had an unpleasant incident with Troubetzkoy during my

first days in Moscow. Upon returning to the city after man-œuvres I had to call on all the officers of the regiment. If no one was at home I would sign my name in the visitors' book and would leave my calling card for the officer's wife. This was the accepted way of paying one's respects. Troubetzkoy was single but, I later found out, was living with a very plain woman and was trying to conceal the fact. Visiting all day long, going out one door and in another, I became somewhat hazy and, forgetting that Troubetzkoy was unmarried, left a card for Princess Troubetzkoy. Next day in the Assembly he shouted at me: 'You are still too young to ridicule me!' He was always suspicious of the cornets, who were inclined to make fun of him. He also had a tendency to snub them, and at one time began to offer them only two limp fingers instead of his whole hand to shake. The cornets then agreed among themselves to take his two fingers with two fingers—it took only one morning for Troubetzkoy to learn his lesson. He did not drink and had no friends—perhaps the two things went together. He was a perfect bore in the Assembly.

Under the same roof with the supply office was the personnel office of which the adjutant of the regiment, Tisheninov, was in charge. It would be difficult to find a soberer, harder-working man. His devotion to duty was complete. For the commander of the regiment he was a find. The papers were ready for signing five minutes too early and never one minute too late. Almost daily he worked till late hours, sometimes falling asleep at his desk. Under these circumstances he could have no home life, and his wife eventually divorced him. But he did not like war and, after a month or so of it, used his many contacts to obtain a transfer to a military office in the rear. His case might serve as an illustration of the fact that many top peacetime officers did not do too well under fire.

Colonel Rot as a young man had been a different kind of an adjutant. He later liked to brag about the fact that when he held the post the papers were pulled out of the office in wheelbarrow loads and destroyed.

There was a current story about this sort of attitude towards paper work. A certain cavalry regiment was commanded by a colonel who could have been Rot's twin. His adjutant, a conscientious young man at first, eventually succumbed to the spirit of his commander. One night on manœuvres, when fortunately only a skeleton of the office was with the regiment, the adjutant, drunk, ordered the office papers burnt. No sooner said than done, and the papers perished in flames. All that he could remember next morning was the fire, and he asked his batman what it was all about. Upon learning the facts he went to the commander to report. The colonel exclaimed: 'Impossible! You didn't do it?' 'Yes, I did,' sadly replied the officer. 'Did you burn all the papers?' 'Yes, all.' 'Nothing is left?' 'Nothing.' 'Then,' said the smiling colonel, 'come to me and let me embrace you.'

We often had guests in the Assembly, invited either by the regiment or by individual officers. By far the largest party was the dinner held on the day of the regiment's anniversary in November. A parade in the enormous City riding school began the day and, because it was also the Russian St. George's day, those Grenadier regiments that had St. George banners were each represented by a single company with banner and orchestra. We paraded dismounted, without topcoats, in blue dolmans and Persian lamb shakos with white plumes. Since the weather at the end of November was cold, the regiment walked to the riding school wearing overcoats. Then these were taken off and piled in an unused part of the building. The first to pass in review were the Grenadiers with their slow, long-striding walk; then we, with the silly, short step of dismounted cavalry. Only the junior cornets returned to the barracks with the ranks; the rest of the officers, hurrying to the Assembly to greet their arriving guests, took carriages.

The tables were decorated with our silver and were set up in all the rooms. As usual, there were no ladies and the guests, besides friends and retired Sumsky Hussars, were the representatives of the army and of the city of Moscow. There were many boring toasts and a long reading of congratulatory telegrams. These were highly unimaginative and, following a set formula, repeated themselves until one would gladly have choked the reader. They ran mostly like this:

'The X battery of the Blank Corps congratulates the Sumsky Regiment on the anniversary of a long life, and surveys the glorious fighting past of the respected regiment with feelings of admiration.'

I sat between the two guests assigned to me, both of whom unfortunately could drink like horses. I had already drunk enough when I was asked officially to down a large tankard of champagne for the Sumsky Hussars without stopping until it was empty. After that I was done for, and do not remember who took me home or who put me to bed.

On that day the soldiers received better food, as well as a dram of vodka and a bottle of beer each. There were no exercises the next day; the Assembly cook also took it easy, and the few officers who came for lunch were reduced to finishing the left-overs.

CHAPTER 6

LIFE IN THE CITY

IN my day, Moscow was conspicuously overshadowed by
the splendours of St. Petersburg where, since the time of its
founder, Peter the Great, the court had resided and where all
the chief government offices were concentrated. Both politic-
ally and socially this city was the centre of the Empire, and
some people there said both snobbishly and jokingly: 'Our
relatives live in Moscow.' But besides these relatives, Moscow
had a population of just under two million.

It was not a handsome city, despite the great fire during
its occupation by Napoleon in 1812 which, it was said, had
beautified it. And it probably had—by allowing many slum
districts to perish—while the reconstruction restored old
churches, the palaces of the nobility, and some historically
important structures. But still, around the turn of the century,
most of the Moscow streets were lined with featureless two- or
three-storey buildings, with a sprinkling of larger, recently
constructed apartment houses. Some private palaces, consistently in the classical style, and many large houses of well-to-do
people, frequently with columned porticos, made certain
small sections of the city rather attractive. An abundance of
old picturesque churches lent interest to some otherwise ugly
streets. Peculiarly enough, a few wooden and even log houses
still remain in Moscow today, despite the colossal building

programme started after the Second World War. These one-family wooden houses, not unlike the *izbas* of the Russian villages, reminded one of the time when all but the most important buildings in Moscow were of wood. Here and there stood quite imposing public or government buildings, such as some of the Grenadier barracks, the old University, the Bolshoi Theatre or the Club of the Nobility of the Province of Moscow.

As a young cornet, I found the club a boring place where squires displayed their marriageable daughters and played cards themselves, while their wives sat along the walls of the ballroom. Neither did I enjoy the Bolshoi in those days. Operetta was much more to my taste than ballet or opera. If invited, however, I occasionally went, primarily, I suspect, to decorate a box with my striking uniform.

As most things in the lives of the officers of my regiment, going to the theatre had its regulations. If one went alone, it was preferred that one sit in the first row; if with a lady, in the third. The exceptions to this rule were the Imperial State Theatres, the Bolshoi and the Maly, where one might sit in any of the first seven rows. All this made sense because we were always in uniform; wearing mufti was not only prohibited in the Russian army, but to do so was a matter for court martial. During the intermission, one might either walk in the foyer or remain standing by one's seat; sitting during *entr'actes* was prohibited. If in the first row, one stood facing the audience and could even lean lightly against the barrier dividing the parterre from the orchestra. In this position one looked correct and even smart, but standing up in the third or seventh row, in the middle of the audience, one felt rather foolish, and in such cases I preferred to walk about.

Where perhaps Moscow outdid St. Petersburg was in eating; in any case few would argue that the best restaurant in Russia was Moscow's Yar. Although open for dinner, with tables in the garden in warm weather, it was particularly famous for its stage programmes at night. It had two large rooms: a very high-ceiled and formal Empire one with green columns, and another much more *intime*, white and pink, in *le Style Nouveau*. Supper after the theatre was served in the first one, and then those who had not had enough moved, around two o'clock in the morning, to the pink one. Both rooms had stages. In the rear, along these two rooms ran a wide corridor, on the other side of which was a long kitchen. The wall on the kitchen side of the corridor was of glass, and patrons were invited to watch the food being prepared. The kitchen was much more than simply enormous; with its chefs and scullions in fresh white and its abundance of copper pans it was gay and attractive as well.

The Yar also had a famous gypsy chorus composed of whole families, fathers and mothers, husbands and wives. After appearing on the stage, the chorus was available for singing in private rooms which were used for holding banquets or for *têtes-à-têtes*. The obviously chic thing to do was to have a private room *a deux* and to hire the gypsies to sing for you. As well as being chic it was costly. Gypsies also sang in another restaurant, the Strelna, on the outskirts of the city. This was a very large orangery to which private rooms had been added. Under the glass roof, among a variety of tropical plants, stood small tables approached by sandy paths. In the midst of the deep snow of a Moscow winter this was a rather exotic way of drinking champagne.

Besides singing at the Yar and the Strelna, the gypsies appeared at parties in private houses. They worked hard, often until six o'clock in the morning, always ending the night with the song, 'To sleep, to sleep, it is time for us to rest.' They lived, as a closely knit tribe, on the outskirts of the city, in the Petrovsky Park, and on the nights when they were free they welcomed their client-friends in their homes. Somehow, I never contracted the gypsy fever, but some of my regimental friends did and later, during the war, they liked to remember their visits to the gypsies, where they had gone armed with flowers for the women, candy for the children, and brandy for the men. The very warm atmosphere of their private lives, the pretty, colourfully dressed girls, and the touching singing proved too much for some young men, and since one could not trifle with these girls there was nothing short of marriage. One night one of our officers, Cornet Leontieff, secretly married an illiterate sixteen-year-old Masha. The affair was the more incongruous in that Leontieff belonged to an aristrocratic Moscow family, in whose house Catherine the Great had been a guest. The marriage was soon annulled on the technical grounds of some irregularity in the secret night-ceremony but, in the meantime, Leontieff had to leave the regiment.

Marrying was a complicated procedure in the regiment. Officially one had to have the permission of the commander, while unofficially the bride had to be approved by all the officers. Since most of us served our whole military life in the same regiment, the regiment of those days constituted a family. A few unusually ambitious officers, interested in making a career in the army, might leave to attend the Academy of the General Staff. A few officers might transfer or retire of their own accord; a few might be thrown out; the others would remain until, in twenty years or so, they received regiments in command. The individual who did not suit this family had to be kept out. This was not a matter of snobbishness, but rather of preserving a congenial atmosphere. So, comparatively few officers of the regiment were married—about ten out of forty in my day—and most of these were senior officers.

The officers' wives were not admitted to our club, and all regimental meals and parties were exclusively stag. But the wives invited some of us to dine at their houses or went out to theatres and restaurants in large companies of their husbands' friends.

A different sort of lady, however, visited the club, but this was only secretly, during the night, if she had a date with the duty officer. I was reminded of this the other day, when I asked a regimental friend living near New York a detail about the location of the officers' club. He called my attention to the fact that the rear wall of it faced a narrow deserted street, and asked: 'Don't you remember how we used to let girls in at night through the windows so that nobody would see them?'

Not wishing to get married, and knowing that I would make a desirable bridegroom, I kept away from girls of good family, no matter how attractive they might be. Most of the married women of my acquaintance were the wives of officers (although not necessarily of my regiment), and there was a taboo code pertaining to them. So far as ennobling feminine company was concerned, I was limited to what was called in the regiment the ladies of our circle. These were not prostitutes, but just ladies of easy virtue, and quite a few of them were amusing, besides being pretty and perhaps even chic. Were it not for the knowledge that they shared their favours, one might have fallen seriously in love with some of these gay and attractive girls.

Not only the brides, but, occasionally, even one's lady friends were disapproved by the regiment. During my first month in Moscow I had just such an unpleasant experience. At a charity bazaar I met a very good-looking woman in her

early thirties, and invited her to the circus next evening. A box
near us was occupied by officers of my regiment who, as they
greeted me, fixed their eyes for a moment on my companion.
In the course of the evening my lady suggested that the following afternoon, when I was finished with my regimental duties,
she would stop for me in her carriage and show me her favourite
parts of the city. And so we parted until the next day. In the
morning, however, the senior colonel took me aside and told
me that the lady with whom I had appeared in public had
the reputation of helping young men financially, and that,
although to be polite I might keep my next appointment with
her, I would have to choose between her and the regiment.
That afternoon I sat in her carriage as if I had swallowed my
sword.

At the Yar, as at all the other restaurants in Moscow, we
hussars were greeted by our regimental march, which the
orchestra would strike up every time one of us entered, abruptly
interrupting whatever it was playing. Pausing at attention for
a moment to accept this salute, while all eyes were turned upon
one, would certainly make me feel self-conscious today, but at
the age of twenty-one it seemed to be normal and proper.

At one time, a part of our regimental orchestra played in
the garden at the Yar during the summer months. According
to regulations, a cavalry regiment had a band of sixteen trumpeters; our learned conductor, Markvardt, however, organised
a large orchestra composed of hired musicians many of whom
were students from the Conservatory of Music. This orchestra,
of perhaps as many as one hundred men, who wore our uniform only when playing, would be divided into smaller bands,
and these played on the stage of the Bolshoi when trumpets
were needed in certain operas or ballets; they played at balls,
at the skating rink, made gramophone records, etc. It was a

combination of business and public relations. When we wanted to have music in our officers' club, then only the sixteen official trumpeters were called in. The income from the orchestra's activity helped to build an indoor riding ring, to buy new uniforms for the regiment, and to treat the men to the unaccustomed luxury of raincoats. This sort of buying was called 'expenditure without expenditure by the government'.

Yar, Maxim, Strelna, and Praga were among a dozen or so restaurants and night-clubs we officers had the right to patronise; all others were prohibited by order of the Commander of the Moscow Military District. This order was partly a result of the animosity towards officers displayed by liberal elements in the population, an animosity that had increased by leaps and bounds after the suppression of the 1905 revolution. Unpleasant incidents, when officers were attacked publicly, and according to their code had to defend their honour with weapons, occurred here and there. Occasionally it was an officer who started the trouble. Thus, for instance, a former officer of my regiment had killed a civilian in a St. Petersburg restaurant because the man refused to rise when the National Anthem was played. As a result, in my day, playing it in restaurants was prohibited.

Traditionally, the most important emblems of status to us officers, as well as to those who wished to demolish it, were our epaulets. If an epaulet was torn off, you were forced to kill, defending not only your own honour but the honour of the whole army as well. If you failed in this you were expected to commit suicide. So, besides the regulation sabre, I always carried a small Browning pistol. I carried it in the pocket of my overcoat on the streets and transferred it to the pocket of my breeches when indoors. The constant switching of this

Browning from one pocket to another is hard to forget. After the Revolution the Red army started without epaulets, which were later restored on, I suspect, much the same basis.

Among the less elegant restaurants on the green-light list were the railway buffets. At the Nicholas Railway Station one could eat fairly well. I dined there on several occasions before taking the night express to St. Petersburg to visit my family for a week-end. This express train took ten hours to cover 400 miles of perfectly straight track laid on level ground, but in those days it seemed incredibly fast.

Once a waiter at this station buffet took it for granted that a hussar would certainly wish vodka, and merely asked me whether I preferred a small or a large carafe. In those days I did not drink much, and on that particular occasion I did not wish to drink at all. But feeling that at that moment the prestige of the regiment rested on my shoulders, I answered: 'A large one,' thinking that I would not have to drink it after all. But once the food and vodka were served, the waiter placed himself behind my chair and immediately poured vodka into my glass. The moment I emptied it the waiter would fill it again. There was no way out. It was service rarely encountered in the modern world. And so it went; I drank glass after glass, playing the role of an old hussar. And thus I got drunk, and then sick on the train, and all because of a waiter who had an idea of what a hussar should be; and his idea, unfortunately, corresponded closely to mine.

This keeping up of what one believed to be the prestige fo the regiment was a full-time occupation, particularly during the first few months, when a young cornet sat on pins and needles afraid of making a *faux pas*.

One night, being out of money, I remained home and was going to bed when Cornet Poliakov, with a lot of wine in him, burst into my apartment and enthusiastically announced: 'I've just bought a wonderful dog of remarkable pedigree, a fantastic purchase; let's celebrate. We'll go to Yar. I have money and I'm inviting you.' Around one o'clock, having had our supper, we were ready to go home when Poliakov, feeling his pockets, declared: 'You know, I forgot my wallet.' The situation was absurd: the bill was not more than thirty-five roubles and two hussars could not pay it. What was to be done? To us it was a matter of regimental prestige. So, although quite sleepy, we moved to a private room, invited gypsies, gave them as much champagne as they wanted and, when the bill had been raised to several hundred roubles, happily signed it. Feeling that our honour had been ingeniously saved we went home.

To look and act like an old hussar from the ballads of the War of 1812 was my consuming ambition in those days. The hussars of the songs and verses of a hundred years before charged with drawn swords all day and drank all night sitting around the camp fire. This seemed to me to be a romantic life.

It was rather easy to lend an old look to my hussar's cap by giving it several aging treatments; but it was much more difficult to change my face which, to my perpetual chagrin, was too youthful even for my age. Once at a horse show in the City riding school, after a successful ride, I was walking complacently along the aisle just behind the boxes. I was pretty certain at that moment that everyone admired me as much as I did myself, when I heard a lady in one of the boxes saying to another: 'Look at that hussar, he's just a baby.' I walked out, and took a cab straight home.

Another time, on manœuvres, an old woman in whose house I spent the night raised her hands as I came in and exclaimed: 'So young, and already in the army!' Even at my favourite theatre I was once reminded of my inappropriate face. The glory of Moscow operetta, I then thought, was a piquant actress, Potopchina, who could transform the most banal libretto and trite music into something quite delightful. In one of the pieces Potopchina sang a hit of the day, '*Pupsik*'— the very name indicating that it was addressed to a baby-like young man. Because of the popularity of the melody, Potopchina, after singing it on the stage, used to descend into the audience and sing it again while walking in the aisles. One evening when I was in the first row, she sat in my lap and sang '*Pupsik*' to me. My acquaintances in the audience made this episode widely known of course, and for a while *Pupsik* became my nickname.

One of my ideals of good looks was Colonel Rot, whose particular fondness for liquor for many, many years was reflected in the colour of his nose; it was a combination of red and blue. I then thought it was just right, just the colour a hussar's nose should be. The wife of one of our officers, a very shy woman, had difficulty in starting a drawing-room conversation. Once, when she was giving a tea, her husband offered her some last-minute advice. 'It is very easy,' he said. 'Just try to remember the interests of the person who happens to be next to you; if you have heard that he likes dogs, say something about dogs; if he likes fishing, ask him about fishing.' At that moment the first guest arrived for tea. It was Colonel Rot. The hostess looked at him, looked at his nose, and cheerfully asked: 'Colonel, would you like to have some vodka?'

Colonel Rot was a wonderful raconteur while there was wine on the table; it was easy to listen to him for a long time. One afternoon, after the routine work in the regiment was over, five or six of us youngsters were called to the officers' mess by

Plate 14 The six sergeant-majors of the Regiment. First on left, Sidorovich, of the 1st squadron.

Plate 15 A conscript saying goodbye to his family. He is wearing the usual Russian civilian cap, not a military one.

Plate 16 A school for non-commissioned officers of another cavalry regiment. The bearing and the faces of these soldiers would be typical of a corresponding group of Sumsky Hussars.

the Colonel, who needed listeners, and the waiters got busy bringing in the bottles. Some three hours later it was decided to go to an operetta. Evidently this was the last that the Colonel could remember. In the meantime a telegram had come from the commander of the regiment announcing his arrival from St. Petersburg at nine o'clock that night. Going to the operetta was cancelled, and we went to the station instead. There we continued to drink in the buffet. Colonel Rot by then was silent, slumbering, and almost unconscious. At intervals a man with a large brass bell in his hand would enter the door, ring the bell, and announce the next train. In the Russian theatre a bell indicated the rising of the curtain, and the Colonel, returning to life for a moment, asked: 'Why this disorder? The bell goes on ringing and the curtain does not go up.'

Soon after my arrival in Moscow, still a tourist, I made the circuit of museums and places of historic interest inside and outside the Kremlin. To my present regret I never made a point of revisiting them later. A life free in comparison with the prison-like one of the military school presented too many opportunities besides what museums had to offer. And I have to admit that during my couple of visits to the Kremlin I was more impressed by the rows of guns captured from Napoleon and lined up in the square than by the ancient churches, by the old Palace of the Tsars, by the treasures of the museums, or by the feeling of the history of early Russia with which the place was imbued.

I have a particularly vivid recollection, however, of a service in one of the Kremlin chapels. At the time of the Revolution of 1905, the Grand Duke Sergei Alexandrovich, the commander of the Moscow Military District, was assassinated. He had been married to the Empress's sister, Elizabeth

Feodorovna. They had both been friends of the regiment. After his death, she founded a religious sisterhood. Once a year, on the eve of the regimental anniversary, we held a memorial service for him in a private chapel in the Kremlin where he was buried. I remember clearly on one such night the touching sight of the white nun who had been a grand duchess, standing in the dark, candlelit chapel among the gold-braided, blue-dolmaned hussars.

One of the pleasures of Russia was the Russian Bath (Turkish in England and America). While a necessity to many, this was a pastime for those who had a tub at home, and a tradition with a great deal of sentiment attached to it for all. Besides, it was supposed to be a cure for almost any ailment. My mother's brother, Sergei Bachmetov, an unimportant clerk in the State Bank, and very typically Russian in his habits, went to the bath once a week with his cronies instead of to the office, and for a whole day. He most sincerely considered this to be his national privilege, and could not be persuaded that it was not. I do not know how he got his job, but I know that he kept it through the influence of my father.

There were, I believe, two *de luxe* baths in Moscow. On the evenings when Cornet Yazvin, with whom I shared an apartment, and I felt that we should economise, we would go to one of them to bathe, not merely in water but in the feeling of complete physical relaxation created by masseurs, chiropodists, men who washed you and boys who served you.

When you arrived at the bath you were assigned a cubicle with two couches. They were of green velvet and covered with white sheets. There you undressed and proceeded to the room where the bathing proper was done. Here you lay on a wooden bench; an attendant, dipping a bag into a large copper dish full of soapy water, would blow into it and create suds with which he little by little built a pile of foam on your body. To lie beneath it was very soothing, warm and soft; one did not wish to move from under this mountain of soap suds. Then the man would wash and massage you simultaneously.

The next stage was the steam-room. There, wooden bleachers, the length of the room, ascended to within a few feet of the ceiling, where there was a platform with benches around it. Buckets of water occasionally thrown over a pile of red-hot stones on a corner hearth created a marvellous steamy heat. The heat rose and, as one ascended the steps, one rose with the heat. Depending on one's taste, one could go up to the fifth or the seventh step, or to the top. Wherever you were, your man gave you a special Russian massage by beating you with birch twigs. The combination of heat and switching produced skin the colour of a boiled lobster, while the air was perfumed by the aroma of the birch leaves brought out by the heat. Then you returned to the preceding room to cool off, and after that stayed for a while in the marble room, where the marble benches were gently heated from inside and dried you off. You ended in the cubicle where you had undressed, and sipped wine while the chiropodist worked on your feet. Thus two or three hours were pleasantly spent.

Most of the officers of my regiment lived in the city proper, and only a handful in the army apartments near our barracks. A few had large houses, others lived with their parents, some rented apartments, a couple stayed in hotels. Leontieff's house, built in the eighteenth century by one of Catherine the Great's favourites, Zouboff, was still surrounded by a small park. In another park, in a cottage on the family property, lived Cornet Vishniakoff and his bosom friend, Cornet Petrjkevich. This was a wild household, and here (I quote from a recently published history of the regiment) gay parties were frequent; *Jenka* (a hot drink) was boiled on crossed-swords, pistols were fired, a new rifle bullet was tried out. Here, the gay Din Din and the loving Nadya were frequent guests.

The adjutant of the regiment had a huge old-fashioned apartment with a ballroom so large that the regimental orchestra and a substantial number of guests could not fill it. It was large enough to exercise a platoon. The beautiful house of Cornet Berg's family was important enough to be requisitioned immediately after the Revolution and assigned to the German Embassy. A very different type of living was exemplified by the sparsely furnished apartment of Cornet Starinkevich, on the blue wall-paper of whose entrance hall was scrawled in large white letters the warning: 'Do not think of the morrow'. And so it went. As varied as the means and tastes of the officers were their modes of living.

My school friend Yazvin and I shared an apartment on the fifth floor of a modern house with an elevator, just a few blocks away from the regiment. We had living and dining rooms, two bedrooms, a kitchen, a bathroom, a room for an orderly, and a balcony. We had both arrived in Moscow with money from our families to furnish whatever we would rent. But the Yar, wine and girls seemed to be more important at the moment, and the money disappeared before a stick of furniture was bought. So when my mother arrived a month or so later to enjoy the looks of the new household, she found us living in a hotel, while the apartment remained pristinely bare. Mother stayed in Moscow for a week, and Yazvin and I were finally able to move into rather cosy quarters. Later, our rooms were further decorated by Yazvin's family's sending us bronze and porcelain bric-à-brac. These were some of the spoils of the Boxer Rebellion in China, in the suppression of which Yazvin's father had taken part. Since Russian troops, along with the troops of other nations, had participated in the plundering of the palaces of Peking, we probably had priceless things on our tables. Of this I am not sure, but of the fact that they were treated very casually, I am.

In spite of the fact that our barracks were within the city, that most of us lived in the city, that some of us were of the city, and that all of us had friends in the city, there was a feeling in the regiment that we were quite apart from the ordinary civilian world. Simply leaving the army compound, that is, walking out through one of its gates, was called 'going to the city', and meant into a different and rather alien world. I imagine a similar feeling exists in every army, but perhaps in our case this sentiment had been accentuated by the Revolution of 1905. Moscow had been one of the centres of rebellion, and because our Grenadiers had either revolted or could not be depended upon, while at least half the Cossack troops had been sent out to the country, the suppression of the revolt, for a few days, anyway, fell on our regiment and the artillery. The revolutionaries printed leaflets with headlines, 'Kill the Sumsky Dragoons' (we were dragoons at the time). A week later two infantry regiments arrived from St. Petersburg, with the army manning the trains because there was a general strike, and the revolution was quelled. But this had taken two to three weeks of skirmishes, in which the artillery demolished houses and the cavalry charged. From then on we naturally had a bad name in liberal circles and among the workers. In our turn, we were suspicious of anyone who might have unorthodox ideas. There was an army joke about a soldier who, when asked who his external enemy was, answered: 'The Germans,' and to the query about his internal enemy replied: 'The university students.'

The feeling of separation from the rest of the world, the living 'behind the iron curtain' so to speak, bred ignorance and hence the assurance of superiority. This, in turn, led to strong resistance to any attempt, however justifiable, of the civil authorities or the police to interfere with what we considered our special life. For example: the city police once arrested and held one of our hussars for attempted rape. The commander of the regiment, incensed at anyone taking such liberties with one of our soldiers, sent me to get him out of the local precinct. 'You may tell them whatever you wish, but be sure to bring him back,' was his order. 'If he is guilty, we will punish him.' In the precinct, our hussar declared that he had been apprehended by mistake and that he had never done such a thing; he swore to this as he crossed himself in front of an icon. Shortly afterwards, he and I were walking back to our barracks. I was rather proud of my part in saving an innocent man. Probably just to break the silence of our walk, I started a conversation quite awkwardly by asking a, by then, superfluous question: 'Now, tell me, did you do it or not?' 'Yes, Your Honour,' came the completely unexpected answer. Later, in the regiment, every one of his immediate superiors who could swing an arm took a crack at him, but to admit that he was guilty, and thus to expose him to official justice and ruin his life, was something few of us would do. He belonged to us: it was for us to punish him, and it was not the business of the silly city police and the yet sillier courts. Perhaps I felt this way more strongly than some of my friends because of the influence of my squadron commander, Prince Menschikov, whom I then admired very much.

Another time a soldier of our squadron, armed with a knife, attacked a sergeant: this was an obvious case for court martial. But Menschikov, trying to save the would-be murderer, acted in his usual original manner. He told the man: 'You were behaving like a dog when you attacked the sergeant, and I shall tie you up like a dog in the stable. You will sit there like a dog on a rope, and if you try to free yourself, I shall bring you to the law.' For a few days the tethered soldier was the joke of the squadron. Although the punishment was profoundly humiliating, Menschikov avoided spoiling the man's future.

We officers could be arrested in the city only by the special officers of the *commandatura*, and there were not enough of these to be permanently stationed in all the places where we could raise hell. Therefore, if an officer misbehaved in the city and the office of the military commander of the town was advised of it, one of its officers, the so-called *platz adjutant*, would be sent to take care of the culprit. But because it took time to telephone the *commandatura*, as well as for the *platz adjutant* to arrive, the misbehaving officer had time to perform his antics. One of our cornets, Pankov, drank much too much. Fortunately, he did it mostly in the officers' club, sitting at the piano and playing most marvellously by a very keen ear. Because the only music he ever heard was the music of military bands, he quite naturally reproduced on the piano the sounds of different brass instruments. When on occasion he changed his routine and, after getting drunk, went to the city, there was invariably a scandal—and one on a large scale, in which many people were involved. Once, standing at the bar of the Hotel Metropol, Pankov looked fiercely (and he had a very fierce look when drunk) at the people around him and ordered: 'Everyone line up!' Everybody meekly obeyed, as people usually do during a hold-up, and both gentlemen and waiters lined up. The line, however, was not to Pankov's liking, for the men did not stand according to their heights, the tallest on the right flank. And so, while somebody was calling the *com-mandatura* and the *platz adjutant* was on his way, Pankov busied himself rearranging the line according to the rules of military formation. For this he was locked up for the next thirty days.

The final incident took place in summer camp near Moscow. One night, when all the senior officers were in the city, a practice alarm was sounded. In such cases the squadrons, which were stationed in different villages a couple of miles apart, proceeded to some centrally located spot. Pankov, angry that his drinking had been interrupted, led his squadron there. Near this spot, in pitch darkness, he heard a voice asking: 'Which squadron?' Still annoyed, Pankov replied: 'Ah, go to hell!' This reply was highly inappropriate, for the asking voice was that of the commander of the brigade. The next day, the general told Pankov: 'Because of this, we must part.' And so Pankov left the regiment and became a civilian. He returned to us, however, during the war, having given his word of honour that he would not drink. He kept his word, brilliantly commanded the 4th squadron, survived the Revolution, went to New York, and succeeded in having his own small business there.

This gay life, many anecdotes of which I have retained in my memory, was only one aspect of a hussar's existence; the other was work. Outsiders, however, never saw the latter, and therefore often formed a point of view uncomplimentary to the army. As a matter of fact, in most cavalry regiments work predominated, circumstances being perhaps the major reason. Except for the guard cavalry, stationed in and around St. Petersburg and Warsaw, and for us in Moscow, there were only a handful of cavalry regiments (not counting the Cossacks) stationed in large places; the rest were quartered on the Austrian and German borders, mostly in villages and small towns where no social life or entertainment outside the regiment was available. Because of their location, some of our cavalry regiments crossed the German border in 1914 within a half-hour after the declaration of war.

Each officer had a twenty-eight-day vacation once a year. He would spend at least part of it in St. Petersburg, Moscow or Warsaw, dressed to kill in his beautiful uniform, and with extra money saved up during the year to throw around. These Uhlans, Dragoons, Hussars, blue, yellow, red or green, with gold or silver braid, were conspicuous in the capitals on any day of the year, creating the false impression that painting the town red was army life. Actually they were only 'sailors off ship'. Most of them spent the rest of the year in barracks, stables, on manœuvres in the deep Russian mud or dust, working with illiterate soldiers, busy with lame horses, missing buttons, lost bayonets and such things, while in some areas, only peasants, small merchants and a few local squires constituted the civilian world around. A small provincial town in the neighbourhood, where a third-class theatrical company might occasionally stop for a couple of days, was all they could hope for during eleven months of the year.

The cost of an officer's life varied from regiment to regiment, depending upon where the regiment was stationed, as well as upon its particular traditions. In Moscow my monthly salary as a cornet, with all extras, amounted to 110 roubles. The rouble was then worth 2s. $1\frac{1}{2}d$. sterling (100 kopecs to the gold rouble), and it may be said to have had in most things double the purchasing value of the £1. Living was cheap in Russia. The price of a pair of the best boots, however, was forty-five roubles, of a dolman over 100, and a bottle of French champagne in a night-club cost twelve roubles. Thus my salary equalled the cost of nine bottles of Cordon Bleu at the Yar.

Obviously, one could not get far on what one earned. The salary was not even sufficient to cover daily life in the regiment proper, that is, meals and liquor in the officers' mess, plus the innumerable little necessary contributions resulting from life in a large city with all sorts of social obligations: a gift to one person, flowers for the funeral of another, a party given for a visiting officer, or the big celebration of the regiment's anniversary, to which many guests were invited, both military and civilian. At the end of each month, instead of receiving a salary, one was presented with a bill by the regimental office. Every one of us had means, some more than others; consequently the officers lived on different scales. But there was a certain minimum, different in different regiments, and when choosing one, the future officer took this important item into consideration. Errors in calculation were made, of course, as in anything else, and occasionally an officer was forced to leave the regiment because his private means were insufficient.

CHAPTER 7

TRAINING OF THE REGIMENT

A LTHOUGH it was easy to foresee that in the next war there would be little place for mounted charges and that the cavalry would be reduced to scouting, to the occasional pursuit of the defeated enemy, and to dismounted combat, the spirit of the Russian cavalry still remained that of charging with drawn swords. The fact that we had ever been Dragoons was mostly forgotten. A romantic attitude towards the picturesque battles of the past still prevailed among us before the First World War. So, while a great deal of time was spent learning and teaching how to fight as infantry, the emotional stress was still on fighting in the saddle. This, of course, is why we took tactical discussions and anything else that smelt of modern warfare so lightly. Eventually we were to be very much disillusioned, but in the winter of 1913–14 we were still professing that the principal weapon of a cavalryman is his horse. Therefore, learning to ride was an important item on the programme of exercises conducted in the regiment.

The method of riding in the Russian cavalry was of the manège type, which today is usually called Dressage. It had been practised in the Russian army for nearly a hundred years, although it came originally from western Europe. This artificial system worked well on the parade ground, but not across country, and the experiences of war disappointed even its most ardent exponents. Very early in the war we began a pragmatic return to the natural methods of the born horsemen of the eastern European plains.

Equestrian sport was not particularly developed in the regiment and, as a matter of fact, the commander, Groten, did not favour it. Preoccupation with sport obviously took up too much time, and the officer who indulged in it was at least in part emotionally lost to the ranks. Some ten officers, however, did participate in jumping competitions and two or three in military steeplechases. Groten called them gladiators. About half a dozen officers kept horses on the race track, but these were ridden by professional jockeys.

The Italian method of riding, still a novelty then, was popular among young officers, but the old-timers' ideas were not to be changed. One of the senior cornets, Vladimir Sokolov, volunteered to teach me the new system. Looking back on it now, I realise that what this consisted of to him was no more than riding with shorter stirrups, having the body inclined forward and out of the saddle at a gallop and over fences, and keeping the horse free and extended. But for those days these were great innovations.

During the winter only the new recruits were given riding lessons proper. The old soldiers merely hacked their horses, and the best riders continued the schooling of young horses. These already had had one year of training in special reserve regiments, which were training depots. In the winter of 1913–14, the war that was to start the following summer was anticipated. Hence an exception was made and about 100 young horses came to us without preliminary schooling in the reserve regiment. Two officers and a group of specially selected hussars were given the job of breaking and schooling them. Those that had been bought from stud farms were not too difficult, but the others that came from the herds on the Don prairies were wild beasts. A tramway passed our exercise field, and whenever a trolley car appeared these horses, even under riders, would scatter all over the place like a handful of peas dropped on the floor. In spite of all their rearing and throwing themselves on the ground, they were in the ranks by spring.

Some of the hacking trips for the old horses were supposed to be long enough to keep them in condition. For this they had to be taken to the country, to fields outside Moscow. In the 1st Squadron, in which I served as cornet, these long field trips were not practised, because the main concern of the commander and his sergeant-major was putting fat on the horses, not taking it off. Ten or fifteen minutes' walk from our barracks there was an old convent, called the Girls' New Convent (Novodevichy). The area around it, now much reduced by the encroaching city, was still called the Convent Field. Once, during lunch in the Assembly the commander of our division, General Gourko, asked Menschikov: 'Do your men ever ride in the fields during the winter?' 'Yes, Your Excellency,' answered the latter. 'And whereabouts?' 'In the Convent Field,' replied Menschikov with a smile. And as a matter of fact, this was as far as our horses went, unless sending them a greater distance could not be avoided.

We had two indoor riding rings, but because of insufficient space in the stable one of them was used for storing hay. The remaining ring was not big enough to serve all our needs, so most of our riding lessons were in outdoor rings. A layer of straw manure was laid as a track in each ring so that the horses would not slip on the ice. As a result of the periodic clearing of freshly fallen snow each ring was eventually surrounded by a snow wall.

The earliest lesson in the indoor ring started at seven o'clock.

It was completely dark at that hour during the winter. It was also particularly cold in the ring then, and as the steam from the horses turned into fog it would fill the ring, making the riders almost invisible. Each squadron took its turn at this undesirable hour; otherwise riding began at nine o'clock.

Whether the riding lessons started at seven or at nine, being late was not regarded kindly. Every squadron commander had his own tactful way of expressing his disapproval. Menschikov, not waiting for excuses, would say: 'It's all right; it can happen to anyone'; Captain Markov, the commander of the 2nd, would silently point to the time on his watch; Captain Lazarev, the commander of the 4th, used to say: 'You will get me in trouble, my friend.' On the other hand, if a cornet was on time but had obviously had a sleepless night, Menschikov would be quite fatherly, saying: 'You look as if you have a cold. Go home and take the day off.'

All the exercises were supervised by squadron commanders and sergeant-majors; next in importance were the platoon sergeants. We junior officers did not count for much, although we actually did the teaching.

The sergeant-major of the 1st Squadron, Nicolai Sidorovich, was a highly respected man. The officers of the squadron called him Nicolai Ivanovich (Ivanovich meaning son of Ivan), as if he were their social equal; to Menschikov alone he was simply Sidorovich. He was a handsome blond man with rosy cheeks and upturned moustache. The word 'smart' motivated his whole life, which was devoted to turning out smart-looking horses and smart-looking men and making the latter behave in a smart manner. He was a typical peacetime sergeant and was out of place in war. He had little sense of humour and only one joke, which he repeated constantly. Each time that the squadron was mounted after staying overnight in a village he would ask, addressing the formation: 'Have you made a list of the things you left behind?'

When the squadron proceeded along the road in a column of three the sergeant rode at the tail of the column with an officer beside him. On many occasions I rode next to Sidorovich, and so heard his few stories over and over again. The one that he particularly liked to repeat was about his trip to Denmark as a member of the delegation to the King's funeral. There, the host assigned to him was a sergeant of the Danish cavalry, and in the evenings they drank together. Since they had no common language, there was nothing else to do. To Sidorovich the great joke of the story was that the Danish sergeant could not begin to compete with him in drinking. In the regiment, however, he drank only after sunset and never got drunk. If he was called up by an officer late in the evening he would first chew some sort of deodorising stuff which smelt of synthetic violets.

During my first year in the regiment, if there was no set programme for a part of the day, I never dared to decide what to practise next without asking the sergeant. Our conversation would run like this: 'Nikolai Ivanovich, what shall I do now?' Sidorovich would stiffen up and report: 'Whatever you wish, Your Honour.' Then, after a moment of silence, he would add: 'I would like to report that we haven't had any sword exercises for quite a while.' 'All right, let us have the swords.' At this point of the conversation, Sidorovich would make an extra effort to stiffen himself and ask, as if surprised: 'Is it your order to have practice with the swords?' Thus the formalities were observed, but he still ruled both the squadron and me.

Morning exercises normally lasted until eleven o'clock. The officers' riding was scheduled almost daily at noon, usually in the covered ring. At one o'clock exercises with the soldiers were resumed and went on until four o'clock. After this the hussars had to clean and feed the horses again, while we officers, about twice a week, attended various lectures and discussions.

The Russian cavalry soldier was armed with a sword, a lance and a rifle; the officer with a sword and a revolver.

The cavalry rifle (not a carbine) was somewhat shorter and lighter than the infantry one, although of the same model. Like all standard rifles of the time, it was bolt action and had a magazine for five shots. When the soldier was mounted it was worn slung across his back; for dismounted action he had a bayonet which was ordinarily carried inserted in brass loops on the scabbard of his sword.

In charge of the regiment's rifles was the master-at-arms, a military clerk, who was supervised by an officer. The latter, Captain Boris Govorov, was a charming man, with a delightful quiet sense of humour, typical of which was a little incident during one of the periodic reports of the 'Host' of the Assembly. The report ran thus: '300 roubles and 63 kopecs were spent on purchasing hors d'œuvres, 1,200 roubles and 45 kopecs on wine, etc.' At one point Govorov rose and in a shy voice asked: 'I beg your pardon, how many kopecs did you say?'

With his calm sensitive character he was a perennial intermediary between the senior and junior officers. All the cornets went to him when in trouble. He never changed his method of soothing upset young officers. He would offer wine to the cornet and sit drinking and listening silently to his complaints. When the cornet had got everything that he had against Groten or Troubetzkoy off his chest and felt more peaceful, Govorov would say: 'Ah, forget it all; it is not with Troubetzkoy, but with good people that you and I will spend our lives. Let me pour you a little more wine.'

Plate 17   Shoeing a horse from the steppes.

Plate 18   Swimming horses at camp.

Plate 19 Gipsy chorus dressed for a gala occasion, Moscow, late 19th century.

He arranged things as well at home as in the barracks. Once, stopping uninvited at his house in Moscow, I was told by the chambermaid that the captain was in the nursery. There I found Govorov sitting on the floor with his two little daughters in front of a large toy kitchen whose stove could actually cook. As I came in the door one girl was saying to the other: 'Liza, bring Papa some vodka from the icebox; the pancakes are ready.' He arranged things as well on the battlefield and had an excellent war record.

Govorov had a brother, Constantine, who had served in the regiment for a few years before I joined it. During the Revolution of 1905 a *provocateur* in one of the squadrons threw a dead mouse into the soup on the stove while the cook was absent for a moment. Constantine Govorov, as the officer on duty, was advised that the hussars were refusing to eat the soup. When he arrived in the squadron he was shown the bowl of soup with the cooked mouse in it. He calmly took the mouse out with his fingers and ate it, fur and all, saying that it was just a piece of meat. Thus, the potential mutiny never got going and the grateful regiment mentioned this episode in its official history. Fifteen years later he was shot by the Bolsheviks.

But to return to the rifles: the study of the handling and operation of a rifle consisted in taking the mechanism apart, cleaning and reassembling it. We had rifle drill and target practice, and had to learn to gauge the distance between the firing line and the target. Our target practice was normally held during the summer. For this we had a special shooting ground in the camp just outside Moscow. Because the war of the following summer was already expected, teaching the new recruits to shoot started in 1914 during very cold January weather. The shooting ground was about an hour and a half away from the barracks. The young soldiers with their officers would leave in the dark and return in the dark. It was only thanks to careful inspection of the men's clothing that frostbite was avoided.

Before the shooting exercises began all our rifles were adjusted to the new sharp-pointed bullet. The adjustment of the peep sight was made by the best shots in the regiment. They stood in a long trench, with rifles braced on stands, and shot at regular round targets. On the basis of inaccuracies thus observed, the master-at-arms shifted the sight in one direction or the other with a hammer, and the rifle was tried again. Finally each hussar received a card with a description of the characteristics of his rifle.

Our sword was excellently designed and of very hard steel. One Saturday shortly before graduating from cavalry school I bought myself an officer's sabre. When not on duty, we officers carried a sabre, which was more curved than the sword and had an all-metal shiny scabbard. It hung on long leather straps faced with gilt, and was attached to a narrow belt worn under the dolman; it trailed on the ground unless carried in the hand. Being only twenty, I naturally could not be satisfied with the ordinary standard blade and wanted to have something more exclusive. The one I bought had a blade of the famous Damascus steel. Returning to my parents' house for dinner, I found my sister's godfather, General Vladimir Kondratiev, there. A very practical man, the general looked at my blade and said: 'Well, let's put it to the test. I have an ordinary Russian blade. Let's strike the swords against each other, and see which one is the harder.' We did so and from then on my blade had a nick in it while his remained unscarred.

Besides teaching our men how to draw the sword and how to sheath it quickly, how to hold it when saluting or when on sentinel duty, we naturally taught them how to use it for fighting. The first lessons in using the sword to kill were given while the men were dismounted. Later, lessons were conducted in the saddle, at slow gaits, eventually increasing the speed to a gallop. During these drills the hussars sliced clay pyramids raised on stands to the height of a dismounted man's head, as well as long twigs set in special holders. If the sword was swung at the correct angle and with the correct strength and timing, the blade would pass through the clay pyramid without toppling the upper part. The pyramid would remain seemingly untouched, and one would only hear the peculiar metallic sound of the whistling blade. As a result of these exercises some of our horses had the tips of their ears cut off.

A colourful example of artistry with cold weapons (swords and lances) took place early in the war. A Cossack corporal, Kruchkov, with two or three other mounted Cossacks, stumbled upon a German cavalry scouting party of twelve men. He immediately gave the order to attack, and the Cossacks accounted for eleven Germans—Kruchkov himself doing most of the killing.

I met Kruchkov at an infantry corps headquarters where he was serving as messenger. He looked just right for what he had done. On the day I was there a popular folk-song singer, Plevitzkaya, dined with the staff and sang during the meal. She was on tour entertaining the troops. She wanted to have her picture taken with Kruchkov, who refused, saying: 'I am a married man and it is not proper for me to be photographed with another woman.'

Our lance was a long, light metal tube with a steel point. At its base there was a small leather loop which went over a man's foot when he was mounted and on the march. There was another large loop attached near the middle of the lance for hanging it on the arm. When at attention this last loop was not used, but the soldier held the lance vertically in his right hand. In preparation for action it was taken off the foot and held inclined at an angle of forty-five degrees by the right hand placed on the thigh. For the charge the lance was switched to a horizontal position. Only half of the men of the squadron—those who would form the first line if the squadron were to open formation in two lines—carried lances. In a charge at full gallop the lances were intended only for the first shock; once they hit (or pierced) the enemy they had to be dropped, otherwise the force of the impact would have dislocated the lancer's shoulder. As soon as he had dropped his lance he drew his sword.

In individual skirmishes without speed, the lance could be used effectively in quite a different manner. It was well balanced and easy to rotate; by doing this rapidly above the head or to either side the soldier was able to parry sword blows and protect both himself and his horse. At slow gaits it could also be used to pierce an enemy who was either on foot or already prostrate, and could be drawn out again. Because I was skilful with the lance I enjoyed teaching and demonstrating this fancy work. I do not remember, however, a single case when the lance was thus used in actual fighting.

During the war, particularly when we were operating in forests, lances were often a nuisance, and at times it was hard to keep the soldiers from abandoning them.

The assertion of some that the lance is a powerful weapon may be argued, but unquestionably it is able to produce a demoralising effect. To see a long row of lowered lances coming towards you at full gallop must be an unpleasant experience. To accustom our infantry (the Germans also had lances) to this, we practised combined exercises, during which the infantry soldiers stood in a single line, about ten feet apart, and we charged in between them. The command for a charge was: 'Swords out, lances for the fight, gallop, march, march.' We could begin a charge from far away at a trot with lances on the thigh, and follow it with a canter, but it was the last command that would start the gallop and unleash the 'hurrah'.

During the winter, while the young soldiers did not yet ride sufficiently well, we practised all formation exercises dismounted, pretending that we were on horseback; these exercises were called 'on foot as if mounted'. Only early in the spring did mounted formation exercises begin. We first practised by platoons, later by squadrons, and finally with the whole regiment.

The commander could give orders for the various changes in the formation of the mounted regiment by voice commands, by certain movements of the drawn sword, or by trumpet signals. There were about twenty of the latter, mostly short, and some resembling each other; one had to have a good ear to learn to distinguish between them. While it was the business of the officers to know them, a familiarity with them was also desirable in the soldiers. The lessons in signals were given in the barracks, with the soldiers sitting on their cots, singing the signals together. The rather stiff official words were hard for our men to memorise, so there was another set of dirty words for some signals, which were both easier to remember and more cheerful. The words in the latter category for the signal to mount, for instance, were: 'The devil got hold of me and I mounted a nun.' This kind of singing directed by an officer was quite a show.

Sitting on the same cots, the soldiers learned the elementary facts concerning the structure of the division, learned who the commanders of the military district, the corps, the division, and the brigade were, what the duties of a sentinel were, and in what discipline consisted, etc. The standard answers which they had to memorise were as follows: 'discipline consists in the precise execution of the orders of a superior', 'a soldier placed at a post with a firearm or drawn cold-arm is called a sentinel', 'a sentinel is an inviolable person'. Such words were not easy for illiterate peasant boys to grasp. They sat on their beds with glassy eyes, and were mentally exhausted at the end of each lesson. In between these lessons given by the officer, the corporals and platoon sergeants conducted their own 100 per cent pragmatic instruction, which aimed primarily at preventing the soldier from doing something absurd while on duty. These two kinds of lessons were sometimes confused in the soldiers' minds. Once a hussar, instead of answering the question, 'What are a sentinel's duties?' with 'The sentinel must vigilantly guard his post and everything committed to his surveillance,' answered: 'The sentinel must not drink, smoke, whistle, or piss.'

In 1912 a special machine-gun troop was formed in our division; it was quartered with our regiment, and its commander was a Sumsky hussar. It had only eight Maxims for four thousand men. Later, during the war, each regiment had its own four machine guns. At the end of 1913, Yazvin, with whom I lived, was transferred from the 1st squadron to this machine-gun troop. Because the name of its commander was Shwed, which in Russian means a Swede, we called the machine-gun troop the Swedish army. Probably just because this 'army' was something new, stories were invented about it. A son was born to Shwed, and he announced the event to his troop by saying: 'There were a hundred and fifty machine gunners and now there are a hundred and fifty-one.' To this someone added that the soldiers replied in unison: 'Glad to do it, Your Honour.'

Early in May we moved to camp. The regiment was stationed in five villages. The 1st Squadron, along with the machine-gun troop, occupied the village of Mnevniki. Unfortunately for me, it was near the Moscow river and one of my senior officers, Ongirski, was a fanatic about physical education. He tortured me every morning by making me join him in running to the river, having a plunge, and running back again, all this almost naked and before breakfast. I simply hated it, and although I could not notice any improvement in my health I did not dare to disobey.

The officers' Assembly was in a village about two miles away; communication between the squadrons was exclusively on horseback. The average distance of these villages from the outskirts of Moscow was about four miles. To go to the city one had to ride a horse to the city limits where one could get a cab, while the orderly took the horse back to camp. But when returning it was easy to find a driver who did not mind going to the country. And it was still country, despite its proximity to Moscow. The rural aspect of part of our territory was spoiled, however, by many summer cottages, whose inhabitants periodically complained that we made too much dust as we passed by. In the villages three or four soldiers were billeted to a house and its barn. In front of each house they set up a tall pole crowned by a framework of twisted straw, from which hung as many tassels as there were horses in the yard.

The day in camp began early. By seven-thirty in the morning our squadrons were already on the march in order to reach the point of assembly by eight o'clock. Then, on the enormous Hodinka field, we practised formation exercises, still by squadrons early in the summer, and later by the regiment. To manipulate with nearly 1,000 horses so that the regiment preserved the aspect of a solid mass while changing gaits, turning and opening and closing formation was not an easy matter. A turn in open formation will give an example: during this the regiment would be drawn up in two lines, with about 450 horses to each line and the command would be given to wheel by the right flank. While executing this, a platoon or two on the left flank would be turning slowly in place, the next platoon towards the right would be moving at a slow walk, the next somewhat faster, the next perhaps trotting, while at least one squadron on the right flank would be galloping at a good clip. In the process of making such a turn it was easy to spread, revealing intervals not merely between individual men but between platoons as well. To avoid gaps both flanks had to exert pressure towards the centre. And if, during the turn, the lines remained beautifully solid it meant that somewhere in the middle soldiers were swearing and horses grunting.

One of the very effective changes of formation that was often used as a demonstration for important visitors consisted in the following: the regiment would begin by galloping in open formation towards the inspecting group. Then, while still quite far away, the order 'Halt and dismount' would be given (two out of every three men dismounted). In a matter of seconds, the advancing dismounted lines, bayonets fixed, would appear from clouds of dust, while in the rear one could see the led horses galloping away. Then in a couple of minutes the trumpet would sound another order, and the horses would be brought back to the dismounted soldiers, who would quickly mount and charge mounted, coming to an abrupt halt before the visitors. It all may sound easy, but it took a lot of drilling.

Whenever a commander of the regiment wanted to speak to the officers, either to explain the next lesson or to give them hell for bad execution of the previous one, his trumpeter would sound a special signal, the words for which were: 'Assemble to discuss the lesson.' When they heard it, the officers would leave the lines at a gallop and ride to the commander.

An exercise that required quick thinking on the part of the commander and quick execution on the part of the ranks was an attack on an unexpected enemy. The targets representing cavalry, infantry, artillery or mixed formations would suddenly appear on one side of the marching column. Groten called them 'puppets'; they were red for infantry and blue for cavalry. According to the type of enemy, the commander had to change the formation of his unit and attack either in solid or dispersed lines.

Before Groten received command of the regiment in 1912, the former commander, Nilov, would always address the formation after its successful performance of the regimental exercises by saying: 'Thank you, lads; a dram of vodka for each.' Later, when vodka was prohibited and beer took its place, he once let his tongue slip and said: 'A bottle of vodka for each.' Everyone smiled, wishing the error were truth. Such gifts were made from the officer's own pocket.

But it was far from always that exercises or even reviews went smoothly. We had particular difficulty in 1912 when some of the commands were changed and dispersed formations added. One such sad episode is described in the official history of the Sumsky Hussars.

'At the end of September 1912, the regiment was assigned to exhibit formation exercises to the United States military mission. On that day the regiment was commanded by Colonel Rachmaninov. Wishing to change the open formation to a platoon column . . . Rachmaninov gave one of the new commands. The results were disastrous . . . fortunately, it happened far away from the Americans. Then Rachmaninov wanted to approach the Americans in open formation and could not succeed in doing so. The regiment was galloping all over the field and always missing the visitors. The latter were mounted on extra-calm old horses who knew everything. One of the Americans, obviously tired of seeing only a cloud of dust, attempted to approach the regiment. Due to bad luck he found himself straight in front of the centre of the regiment which was wheeling . . . the American wanted to turn back, but his horse pulled him towards the other horses. For a while he galloped in the line of officers, then in the first line of the regiment, then in the second, and finally behind the formation.'

On some mornings in camp shooting was practised instead of formation exercises; it started early and the squadrons left their quarters at the crack of dawn.

The afternoon hours were rather easy; the horses were taken to the Moscow river to swim, and some time was devoted to the study of 'field service', such as how to place and conduct advanced posts to protect the regiment during the night. The hussars, pretending that they were at war, lay on the ground, hiding behind bushes, talking, and even napping. It was work only for the officers and non-coms who directed it all. The work was particularly designed for the recent graduates from the regimental non-com. school. At the same time the scouts practised in the field what they had learned in the barracks during the winter. But now, besides putting the standard 'field service regulations' into practice, they learned how to cope resourcefully with various situations. For example: if a small body of the enemy's infantry is expected shortly to pass along a narrow path in the woods and you wish to count them and learn their equipment, you climb a tree above the path. To make sure that no one will look up, you half break two or three saplings, about twenty feet apart, and lean them across the path, thus forcing the men to bend over while walking under them.

Here and there time was wasted studying something that turned out to be impractical in war, such as heliograph communications, which consisted in sending Morse code messages by blinking light off a mirror. Suspecting its impracticality, we did not take it seriously, but some of the generals did. Nevertheless, we did not spend much time teaching the soldiers how to use it. I remember I was once standing beside this apparatus when an inspecting general wrote a message on a piece of paper and asked to have it heliographed to another station not too far away. Our heliograph began to blink immediately, but we did not trust the soldiers' ability to make it work. To make sure there would be no mistake, we had the message copied while the general's back was turned, and a soldier was sent at full speed with it to the receiving station. A few minutes later when it was delivered back to the general he naturally thought it had been a perfect transmission.

While stationed in the villages and off duty, the soldiers led almost the normal life of Russian peasants. Many of them became friends of the families with whom they were quartered and helped them with their work. There were even a few love affairs and, consequently, fights with the local boys. Later in the winter the squadron commanders would occasionally receive letters of complaint from the jilted girls.

In a body of over a thousand men and horses a certain number of accidents or undesirable incidents would naturally occur. The commander, Colonel Groten, was invariably over-upset by them. In May 1914, when we were going to camp, the

Moscow river was in flood and the bridge near the 2nd Squadron's village was practically at water level. The squadron commander, Captain Markov, as a matter of precaution decided to have his men lead the horses across the bridge. One frightened young horse fell into the river. The current quickly pulled him under the bridge and he drowned. Groten was very distressed by this incident. Shortly afterwards, another horse got loose, unsuccessfully jumped a village fence and eviscerated himself with the sharp end of an upright post; this horse was also lost. By now Groten was raving. Before he even had a chance to calm down, an arrested hussar escaped from the guard-house by digging a trench under the wall. At this news, Groten, in despair, wrote a report of resignation and left on leave. While he was away, the Emperor, who had always liked him, decided to make him a *flugel-adjutant*, that is, a member of the Imperial suite. Because of this high honour, Groten did not feel he could possibly resign, so he returned to the regiment. I think the Sumsky Hussars was the only line cavalry regiment of the time commanded by a man who had such a distinction.

At the beginning of July the regiment usually moved to Klementievo, some sixty miles away from Moscow, to take part in the so-called Cavalry Assembly, in which eight cavalry regiments participated. These manœuvres ended yearly with a mounted attack by one group of four regiments against the other four. The exercises lasted for about two weeks, after which the big manœuvres began; these ended with our return to Moscow early in September.

In 1914, in anticipation of war, the Cavalry Assembly was cancelled and instead, on 26 July (from now on all dates will be according to the western calendar), we were ordered to our barracks in Moscow; the pre-mobilisation period had begun.

Horses were re-shod, saddles and bridles inspected, dolmans, shakos and red breeches (we had dark blue ones for war) were stored away. On the other hand, the wartime equipment we were to use was made ready for distribution. The soldiers' chests were labelled with the names of their nearest relatives and also put away. So was the officers' club's and the barracks' furniture, while our silver was taken to the vaults of the State Bank. The six old standards of the regiment were placed in the Historical Museum.

On 28 July, Austria declared war on Serbia. Late in the evening of the 30th, the regiment was informed by a telephone call from the division staff that a messenger with a secret packet was on his way to us. He arrived fifteen minutes later. During this time most of us assembled in the barracks. The packet contained mobilisation orders, the zero hour was midnight. These parted us from our Grenadiers; while we were to proceed to the East Prussian border, they were to move to the Austrian front. Each officer of the regiment received a sealed envelope containing the long-prepared schedule of what he was to do from then on, hour by hour, for the next thirty-six hours, until the regiment left the barracks to board the trains.

The commanders of the squadrons distributed cartridges, first-aid kits, horse blankets, sailcloth pails, hay nets, new horse brushes, extra horseshoes, extra pairs of boots for the men, two extra shirts apiece, and such things. From then on, the regiment had to carry everything that it would need. The saddle and pack together weighed sixty-five pounds.

Among the items distributed were cans of emergency rations; these were to be consumed only in case of extreme hunger. Within an hour, empty cans littered the courtyard. This was probably simply the result of a childish curiosity to taste what was in cans, which the soldiers had never seen before.

Even Cornet Constantine Sokolov, when he noticed the date on the cans—1904—could not resist opening one; he found that it contained soup with a piece of meat in it. Due hell was raised, the eaten rations were replaced, and we forgot about it —there were more important things to attend to. But I remembered this incident a couple of months later, when we picked up a hundred or so Germans belonging to a unit defeated some time before. These men had been by-passed by the Russian infantry and had been hiding in the woods all that time. They were exhausted and hungry, but their emergency rations were still untouched. It was a kind of discipline that did not permit of any human feelings. I preferred commanding our men.

My parents lived in St. Petersburg. There was then a long-distance telephone line between the two cities, but only from a central station. I did not have time to go there, so instead I wrote a short letter about our imminent departure for war. I know that were my parents to have come to Moscow, the farewell would have been quite unemotional. I am certain that neither of them would have told me: 'Be careful.' My going to war sooner or later was expected: this was what I had been trained for; there was nothing extraordinary about it. But I am also certain that they would have said 'Good luck', and 'God preserve you.'

Yazvin and I had no time either to do anything about our apartment. We just walked out of it as if we were leaving it for half an hour. Later, a lady friend of mine kindly had our belongings packed and stored for us.

On the morning of 1 August, the regiment, dressed in fresh, newly issued field uniforms, lined up on our exercise field. After the blessing of the ranks, the commander of the division, General Gourko, said a few words about the coming

war, and then the order: 'First echelon . . .' was given. The
1st Squadron and two platoons of the 2nd, under the command of Colonel Rachmaninov, began to move towards one
of the Moscow railway stations.

Few people came to say goodbye to us, for most of our
relatives, friends and acquaintances were in the country that
hot July. Nor did anyone on the streets, except the usual small
boys, particularly notice the column of the first echelon; there
was nothing unusual in seeing hussars riding in the streets.
The rumours of a possible war, however, quickly made people
realise where we were going, and the next echelons drew some
cheers. The machine-gun unit was halted on one of the streets
by a man with an icon in his hands. He raised it, blessed the
troops with it, and presented it to the commander.

The only ones at the small station to bid us farewell were
Princess Menschikov, Mrs. Govorov and a young girl.

The train consisted of wooden cattle trucks, painted dark
red and bearing the inscription: '40 men, 8 horses'. The '40
men' part was for the infantry, while we placed four horses
at each end of the car facing the centre. The space in between
the two rows of horses was sufficiently large for saddles, equipment, hay, and the eight hussars. The latter could either sit on
the bales or break them open to lie down on the loose hay.
For the officers there was a passenger carriage.

Our horses, who were unaccustomed to being transported in
railway cars, gave us a lot of trouble in loading, and one of the
cornets was kicked in the head and wounded so seriously that
he had to be left behind to spend two months in hospital.

At the station of Rjev, about three hours from Moscow,
every echelon was met by a grey-headed, but still erect, old
man in tears. He was one of our retired sergeant-majors.

By 3 August, when the head echelons were approaching their

destination, the little town of Suvalki, near the German border, proclamations with the declaration of war had already been pasted on walls. War had been declared while we were in transit.

As we were moving towards the border, the local population was beginning to move away from it. Their carts, packed with their most precious or necessary possessions, and their cows and dogs around them, could be seen on all the roads leading toward the interior. This was my first glimpse of a later common sight, war refugees.

The First World War

CHAPTER 8

BAPTISM BY FIRE

THE little town of Suvalki, about twelve miles from the border of East Prussia, was the permanent station of two cavalry regiments. When the 1st Cavalry Division assembled in this town on 6 August these two regiments had already gone to the border. Their barracks were empty, and for the next six days our regiment occupied the excellent quarters of the 2nd Dragoons. Not much happened during these first days and we young officers had plenty of time to become intimately acquainted with a first-class restaurant in the town. Such a thing could exist in this small community only because cavalry was stationed here.

On the 9 August, the commander of the division, General Gourko, ordered a squadron from each of the four regiments to cross the border for a reconnaissance along four different routes. He also expressed the hope that they would be able to blow up some sections of the railroad between the German towns of Markgrabovo and Goldap. The four squadron commanders decided among themselves that the most important thing was to damage the railroad. In order to be strong enough when nearing the track, which they expected to be defended, they disobeyed Gourko's orders and marched together. They did meet with strong resistance, and returned to Suvalki after having neither accomplished the reconnaissance

131

assignment on a wide front nor damaged the railroad. For failure to execute his orders exactly as he gave them Gourko took their commissions away from three of the squadron commanders. The commander of the 4th Squadron of the Sumsky Hussars, Captain Lazarev, was not punished, because he had moved along the road by which he had been ordered to go; the others had joined him. It was with this unfortunate incident that the war action of our division began.

Lazarev, although not punished, was much impressed by Gourko's denunciation of the squadron commanders' actions. We always thought that his death three days later, as the result of an unnecessarily dramatic exposure of himself, had some emotional connection with it. Perhaps he wanted to show Gourko what kind of an officer he was.

On 10 August the individual squadrons of our division began to take turns guarding the border. It was our turn two days later and we moved to the village of Bakalarjevo. A road going through it crossed the border just below the hill on which the village stood. The border was a narrow ditch, winding through pleasant pastoral country. At the spot where the road crossed the ditch there were barriers and the empty houses of the Russian and German border guards. An uprooted pole topped by the German Eagle lay in the grass: obviously Russian scouts had already been in East Prussia. Neat German farms and villages, but little life, could be seen on the other side of the border.

Captain Menschikov ordered the senior cornet of the squadron to take twelve men (the usual size of an officer's scouting party) across the border and find out whether there were German troops in our vicinity. Cornet Snejkov and I asked permission to join the scouts—it all was so new and exciting. The possibility that we might encounter an ambush and three officers could perish unnecessarily did not occur to anyone. The war was not yet real. All three of us felt that at last we were participating in a true adventure. We were like children playing 'hide and go seek', certain (and half-way hoping) we were going to be discovered at any moment. We moved cautiously, as if stalking our prey, ready to pull out our swords or revolvers at the slightest noise.

Our romantic attitude was soon shattered. A quarter of a mile inside Germany all we encountered was a Russian infantry soldier returning unconcernedly to Russian territory with a heavy load of stolen German geese. This brought us back to reality and, after riding rapidly through a couple of villages and several farms without meeting any German troops, we returned to our squadron.

Late the same evening we received a sealed envelope, to be opened at midnight. It contained an order for our participation next day in a move into Germany. All we then learned from this order was that we were to attack; we were not informed that it was to be merely a reconnaissance in force, after which we were to return to Russia. It was only later that we found out about Gourko's plans for this action. He wished to attempt the capture of a German town, Markgrabovo, about seven miles away from our village, just to see how strong the German resistance would be. The operation was simply scouting on a very large scale. Our division in full, plus a regiment of Chasseurs, was assigned for this exploit. The Chasseur line regiments were stationed on the border and were always in a fully mobilised state—as was the cavalry. They were therefore available for action before the regular infantry regiments, which needed time to put the arriving reactivated reservists into the ranks, nearly doubling their size.

Our squadron and two platoons of Chasseurs were given the

THE FIRST WORLD WAR

job of guarding the left flank of our troops, who were to advance on a broad front. We were not to take part in the actual attack on Markgrabovo. We started while it was still dark. As the mounted squadron was about to move off, Captain Menschikov, on his horse at the head of the formation, took off his cap and crossed himself. I was not very religious and not in the habit of doing so myself, but I looked around and saw that all the men were also crossing themselves; just to be on the safe side I did so too.

For more than an hour we moved in complete darkness, our Chasseurs some three hundred yards ahead of us. While we marched in a column along a narrow dirt road, the infantry moved across country in open battle formation. They occasionally varied it, changed direction, halted when alarmed, then resumed their advance; once they annihilated a small German infantry detachment. The signals for these manœuvres were varied bird calls, rather than regular voice commands. The calls sounded strange in the stillness of the night. The performance of these two platoons earned such respect from our men that when we veered further to the left and separated from the Chasseurs some of the hussars became alarmed. 'Have we left them for good? Are we going to join them again?' they whispered.

At the break of day we were fired upon by a small German advance unit. Menschikov ordered me to dismount my platoon and dislodge the Germans. I chose to run part of the way towards the enemy through a small wood. Although they could not see us there, they had probably observed us entering it and they fired at it. Bullets whistled past and struck the tree trunks with the characteristic sound so familiar to us all later on. Never having been on the target end of the shooting ground, I was unfamiliar with it. 'What is it, Your Honour?' asked the corporal who was running by my side. Occupied by other thoughts, I innocently answered: 'I *suppose* they are bullets.' None of my soldiers was hit, and bullets still remained for a while an abstract notion. When we reached the place from where the Germans had fired there was no one there.

This is how I first heard bullets 'singing'. In a popular army joke a soldier was asked whether he had ever heard the whistle of a bullet. 'Twice,' he replied, 'the first time when it passed me, and the second time when I passed it.'

The fact that on this day our squadron did not encounter any German soldiers face to face gave our sergeant-major, Sidoro-vich, the idea that we were not fighting the German army but had merely been fired upon by the 'peaceful population'. True enough, some German civilians did fire at our small units on their own initiative.

Around seven o'clock in the morning our squadron reached the objective for the day, a large German farm on a hill. From it we had an excellent view of the town of Markgrabovo. Our division was moving towards the town, with the main body of the Sumsky regiment on its left flank, nearest our squadron. Since we did not have much to do but send short-distance scouting parties to our left we were only spectators most of the time.

The attack on Markgrabovo started in rolling open country and progressed along narrow strips of land between the numerous lakes that lay in front of the town. These necks of land were the only approaches to it.

Much of what we saw from the hill had the character of the nineteenth-century actions so dramatically painted on the large canvases of the period. At times our dismounted hussars marched as if they were on the exercise ground; two guns of our battery galloped forward to take a position in an open field just behind our firing lines; artillery roared; shrapnel burst; machine guns spat bullets; and still our men marched forward. From where we were it all looked like a war game. It was more beautiful than frightening, and the knowledge that we were witnessing people killing each other penetrated neither my brain nor my heart.

That afternoon a hussar arrived with a message from Groten. As he delivered the envelope with one hand and saluted with the other he spat blood. When asked what was the matter with him, he replied that he was wounded in the chest. This was a shock to us all. 'Is anyone else wounded in the regiment?' asked Menschikov. 'Several, Your Grace—some of the officers too: Lieutenant-Colonel Adamovich is badly wounded and is unconscious; Cornet Horoujinski is dying, and Captain Lazarev was killed outright.' It was only then that I fully realised for the first time since we reached the border that I was in a war and that it would be different from the most realistic manœuvres.

Later we learned what had happened to the regiment on the outskirts of Markgrabovo. Our cavalry division did not have any trouble pushing back the German advance units, and arrived at the lakes well ahead of the infantry. It immediately began the attack. Our regiment advanced with three squadrons, while two squadrons were kept in reserve. Our 4th Squadron was on the very left; and to the right of it was the 6th. My friend Yazvin, with a two-machine-gun unit, was with the latter. Lieutenant-Colonel Adamovich was in command of this group. The 4th Squadron, commanded by Captain Lazarev, attacked via the southern neck, along which ran the road to the town. This was probably why the hussars there met particularly heavy fire. At least on one occasion the squadron was checked by it. Lazarev asked for machine guns, but these were refused by the brigade commander, General Nilov, who preferred to keep them in reserve.

The first officer to be wounded was Adamovich. While on the train *en route* to the border he had said that he was not afraid of death, but of being crippled by a serious wound. This is exactly what happened to him, and he never returned to the regiment.

In order to spur his squadron to move ahead again, Captain Lazarev appeared mounted among his men, who were pinned to the ground by German fire. He made an easy target, and was soon killed while his mare, 'Rogneda', was munching hay from a stack beside which he had halted for a moment. Constantine Sokolov, just a year my senior and my life-long friend, assumed command. He had barely done so when he was advised that Cornet Horoujinski was mortally wounded. The latter had been my 'beast' in the 'Glorious School' and had joined the regiment only three days before.

The town of Markgrabovo was not strongly defended and the Germans evidently did not intend to make an issue of it. They received only one train-load of reinforcements during the battle. They concentrated their fire on the left flank of our regiment, as they did not have enough troops to defend their centre and their other flank. Other regiments of our division soon penetrated the town and, when the infantry finally came up, it entered almost without firing a shot.

Once the mission was accomplished, the order to retreat was given. The returning 4th Squadron found only a few of its horses where it had dismounted. While the men of the 4th had been fighting on the neck, the German artillery had scattered most of their mounts. One of the remaining horses was ridden by a hussar who was holding the moaning and dying Cornet Horoujinski in his arms. Most of the squadron continued its march to the rear on foot. A mile or so farther on the hussars saw the rest of their horses coming to them at a brisk trot. The horses were being led under the command of Rachmaninov, who had been instrumental in reassembling them.

This short and unimportant battle of Markgrabovo was the regimental baptism by fire. We were all depressed by its results. We did not know, of course, that it was only a reconnaissance; and the retreat after the action even seemed to be a defeat. The loss of three officers, two of whom were old friends to many of us, naturally contributed to our low spirits. Both Lazarev and Horoujinski were buried in Suvalki.

During our return to Russia our squadron was on the far right of the formation, and Menschikov sent my platoon still farther to the right to guard our flank. Thus I was moving close to the border and occasionally very near the winding ditch. At one point a few bullets whistled over and shots were heard on our right. Some of my men, pointing to a farm, shouted: 'There they are! There they are!' A couple of figures moved between the buildings. I quickly ordered about twenty men to dismount and we ran towards the farm. The enemy bullets were still flying overhead when I stumbled into a ditch leading in the direction of the farm. I ordered my men to use it for cover. It was only the next day that I realised to my horror that the ditch was probably the border, and that the farm was a few yards from it on the *Russian* side. At that moment I did not have time to think; I was attacking under fire. As we neared the farm the firing ceased, and when we entered it we could find no one. So all we could do was to set fire to it, as our troops had been doing all day long under similar circumstances. The scene on the German side of the border was quite frightening. For miles, farms, haystacks, and barns were burning. Later on, some apologists such as General Gourko tried to explain these fires by attributing them to the Germans, who were supposed to have started them as signals to indicate the advance of our troops. I doubt this, but even if it were so in some cases, I personally know of many others where fires were started by us.

Our burning of the Russian farm was something else though, and two days later I had an unpleasant experience. An adjutant from the staff arrived in the regiment to find out who it was, mounted on black horses, who had set fire to a Russian farm. I had a hard time arguing that my platoon had been fired at from the farm no matter who owned it. For the next few days I looked suspiciously at any ditch.

Another six months of fighting in this area rendered the question of the exact position of the border of no practical interest. Almost every structure on both sides had been destroyed.

CHAPTER 9

THE INVASION OF EAST PRUSSIA

O N 16 August the 1st Cavalry Division again crossed the German border. It had orders to guard the left flank of the 4th infantry corps, which was to start the advance the next day.

The first small town that we went through on entering East Prussia was Marunsken. It had a substantial cheese factory, and in a matter of minutes whole cheeses were hanging from almost every saddle. In the cavalry we were used to all kinds of odours but never before nor later did we smell like this. For our soldiers this was the beginning of luxurious eating that was to last for the next two or three weeks. German sausages, ham, pork, chicken and goose were on the daily menu. Sergeant Sidorovich could not possibly approve of such high living; he was soon predicting that the day would come when we would pay dearly for these pigs and fowl.

On the left flank of the 4th Infantry Corps was a foot regiment commanded by Colonel Komarov. He was an old friend of the family's and, knowing that we would send him a liaison officer, he asked that I be sent. His note arrived a couple of hours too late: Cornet Gukovski, also of the 1st Squadron, was already on his way. This was the first instance of my good luck, which consistently remained with me through the war and later through the Revolution. In a day or two Komarov's regiment was in an unfortunate battle in which it suffered extremely heavy losses. Komarov himself was killed and our Gukovski wounded. His fate could easily have been mine.

About three days later, however, I was sent as liaison officer to an infantry division of the same corps, which was heavily engaged at the town of Gumbinen. I reached it a couple of hours after it had defeated a German infantry division. When I arrived, the Germans were in full retreat and the scene of the battle was quiet. The Red Cross men were walking over it, picking up both Russian and German casualties. They had an easy task finding them. The countryside was littered with dead and wounded. I was told that at one point, when in view of each other and after hours of heavy fire, during which the advancing Russians were getting closer and closer to the Germans, both sides rose, closed ranks and charged, with music and flying colours. This had been a big and bloody battle, involving several divisions on both sides; what I have described here was only a small part of it.

It often happens that one forgets big things and remembers details; two have stuck in my mind. Nearly every mildly wounded German lay on a stretcher smoking a cigar. Although I knew that these were cheap German cigars, they nevertheless represented a standard of living not known in the Russian army. The other little picture still vivid in my memory is of a dead Russian soldier. He was a big man and had been killed before the final charge. He was evidently also a brave man, for he lay considerably ahead of the final firing line of his company. Judging by the large heap of used cartridges that lay by his side, he had remained on the spot for quite a while, probably unable to move forward and thus busy shooting. Since then I have seen and forgotten thousands of dead bodies, but this one I remember as though I saw it only yesterday.

After the defeat at Gumbinen, the Germans began a retreat so as to disengage themselves from the Russian 1st Army, because the Russian 2nd Army was then entering East Prussia from the south; the Germans had to evade the pincers. On the other hand our 1st Army, due to difficulties in transportation of supplies, was unable to pursue them. Once the Russian infantry had halted for a few days, the Germans seized the opportunity to transfer their troops to the southern East Prussian front, where within a week they defeated the 2nd Army. This German victory is commonly known as the Battle of Tannenberg. Meanwhile, only the cavalry of the northern army kept in touch with the screen spread by the German cavalry and fast-moving infantry on bicycles. Behind this screen the main body of the German army was moving south. Constant moving forward to push the German screen back and perpetual reconnaissance on a front of thirty-five miles was keeping our division busy.

Officers' scouting parties of twelve soldiers (there were also corporals' scouting parties composed of six men) usually went out for approximately forty-eight hours. This meant two days without sleep. Often after only twenty-four hours of comparative rest with the regiment, a cornet went scouting again. These scouting parties, or sometimes scouting squadrons, went as far as twenty miles from the regiment. The regiment itself was moving at the same time, and not necessarily along a predetermined route. Nor did the scouting party follow a straight line. Fired at from a wood, one tried to circle it to the right or left, only to be headed off again by another German unit hidden among farm buildings. Scouts frequently felt like chased rabbits. So the scouting usually proceeded in a zigzag fashion. Even with the help of a map it often took a few minutes to orient oneself. Except for a corporal and a couple of trained scouts, the men of the party were ordinary soldiers, who served as messengers.

After collecting a certain amount of information the commander of the scouting party would send a report to the regiment. The messenger was usually illiterate, and there was no use in showing him on the map where we were and where the regiment probably was by then. So he was merely told: 'Take it to the commander of the regiment.' The hour of the messenger's departure was marked on the envelope, as was subsequently his hour of arrival. Surprisingly often he must have ridden as the crow flies. How was this done? What kind of homing-pigeon instinct does a real country lad have?

A big problem in scouting was how to take care of the wounded. The regiment had only one Red Cross wagon, which naturally remained with the main body. The one doctor who served the whole regiment stayed with this wagon. And each squadron had one male trained nurse who remained with the squadron. First-aid kits were all that was available to us for the scouting parties. Even when these were sufficient, there was still the problem of how to deliver the man to our lines. We usually strapped the wounded man to the saddle and dispatched him with another hussar in the direction of the regiment. After this, all one could do was to hope.

It was easier to handle the matter of wounded horses, at least during the early days of the invasion of East Prussia. At that period of the rapid advance of our cavalry much of the country had not yet been evacuated, and German horses at pasture were a common sight. In lucky circumstances one just left a not fatally wounded or a merely lame horse behind and saddled up a German horse. If the latter was of a riding type the exchange might even be advantageous.

During our first week in Germany the regiment passed a

stud farm. It was towards evening, and we soon halted for the night. Groten, thinking of the well-bred horses we had just seen, ordered me to take my platoon and go back to the farm to collect some of them. With thirty men I did not have much trouble in rounding up some thirty or forty animals. With the herd inside and the hussars outside, using the blunt ends of their lances to prevent escapes, we began to move towards the regiment. It was almost dark by then although the western sky still held a little light. Suddenly, on a hill to our right, the silhouettes of German cavalrymen appeared. We knew they were Germans from the fact that we did not see rifles on their backs (these were carried on the saddles) and from the shape of their lances. The German lance, below its point, had a ball to prevent it from penetrating deeply. These balls showed against the light sky. It was a scouting party of ten or fifteen men. I doubt if they, gazing into the dark valley where we were, could distinguish mounted from dismounted horses, and so we must have seemed some seventy strong. My men shouted: 'Germans! Get them!' Before I knew what I was doing I shouted in my turn: 'Hurrah!' and we were off. It was a sort of 'tally ho!' The Germans immediately disappeared and we halted: we could not possibly pursue them in the dark. Our sortie had not lasted two minutes, but in the course of it we had lost half the German horse. I felt quite foolish when it was all over, and when I delivered some fifteen horses to Groten I never mentioned what had happened to the others. Groten gave one of the mares to me. In the parlance of the Russian army she was a gift 'from the grateful population'. She was well bred, with the Trakehner brand, chestnut in colour, four years old and had a nasty disposition. All through the war she carried my personal pack and hence was in the charge of my batman, Kourovski, who simply hated her.

This most inappropriate attempt of mine to charge was probably inspired by what I had heard the day before. It was a story about the first cavalry charge in our division, which occurred in the following manner: a Cossack platoon was returning to its regiment after spending the night in the guard line ahead of the division. A German half-squadron (two platoons) suddenly appeared and opened formation for an attack. The Cossacks were tired and sleepy and, being outnumbered two to one, were not particularly anxious to accept battle. The Germans, on the other hand, knowing their territory and seeing that the Cossacks were heading for a swamp, did not press the attack. They simply followed the Cossacks at a trot, but remained in formation for a charge. When the Cossacks came to the swamp and realised there was no choice, they turned and charged. At that moment the two German platoons were standing in open formation on a hill overlooking the swamp. The Cossacks charged uphill and their horses were down to a slow canter by the time they hit the German line. Just the same, their victory was complete.

Something like fifteen minutes later two Cossacks, who were galloping to their regiment to report the skirmish, passed our squadron on the road and halted to gossip. 'You should go there, to the field. You never saw such a sight; it's strewn with dead Germans and dead horses. None of them escaped.' I became very excited when I heard this, but asked about the Cossack losses. 'Oh, we have only a few men wounded, that's all.' My spirits rose like mercury in a thermometer. If it was as easy as that to charge the Germans I also wanted to do it right away. 'And what about your officers?' somebody asked. 'Officers?' said one of the Cossacks, 'Both officers were killed.' My spirits sank.

Some of this was the usual exaggeration of eye-witnesses.

The Germans left only thirty-seven bodies on the field; so quite a few of them must have escaped, although I presume many were wounded. And the Cossack officers were not killed but only wounded. It was true, however, that the platoon suffered few losses. It was the first on-the-spot story of such action that I had ever heard.

A couple of days later a platoon from our regiment charged mounted into a village occupied by a small infantry unit and chased the latter out. The next day I took part in a similar but totally unsuccessful action. Two squadrons, the 1st and the 6th, commanded by Colonel Rachmaninov, were halted by rifle-fire from a village. Our orders for the day were to proceed with speed, and so Rachmaninov immediately opened formation and charged. The village was strongly occupied, and lively shooting turned us back. The fleeing squadrons veered to the right and galloped across a ploughed field. The shooting was considerably weaker on this side of the village. Cornet Ongirski, who had tortured me in camp with physical education, was wounded at that moment. The sergeant-major (W.O. 1 or 2) of the 6th Squadron was also wounded and fell off his horse near me. I halted and ordered two hussars to halt also and help me. Two of us put the sergeant in the arms of the third man who remained mounted. While we were thus engaged, bullets hit the ground very close to us, raising little puffs of dust. It seemed to me that we were incredibly slow in doing our job, and the few bullets seemed to grow into a storm around us. 'Why was I so stupid as to stop to help the sergeant? I barely know him. What is he to me?' passed through my mind. In reality we were working fast, and in no time we were galloping after our squadrons with the sergeant lying across the saddle. He survived. So did Ongirski. The 1st Squadron had lost Gukovski just a week earlier, and now Ongirski—

146

Menschikov was in a bad mood. Sergeant Sidorovich was repeating: 'Beware of the peaceful population.' As if to substantiate his suspicions, Cornet Budzko, although not in action, was wounded by a shot from a thicket. The regiment lost him for good; he was afterwards sent to Washington, D.C. as an assistant to the military attaché.

About the same time I took part in another exploit under the command of Colonel Rachmaninov. This was blowing up a railroad track. Each squadron had its explosives carried by a pack horse. I was in charge of those of the 1st Squadron. For this particular operation all six packs were assigned, each with an officer and four men. We had no trouble reaching the railway, but we fully expected that we would be fired upon once we were on top of the embankment. While we were still protected by the latter, Rachmaninov gave the following instructions: 'We will scale the embankment, keeping a distance of about 600 feet between our groups. As soon as any one of you has attached the T.N.T. to the rails, and is ready to light the fuse, he will stand up with a handkerchief in his raised hand. I shall be standing up all the time, about in the middle, with my arm raised holding a handkerchief. When I see that all of your handkerchiefs are up, I shall lower mine and then simultaneously you will light the fuses.' It was probably his artistic temperament that made him wish to achieve the dramatic effect of six co-ordinated explosions. Perhaps he also thought it would be safer this way, the chances of being hit by the fragments of an earlier explosion being eliminated. Whatever he had in mind, the plan did not work. The moment our heads were above the protecting ridge the bullets began to whistle; standing up made no sense. We quickly began to light the fuses on our own initiative and scrambled down the embankment. But Rachmaninov stood on the track like a candle for quite a while; why he was not hit I do not know.

It was during this period that a little incident took place where my inefficiency saved the day. At the very beginning of our invasion of East Prussia three large trucks were attached to our division to bring us supplies. For some reason, their service was terminated within the first couple of weeks. One night my platoon stayed at a small farm by the side of the road, as part of a chain of such units guarding the resting division. The three trucks overshot the Russian front line—an easy thing to do, since there was no definite line and the gaps were numerous and large. The drivers soon discovered their mistake and tried to return by a different route. This was the road that my platoon was watching. Late that night a sentinel ran into the house where I was sitting and reported that German armoured cars were coming. In a second I was outside and listening to the rumble of approaching motors. In another, my platoon was down in a firing line and I was trying to figure out the best way to disable an armoured car. Where was its vulnerable spot? At what part should one aim? Not knowing a damned thing about such vehicles, I decided to shoot at the wheels: no wheels, no moving. My platoon sergeant thought my guess made sense, and we ordered the men to shoot just slightly above the ground. When the 'armoured cars' were close enough so that we could almost distinguish the silhouette of the first one, I gave the command: 'Platoon, fire.' Our rifles fired one volley, and from the direction of the trucks I heard a Russian voice shouting: 'Turn round—the Germans are here!' This was followed by every bad word in the Russian vocabulary. Fortunately I had fired low, and no one was hurt.

On 23 August the division approached the town of Anger-burg. It was occupied by German cavalry. The Sumsky

Hussars were in the vanguard. Two of our squadrons attacked the town on foot and pushed the Germans out of it. The 'peaceful population' actually took part in this skirmish, and one hussar was wounded in the face by a shot gun. His face, with blood streaming from the quantity of little holes in it, looked terrifying. When they saw it, the hussars went wild, and several civilians in the town were killed before order could be restored in the squadrons.

Speaking of killing civilians, an unfortunate army staff order was issued about this time. It concerned Germans on bicycles. There was no question that many of them actually were spies, but the order was so worded that any man on a bicycle might be considered such. Furthermore, the text of the order could be interpreted so that every Russian soldier on his own had the right to kill a cyclist. Many murders were thus committed. I once overheard one of my hussars telling another: 'I shot him; he fell down and his legs jerked for a while as if he was kicking his boots off.' Many officers protested against this order; perhaps their protests played a part in its early cancellation or revision, I do not remember which it was.

After the fight for Angerburg was over, Colonel Rachmaninov was walking down a street and saw at a distance a crowd of hussars standing in front of a shop. As Rachmaninov approached they ran away. Obviously something was going on. The door had been broken in and everything was topsy-turvy. The place was being looted. As Rachmaninov entered he heard voices below; he walked to the head of the stairs leading to the cellar and, swearing loudly, ordered the thieves to come up. The first to appear was the commander of our brigade, who asked in a mild tone: 'Now, why do you use such foul language, Colonel?'

Later, Rachmaninov discovered a huge rusty key and tried

to convince everyone that it was the key to the town. Although we were sceptical about this, he saved the key for our museum; he was always a diligent curator.

Like every army under the sun, we looted and destroyed, and later hated to admit it. Once, upon entering an empty house in a small German town, I saw one of the hussars of my platoon sitting at a piano ripping the keys out. This was not easy to do and required force, which my soldier methodically applied. I called him by name; he jumped up and stood at attention. 'Why are you destroying the piano?' He looked at me as if I were asking a foolish question. 'It's German,' was his reply. My friend, Cornet Constantine Sokolov, once witnessed one of our men systematically smashing gramophone records, one after another. His reason was: 'There are no needles to play them.'

In the meantime, the German screen was withdrawing rapidly; we followed at an equal pace, always hanging on their heels. For instance, on 25 August the division moved ahead seventeen miles. On the previous day Cornet Georgiadi had been wounded while on a scouting mission. He, like the killed Horoujinski, had joined the regiment in Suvalki; his luck had held only ten days longer.

Advancing rapidly, we sometimes passed villages and small towns where life was almost normal. Once, my scouting party cut right across a long narrow one-street village. When I reached this main street I halted on a corner because another scouting party of ours was to cross it farther on our left and I wanted to line up with it before proceeding further. The party was already there and a woman ran from it towards us in a panic, shouting to me in German and addressing me as 'Herr Leutnant'. Pointing behind her she cried: 'Kosaken, Kosaken!' Then she looked at me, looked at my men, raised her arms in terror, and ran away. Evidently a German cavalry unit had stood in our place on this very corner a few minutes before.

On 27 August the division, with Uhlans in the van-guard, successfully fought German infantry and captured a strategic railroad junction, Korshen. The order was given to blow up the station. I took part in this picnic. Soon wine was discovered in the station warehouse and another kind of picnic took place.

Next day we resumed our advance and, if all went well, we were to spend that night in a little town called Santopen, in the vicinity of which the Germans were not expected to be. The division was marching in a column along the road as it approached the town. The Hussars were in the vanguard. A mile or so to the right and to the left of the column each regiment had a platoon guarding its flanks. Snejkov was on the right of our regiment and I on the left. About a quarter of a mile in my rear was a platoon of Cossacks. At one point I heard shots behind me just where the Cossack platoon should have been. I decided to go back to see if they needed help, and sent a messenger to inform the regiment about it. The dismounted Cossacks were firing in a leisurely manner at two farms on a crest, several hundred yards apart. A few bullets came from them towards us. In the meantime another Cossack platoon arrived. Altogether we had at least seventy-five men. Once in a while a German horseman or two would gallop between the farms. Obviously they were occupied by cavalry. We decided that at most that one squadron could be hidden behind the buildings, only twice as many men as we had. The Cossacks, from the personal experience of a few days before, argued that this ratio was of no importance, and so we decided to charge, which was none of our business. We were there to report, or even to hold back the enemy; we were not there to take the initiative, but the situation looked too tempting. It never occurred to us that besides the cavalry there might be infantry. And it was there, in force, supported by artillery. As a matter of fact, this was the head of a substantial German column, one and a half miles long, as our scouts soon afterwards reported to Gourko.

It took us just a second to make the plan of attack. One of the Cossack platoons was to go against the right farm, the other against the left, and I in between. Because the distance was considerable and uphill, we decided to go at a trot as far as possible. So we mounted, opened a dispersed formation (about ten to twenty feet between soldiers strung in a line) and trotted up the hill. The Germans increased their fire somewhat—just enough to make us suspicious that perhaps there were more troops around the farms than we had calculated. On our run to the farms we had to cross two or three minor rises; we halted behind one of these to confer. At the same time, we dismounted and opened fire. The German fire diminished again. Later, I realised that they were playing cat-and-mouse with us. The diminished shooting made us believe that they were weak and that we, excited when starting the charge, had heard what did not exist. Wishful thinking can even operate in circumstances such as these. We thought: 'Now we are much closer to the farms and we can start moving at a canter and change to a gallop in short order. In two or three minutes we will be there.' We remounted and moved ahead.

The lookouts galloped in pairs on the right and left of our line and ahead of it. Suddenly, the left pair turned back shouting 'Infantry!'; they had seen German foot soldiers. They swung their rifles from their shoulders, dropped their reins, fired at the farms, shouted 'Infantry!' again in our direction, and again fired. Before they had fired more than twice the Germans stopped pretending, and pandemonium broke loose. Machine guns opened fire with the riflemen, and shrapnel began to burst above our heads. We had not expected anything like this. The surprise was overwhelming, and all three platoons turned back. How I turned I do not remember. This was the only instance when I experienced such a complete black-out: I was in a panic. Surprisingly, my platoon did not suffer much, but I don't know about the Cossacks.

While we were still trotting towards the farms, our regiment was entering Santopen and as it reached the square before the church shells began to burst near it. This was while we were running back in panic. The Germans had opened fire simultaneously at our three platoons and at the main column. A few people stood in front of the church. Groten, upset by the accuracy of the shelling, asked these people in German whether there was an observer in the belfry. They all swore that there was no one up there. But the German artillery continued to be accurate and Groten continued to be suspicious. Disregarding the assertion of the Germans that there was no one in the tower, he ordered his trumpeter, Bondarovich, to go up in it. Bondarovich went up while the Germans were still protesting that nobody was there. Then a shot was heard from above. Obviously, Bondarovich had found someone. Groten completely lost his temper and shouted: 'They are all spies, shoot them!' In a moment they were all dead. Bondarovich came down to report that he had not found anyone. 'Then what was the shot about?' asked Groten, pale. 'I had a cartridge in the barrel, and the trigger of my rifle is touchy; it caught on something while I was climbing the belfry,' answered the trumpeter.

The presence of German forces in this region was completely

unexpected, and the staff of our division refused to believe in their existence. For a while Gourko was certain that the firing artillery was Russian. He called the trumpeters and ordered them to play a signal, 'Halt the action'. It was played; the bugle sounds died away but shells continued to burst. Then Gourko sent an officer to this supposedly Russian battery with an order to stop the foolish firing. The officer galloped off and soon found himself being shot at. He returned with the surprising news that he had seen German helmets. After this, the division deployed for battle, and our artillery opened fire. The Germans did not accept the challenge, but retreated.

In the meantime my fleeing platoon, in complete disorder and spread over a considerable front, reached the wood where, still dumbfounded, we lost each other for a while. I walked through the narrow strip of forest and found myself all alone in a field overlooking Santopen. Knowing that sooner or later my men would emerge from the same neck of the wood, I dismounted and sat on a large boulder to wait for them. My horse was winded and needed a rest. German shells were flying overhead towards my regiment. A few minutes later our battery began to answer. A scouting party of one of our regiments trotted past me. The officer looked at me in surprise and asked: 'What are you doing here alone? There are German cavalry scouts in the vicinity.' My horse's condition was such that for the next few minutes at least I could not possibly escape mounted men. I decided to commit suicide rather than be captured. I pulled out my revolver, and, holding it in one hand and the reins in the other, remained sitting on the stone. Soon a couple of my soldiers approached me with bashful smiles. As bashfully, I said to them: 'Glad to see you alive.' Then more and more of my men rode out of different sections of the wood. Gradually, almost the entire platoon assembled:

we had only two or three wounded. Several little valleys between the ridges we had crossed had probably saved us. We walked towards the regiment. Behind me a conversation began, at first in low voices, but soon turning into a heated argument. 'Why did we run?' 'I turned when I saw a couple of other fellows turning,' said one hussar. 'Ah, shut up!' several men stopped him. 'We all turned, and the Cossacks turned, and "his honour" turned, and we all turned at once,' my soldiers were saying, interrupting each other. 'If it had only been a matter of fighting cavalry we would have got there and laid them flat, but infantry is another story.' This was both a good excuse and a fact.

This Santopen episode was satirically described in verse which fitted the music of a popular polka. Occasionally, after a few drinks, we enjoyed singing it together. The author was a private, Wilenkin, who, later on in the war, in the same polka rhythm, humorously commemorated some of our other experiences. Here is an approximate translation of the beginning of the song about Santopen:

> 'Grey from dusty going,
> We were sore and weary
> And we longed only for sleep.
> From behind the haystacks
> Rose the town, Santopen,
> And its beds in which to creep.
> We dream of curtained windows;
> Quickly, quartermasters,
> Set our lodgings for the night.
> Surprised on a sudden
> By heavy shells exploding,
> Shrapnel bursting left and right . . .'

You have to take my word that these verses were much better in the Russian original.

The author, Alexander Wilenkin, was a Moscow lawyer, and had served his military term in the regiment. He was in his thirties and a very cultivated man; many of us knew him socially. The moment war was declared he volunteered, and arrived in our regiment as a private. The fact that he was Jewish complicated the situation, for a Jew could not be even a non-commissioned officer in the Russian army of the time. This is where the independent and extremely *non-bourgeois* spirit of the regiment manifested itself. It was decided that he would be given the post of permanent messenger to the commander of the regiment, and would live and eat with us officers.

He behaved very bravely and had more decorations than any other soldier in the regiment—seven out of a possible eight. The eighth he also earned several times over but was told that he would not receive it because of his privileged treatment. His bravery was not based on a lack of imagination, as the bravery of my orderly, Kaurkhin, was. It also differed from the bravery of Groten, which was founded on fatalism and faith. The basis of Wilenkin's bravery was great will power. He would take big chances, although pale and biting his lips. When doing this he usually posed; he was a romantic and a poet. For instance, once the dismounted regiment was about to come out of a forest; the Germans knew what to expect and were shelling the edge of the wood. Colonel Groten was there, weighing the pros and cons for the regiment's advance. His adjutant, Snejkov, I as the regimental Communications Commander and Wilenkin as messenger stood by his side. The shrapnel and shells burst in volleys every half-minute or so and right above our heads; the bullets and fragments flew into the forest. It was not pleasant, but Groten, looking through his binoculars, was unperturbed. Wilenkin saw an opportunity to display his sang-froid. He felt in his pocket for a bar of chocolate and, just as the next volley of shrapnel burst, quickly took it out and offered it, asking: 'Colonel, would you like a piece of chocolate?' Groten, still looking through his binoculars, simply replied: 'Go to hell.' He did not have to act a part.

Wilenkin's will power was such that even when he was wounded and sitting on a fallen tree being bandaged, he wrote verses about how he had been hit.

Bravery was thus described in one of the army's old stories: 'Everyone runs in battle, but the direction in which one runs makes the difference between a hero and a coward.'

CHAPTER 10

THE RAID AND THE RETREAT

THE state of our division after two weeks of constant moving, skirmishing and reconnoitring is best described in a recorded telephone conversation between the staff of the front and our 1st Army. To the question: 'Where is the cavalry?' the staff commander of our army answered: 'I have precise information that Gourko spent the night at Henrichsdorf. The cavalry is exhausted, and if we do not pull it out we may lose it.'

This conversation took place a few hours before three regiments of our division were to start on a raid through the German rear; it was to last sixty-three hours.

The purpose of the raid was to penetrate into the region of the town of Allenstein in order to establish contact between two Russian armies, the northern and the southern. There was a gap of about fifty miles between them, and their commanders had not even had day-by-day information of each other's progress. So while the staff of the 1st Army (the northern) believed on August 30th that the 2nd Army (the southern) had advanced approximately as far as Allenstein, in actuality the latter had suffered total defeat the day before. Its commander, General Samsonov, had committed suicide during the night of 29–30 August. Any Russians in Allenstein were prisoners. But if the 2nd Army was still fighting, as we assumed it was, then our appearance in the German rear could be helpful.

Three or four cavalry divisions were to proceed to Allenstein. The orders for the raid were received by Gourko on the afternoon of August 30th, twenty-four hours after all was over in the south. In the course of the next twelve hours or so, information was received by the 1st Army staff of the defeat of the 2nd Army, and the raid was cancelled. The cancellation order never reached our particular division, as we had left a couple of hours earlier. Attempts to send messengers after us to halt us were unsuccessful. By that time it was daylight and none of them could get to the German rear.

For the raid, Gourko had at his disposal only three regiments; the Dragoons were away on a special mission. About two and a half squadrons of the three remaining regiments were also away on reconnaissance. This left Gourko with fifteen and a half squadrons (which had already suffered substantial losses), six machine guns and a battery of six three-inch guns.

To reach Allenstein we had to break through the German screen in front of us and penetrate about forty miles behind it. Many small scouting parties were sent out to find gaps in the German lines. An unguarded road through a forest was soon discovered. At 4 a.m. on 31 August the three regiments began the raid. Without firing a single shot we pushed through to the German rear. Shortly afterwards, however, we were checked by German infantry guarding a railroad that we had to cross. The dismounted vanguard quickly dispersed the Germans and we resumed our march. Blowing up railways and cutting telegraph and telephone wires *en route*, we approached Allenstein at about noon. The town could already be clearly seen, when strong German opposition forced Gourko to deploy all his regiments. This was unexpected: instead of making contact with Russian forces we were now fighting German ones. Half an hour or so earlier we had been ordered to get in touch with a Russian Hussar regiment mounted on grey horses. This regiment was supposed to be in the vicinity. Men in pairs were sent in various directions to look for these grey horses. They all reported that there were plenty of German cavalry units all round us, but no grey horses. There was much swearing, and they were all called fools and sent out again to find the Russian hussars. The latter could not be found. We learned later this regiment had never even started on the raid. Bit by bit the suspicion that we were all alone crept into my head.

The 1st Squadron was ordered to protect our battery. The battery took up a position and we, with drawn swords, opened formation behind their left flank. Menschikov was not certain that this was the way to guard artillery, but none of us junior officers had any better idea. Soon afterwards we were happy that we had not dismounted. Our guns opened fire and for a few minutes they shot undisturbed by the Germans. Then, a single shell burst, at a safe distance, but directly in front of us. Our hussars laughed heartily at the poor German marksmanship. The reaction of the battery, however, was different, and the commander gave the order to bring its horses back. In another minute another shell flew over our heads, to burst far behind us. This drew more laughing and joking from our ranks. The artillerymen, on the other hand, knew that the Germans had got our range, and now many men in the battery were anxiously looking in the direction from which the horses would come, firing rapidly at the same time. The horses galloped to their guns. With great skill and seemingly without halting their horses, the artillerymen hooked the guns to the limbers and pulled away. This was the spectacular result of endless drills. We galloped behind them; a minute later, the place where we had stood was virtually ploughed by the bursting shells of a couple of enemy batteries.

At that moment the rear of the powerful German army that had defeated Samsonov's army was in the region of Allenstein. There was no scarcity of German infantry in the vicinity, and arriving reserves constantly pushed us back. One by one, the dismounted lines of our three regiments disengaged themselves and retreated towards their horses. After changing its position once or twice our battery eventually drove to the gradually mounting regiments. At about three o'clock in the afternoon the regiments were completely mounted and, with the battery in the middle, stood in a thick rectangular reserve column. We stopped fighting and were ready to make our escape.

The advancing German infantry was now out of the woods and moving across the field where we stood. They stopped firing at us. They were probably confident that our small force, virtually surrounded and deep in the rear, had no choice but to surrender. I imagine they already considered us their prisoners. There were a couple of minutes of complete silence. Then Gourko galloped forward and, as if on parade, gave the command: 'The division, from the right, by regiments, at regimental distances, forward, walk, march,' and pointed east with his sword to indicate the direction. The thick column moved forward; almost immediately orders to trot, and then to canter, were given.

Taken by surprise, the Germans still did not fire, while some of their soldiers who happened to be in the line of our advance ran aside. When the Germans realised that we were escaping and finally opened fire, it was too late; our regiments were already entering the woods, and only the hussars, who were in the rear, suffered minor losses.

Perhaps we would have failed in this escape if we had not blown up the railway tracks leading to Allenstein. Our scouts reported that a train bringing German infantry to our rear had been stopped by the damaged track and turned back. Why the infantry did not simply detrain and continue on foot is one of those things for which I have no answer.

In about two hours we came to a river which had a boggy bottom and could not be forded. The only means of crossing it was a narrow dam, and we needed time to get across. While the Uhlans and the Cossacks were slowly getting to the other side of the river, the Hussars held back the pursuing Germans. The last platoon to cross the river blew up the dam. For a while the Germans lost us.

It was getting dark and because there were no Germans in our immediate vicinity, Gourko took the opportunity to rest his men and horses. The respite could not be long, for the Germans were hunting us. A prolonged halt would surely have resulted in our being surrounded. And so in two hours we were moving again. At one point the Germans were expecting us and had illuminated the road with searchlights.

Our division halted in the woods and scouts were sent to search the area. They soon reported that there were ravines ahead that could not be negotiated by the artillery. Gourko then told the assembled senior officers that, although the regiments could negotiate the terrain, the guns would have to be left behind. 'Let's not leave them,' was the unanimous answer. 'We'll carry them over by hand.'

While this conference was going on, the squadron commanders made a big mistake: they let their men dismount. They all fell to the ground exhausted, and immediately went to sleep. When the order to move was given we had a hard time waking the unconscious men. As soon as they staggered to their feet and we began the trek across country, we ran into deep ditches and steep ravines. Crossing each of them meant a prolonged halt, and only those squadrons that were to help the artillery carry the guns were allowed to dismount; the rest of our men remained in their saddles fast asleep, with their faces buried in their horses' manes. Under such conditions our progress was very slow; we covered only five and a half miles in three hours. The Germans, knowing the terrain, did not expect us to take this route, and for the time being lost us again. We kept moving all night.

By nine o'clock in the morning a light rain was falling. Gourko, hoping that we had really shaken off the pursuing Germans, ordered the regiments to halt and unsaddle. The moment the saddles were on the ground, our scouts reported that a considerable German force, composed of cavalry, infantry and artillery was approaching us. On went the saddles, and the tired division moved off again. Since our regiment was the rear-guard, it had to delay the Germans for a few minutes, and during these minutes we faced heavy fire. The habitually brave Gourko chose to remain with us, as he always got himself into the hottest spots he could find. At last we broke off the action and rode to join our other regiments. Before we had covered a mile, more German firing lines appeared on the crests overlooking the road. The Germans had evidently prepared a pincer action. The regiment opened in dispersed formation for a charge against the German infantry, but the mild rain turned miraculously into a blinding cloudburst which completely hid us from the enemy. Behind this curtain we turned back and disappeared into the woods to join our Uhlans and Cossacks. Luck was again on our side.

On the evening of September 1st it seemed as though the Germans had really lost us, and Gourko decided to rest his regiments. We certainly needed it. During the last thirty-nine hours the division as a whole had travelled something like seventy-five miles. The scouts and lookouts had covered much more ground and a good half of the horses had by now taken part in these activities. We had also been in several skirmishes and one short battle at Allenstein. Both men and horses were dead on their feet. Our horses carried an average weight of 225 pounds.

Early the next morning we had to chase away some German cavalry scouts. Once discovered, we moved on again; we were still quite a distance from our infantry lines. We finally reached them that evening.

In the meantime, the Germans were still hunting us; some cavalry and small units of infantry appeared here and there; the word 'surrounded' was heard from time to time. Once, hesitant about which route to take, the division stopped for a few minutes. While the commanders discussed the problem, our squadron dismounted and Menschikov and his officers sat down and leant against the trees. Suddenly two Cossacks galloped by and, as they passed us, shouted: 'We are surrounded!' Being surrounded again and again was getting on our nerves. None of us said anything, but Menschikov, noticing the depression in our faces, remarked: 'You know, perhaps at this very moment the Germans are in still worse trouble.' At that instant nothing could have cheered me up more than the thought that somebody else was worse off than I was.

That afternoon, Snejkov, with whom I had been riding for a few hours, said to me: 'I'll give three roubles to the first Russian infantryman that we meet.' Infantry meant security to us. Right behind each foot soldier there were thousands of others; with them one felt safe. Even comparative security may seem to be complete after one has been hunted like an animal.

Towards evening we saw a bearded soldier with a rifle sitting under a tree by the side of the road. Snejkov rode up to him and gave him three roubles. 'What for, Your Honour?' asked the soldier. 'Just because I'm damned glad to see you,' said Snejkov. The hussars behind us laughed.

Sixty-three hours had elapsed since we started the raid. The heaviest losses had been sustained by our Uhlans, who also lost two or three officers; we had not lost any. After the raid we had several days' rest, during which we received men and horses to replace our losses. We also received our first mail in three weeks.

Our replacements in men and horses were supplied by the 7th Reserve Regiment, stationed in Tambov. It took care of nine regiments, and during the war it was enormous: thirty-six squadrons, that is, six full regiments. The size of the reserve squadrons periodically sent to us depended upon our needs. For instance, the fourth replacement squadron we received had one hundred men, one hundred and fifty horses, and sixty saddles. In the course of the war we received a total of six reserve squadrons, the equivalent of a full regiment. These men and horses were distributed throughout the regiment.

There was a rumour that for the raid on Allenstein Gourko wanted to recommend the regiment as a unit for a decoration, and that we were to choose one ourselves. The choice would have to be imaginative, for the regiment had all the standard decorations. Someone proposed to ask for a *mentik* for distinction. A *mentik* was the hussar's second jacket, similar to the dolman but often of a different colour. At times it was worn like the dolman, but on special occasions it hung over one shoulder, on top of the dolman. Certain hussar regiments still possessed it in my day, and the Sumsky Hussars had had it until the middle of the nineteenth century. To this proposal of a *mentik* everyone agreed, but then the question of the colour arose. Tastes differ, however, and by evening the best of friends were no longer speaking to each other. Peace was restored by the suggestion that we ask for the *mentik* we had worn during the Napoleonic wars. This was grey with a red lining and its motto was: 'The colour of steel with the enemy's blood on it.' The rumour was only wishful thinking, and it is hard to see why we thought that a decoration might be forthcoming for this raid, during which we had accomplished nothing.

On September 8th, the German army that had defeated the Russians at the battle of Tannenberg turned north and began an attack on our 1st Army. A day or two before this, our cavalry division was ordered to proceed to the newly formed 10th Army, which was short of cavalry. We began to move towards it and were looking forward to a few days of peaceful travelling behind our infantry lines. In a matter of hours, however, Gourko was advised that the 43rd Infantry Division was having a hard time holding the Germans back. We made an extra night's march and on the morning of September 9th were already guarding the left flank of the distressed infantry. The Dragoons were the first to dismount and join the infantry in the firing line. Later, our squadron joined them, too, taking up a position on the left flank.

A little way behind our squadron stood an infantry battery of eight three-inch guns. For a while, fighting took place only on our right and we were left in peace. Forgetting the traditions of the 'Glorious School', I amused myself by hanging around the battery. The battery was firing, and I was intrigued by the mechanics of shooting and by the efficiency of its commander. Soon the German artillery began to search for this battery. At one point the Germans evidently thought that they had got the range and they opened a heavy fire against a point some 400 yards away. The commander of our battery quickly seized this opportunity to fool the Germans and ordered: 'Three guns out!' Three guns became silent, while the others continued a brisk fire. The Germans, who evidently fell into the trap and believed that the three guns were damaged, enthusiastically continued to pound the wrong spot. In a couple of minutes the commander of our battery silenced another two guns, then another two, and finally left only one active. This fired only once every minute or so. On the German side the impression was probably complete that the battery had been destroyed and that, although one gun was still in firing condition, the remaining disorganised gunners could no longer operate it efficiently.

Before all this had happened I was called back to the squadron because our scouts reported a concentration opposite us of both German cavalry and infantry. An attack aimed at turning our flank was expected. True enough, ten minutes had not elapsed since our battery was supposedly silenced when two German squadrons, riding in dispersed formation, appeared on the field in front of us. Probably unaware of our presence, they intended to capture the remains of the destroyed battery. For quite a while we held our fire; when we finally opened it the Germans ran, leaving scores of men and horses on the ground. Almost immediately, however, German infantry lines began to march against our position. Then it was that the 'dead' infantry battery came to life and, helped by one of our own and by our rifles, forced the Germans to pull back in a hurry. I don't like to remember the cases when we had to fire at mounted cavalry; the suffering of innocent animals dragged into human conflict is not a pleasant sight.

This skirmish was merely an insignificant action during a big German push. That night, our infantry received the order to retreat (along with the whole army) and Gourko decided to resume his march to join the 10th Army. But we were halted again because of a gap which developed between two large groups of Russian infantry. We filled this gap and proceeded to retreat with them.

Once during this retreat our division needed a little time to cross a small river. Our 1st Squadron was sent to hold back the German cavalry, which was on our heels. Menschikov sent one platoon ahead and to the left, and proceeded with the remaining three platoons along the road towards the enemy. Soon our scouts reported that a German squadron without lookouts was coming towards us at a trot. Hurriedly, we dismounted on both sides of the road, and our firing lines placed themselves just below the crest of a low hill which the road crossed. Only two men, the range-finders, had their heads above the crest. In low voices they were guessing the constantly diminishing distance between us and the approaching Germans. The distance was getting shorter and shorter and the Germans still rode on to their destruction. When they were quite near, Menschikov rose heavily, took two or three steps towards the crest, and saw them. He took off his cap, crossed himself, and quite informally ordered: 'With God's help, lads, begin.' The hussars rose up, and some standing, others on one knee, opened a running fire. They could hardly miss, and in a matter of minutes many dead and wounded men and horses covered the ground, while the lucky ones fled.

We mounted, went forward, and soon saw another German squadron in the distance. Undoubtedly they saw us, too. The

Germans were still far away, but we assumed the formation for a charge and moved towards them at a trot. In a matter of seconds Menschikov ordered 'Canter', the German squadron turned round and disappeared, and we halted. A minute later we were under heavy fire, probably from the infantry which often followed the German cavalry on bicycles. It was our turn to run away. We galloped back, and in no time found ourselves rather safe behind one of the many ridges of the countryside. We had only one or two wounded; the German aim had not been too accurate. We dismounted again and kept on exchanging fire with the Germans until they brought up a battery. This was when Menschikov looked at his watch and said: 'That's enough. The division must have crossed the river by now.' We mounted and rode away; the Germans did not pursue us.

Riding back to the regiment I was elated. Our squadron had probably delayed a whole German cavalry regiment supported by small units of infantry and a battery. We had inflicted heavy losses on one squadron and made another flee from our impending charge: I could see myself receiving my first war decoration. My dreams were interrupted by an order passed along our column: 'Officers, ride to the commander.' When we were alongside Menschikov, he told us: 'Don't say anything in the regiment about this skirmish. Don't make them think we are brave. If they believe we are, they will keep sending us to the worst spots.' Thus I missed my first opportunity to receive a military cross.

The ease or difficulty with which one received a decoration depended a great deal on the attitude of the commander of the regiment who recommended the officer for this distinction. Some liked to see their officers' chests covered with crosses. Others, like Groten, did not put much value on them. 'Excuse me,' he would say, 'but the best that could happen to you would be not to get one of those big white crosses.' He was referring of course to the crosses on graves. For the battle of Lasdenen he himself received a very high decoration, a sword with the St. George insignia on it. Some thirty years later, when he was a refugee in France, he was asked by the organisation of 'The Cavaliers of the Order of St. George', who were trying to reconstruct the annals of the order, for what deed he had received his decoration. 'Excuse me,' Groten answered in a letter, 'but I myself don't know.'

A day or two later our retreating division, with the Hussars in the rear-guard again, crossed a small river, and I was left behind with a few men to blow up the bridge. It was a wooden bridge of complicated construction in which beams crossed and re-crossed each other. In the 'School' we had studied the various structures of bridges and had been taught their weak points. With this bridge in front of me I was sorry that I had not been a better student. I looked at the bridge in dismay. I did not have any idea where to attach my charge. The first explosion made splinters fly in all directions, but the bridge stood intact. By the time I was attaching the second one the Germans were already running towards the bridge and shooting at me, which did not help my thinking. Again tremendous noise and more splinters, but the bridge stood firm. I did not have time for more tries, and while I was galloping away the German infantry crossed the bridge.

All this happened not far away from the German town of Markgrabovo, the site of our baptism by fire. Next day we recrossed the Russian border and the hard-surfaced German road abruptly turned into a dirt one. 'In Russia, hard roads are sandy,' a hussar in the ranks behind me remarked with good-natured sarcasm.

CHAPTER 11

REOCCUPATION OF EAST PRUSSIA

OUR 1st Army was unable to withstand the German September attack and after almost a month of fighting on German soil we retreated to Russia. There, not far from the border, after another couple of weeks of constant battles, a strong Russian counter-attack developed and forced the Germans to retreat in their turn. At the beginning of October our regiment was again facing Markgrabovo. We now stayed in East Prussia until about the middle of February, when we were pushed out of Germany for good.

During this time much of the fighting was similar to that which we had previously experienced, but here and there episodes or situations stand out.

As usual, we did a great deal of scouting and two of our reconnaissances were outstanding. In command of one of them was Cornet Ivanov, a sombre fellow who said little but who was stubborn and brave. In a forest in the German rear he discovered a very large enemy column moving along the main road towards the front. He hid his horses and men in the thicket and then crawled so close to the road that he could hear the Germans talking. Lying there for many hours, he made notes on all the passing troops. The first two hussars whom he sent with a report to the divisional staff stumbled upon another German column which was also moving toward the Russian lines. One of the hussars remained to watch the column, while the other galloped back with this information to Ivanov. Ivanov then sent his corporal to observe this second column while he himself continued to collect data about the first one. Late in the evening the reports concerning both columns reached the staff of the division and were immediately telegraphed to the army staff. This was not only important information, but it was the first news of the impending German push. Going out with a scouting party next morning, I encountered the returning Ivanov somewhere in no-man's land. He looked exhausted but pleased and, as usual, said little.

The other brilliant reconnaissance was made by Cornet Poliakov. He was the first to advise the staff of an infantry corps that, contrary to the general belief, the Germans were retreating. A captain of this staff wrote about the episode: '. . . Cornet Poliakov came to the staff with his scouting party. He reported that on the previous day he had been in the German rear and had seen Germans pulling back. . . . He could hardly stand on his feet, and told me that he had not eaten for three days. I took him by the arm, gave him a chair, ordered tea, and began to read his notes. In these, with exceptional clarity he had put down his observations, hour by hour. . . .' It was Poliakov whose purchase of a dog, if you remember, I helped celebrate at the Yar.

Such successful reconnaissances led some generals to expect the impossible. Cornet Constantine Sokolov was once called to the divisional staff and ordered to proceed through the German rear to the town of Insterburg to find out how strong the German forces there were. Luckily, General Nilov was present and he inquired: 'And how is he to obtain this information? Is he to ask the commander of the town for it?' The reconnaissance was cancelled.

Soon after our first retreat into Russia a small Russian fortress, Ossovetz, was threatened with isolation. As it was a very modern fortification it was expected to be able to hold out for some time. But before it was completely cut off a new code had to be delivered to it. I was sent with this. It was written on very thin paper and my orders were to swallow it if I found myself in danger of being captured. During the fifteen-mile ride my orderly, Kaurkhin, entertained me with stories of life in his village. As we neared the fortress, the peasants whom we met told us that German cavalry had passed within the hour. From then on we separated; Kaurkhin rode ahead as a lookout, while I kept some 300 yards behind, holding the code in my hand, ready to swallow it. We arrived in Ossovetz after dark, and I was offered the hospitality of the staff for the night. But the fortress depressed me, and I hated the thought of being trapped within its walls. So, after resting and feeding our horses, we rode back into the safety of the dark.

By the end of October our horses were again exhausted and Gourko sent a short wire to the army staff: 'When do we get a rest?' The answer from the commander of the army was also short: 'When the war is over.'

In order to take care of our sick or lightly wounded horses a hospital was formed for the use of the whole division. Menschikov, who was put in charge of it, took Sergeant Sidorovich with him. The hospital was stationed about a hundred miles in the rear. Sick or disabled horses were first led by the soldiers to our wagon transport, which usually was a ten- to twenty-mile walk. How Colonel Troubetzkoy shipped them from there I don't remember.

There were many adventurous boys in their teens who ran away from home to the front. In our regiment they were auto-matically sent to the horse hospital; from there Menschikov

173

shipped them home, saying: 'Go back to school; it's much easier to make war than to study.' There was a case of a boy who joined the regiment under quite different circumstances. Once, in the ruins of a village, one of our squadrons picked up a thirteen-year-old orphan by the name of Peter. His parents had been killed during the shelling of the village, and when the petrified Peter finally came out of hiding the rest of the population had fled. The squadron adopted him. Soon afterwards, when we were stationed in reserve, the platoon sergeant, in whose particular care Peter was placed, began to be concerned about his upbringing. A part of the latter consisted in flogging him every morning. My batman told me about it in this way: 'After the sergeant gets up, he first sees that the horses are fed, then he has his tea, and then he flogs Peter.'

After Menschikov was put in charge of the horse hospital I probably saw him only two or three more times on his visits to the regiment. During the Revolution he was killed by the Bolsheviks.

There were other changes in the 1st Squadron. Cornet Snejkov was appointed regimental adjutant, and somewhat later I also left the squadron to command the Communications Unit. No original officers remained in the squadron. Many men and horses were lost. The regiment soon asked for and received another squadron of replacements.

At the beginning of the war a unit of some twenty men handled the regimental telephones, telegraph, heliograph and the searchlight. It became obvious during the first months of the war that, although the telegraph and the heliograph could be left with the wagon transport, inter-regimental telephone communications should be increased. In January 1915, when the unit was tripled, I was appointed its commander.

To create this new unit each squadron had to contribute about six men and horses. It was an opportunity for the sergeant-majors to get rid of everything that was no good. So the six worst men were mounted on the six worst horses, given the six poorest saddles and the shabbiest equipment, and sent to me with a smile. When I first faced the ranks of my Communications Unit I wanted to weep. The cast-offs of the regiment were in front of me. The new men looked like outlaws; the new horses seemed ready to die the next day and the equipment as if it would fall apart while I was staring at it. The soldiers' only apparent advantage lay in the fact that most of them were literate; a telephone operator had to be able to write messages.

The fact that many of my men did not have particularly high ethics eventually saved my reputation. A couple of days after I received them in command, our regiment spent the night near another cavalry division. The next morning I noticed two good-looking bay horses in my ranks (strict adherence to black had been abandoned during the war). It was easy to guess where they had come from, but at that moment I pretended not to see them. I wanted to think about it. Later on I came to the selfish conclusion that a closed-eyes policy was best. It worked wonders. Little by little, the poor horses, bad saddles, bridles held together by string—all were replaced. In the spring I was complimented by the commander of the division on the excellent appearance of my unit.

For about two years I commanded this unit, and I became very fond of my men. They were brave brigands, and at times I was proud of being the chief brigand. They were also fond of me and twice touchingly expressed their feelings. Once, on my birthday, they presented me with a carriage drawn by a pair of beautiful dappled greys. This equipage had been stolen from a nearby estate. But this was in Russia and unfortunately I felt I had to return the gift. On the other occasion, after the Revolution, when I left this unit to take command of the 1st Squadron, they gave me a piece of legally bought silver. One of the hussars made a speech to the effect that now that they were free (because of the new liberal regime), and not compelled to be nice to me, they particularly wanted to give me this present.

I did not have any junior officers; my next in command was a sergeant named Krasikhin. He was a bright, energetic man, both strict and diplomatic. Without him I would never have been able to do the job as well as it was done. He had particular difficulty maintaining discipline because most of the time his men were dispersed through the squadrons and he could talk to them only by telephone. 'Peter, hit your mug with the receiver!' he often shouted into the phone. Much of the time this could be his only immediate disciplinary measure.

We were supplied with additional telephones, besides which I bought a dozen excellent Swedish field telephones and presented them to the regiment. The regiment also acquired some very simple telephones, which consisted of round inch-thick boxes, used for both speaking and listening. These were issued to the sentinels.

The heavily insulated telephone wires were wound on large metal spools. A mounted hussar would strap a spool to his back and simply trot or canter away while the wire unwound behind him. The end of the wire on one spool was spliced to the head of the wire on the next. We raised the wire above the ground only when it crossed roads. The fast laying of telephone wires enabled us to establish communications between all units of the regiment within an hour after the regiment had

Plate 20 The author with his father, sister and a friend, on leave in the Caucasus in 1914, just before the First World War.

Plate 21   Field kitchen and cooks in transit by rail.

Plate 22   Blowing up a railway track.

taken up a new position or halted for a night's rest. The difficulty was that horsemen riding across country often broke the wires; during a battle, bursting shells did the same. Throughout an engagement my men constantly had to crawl to the wires to repair them, at times exposing themselves more than the firing squadrons. Many of them did their work heroically, and I was never slow in applying for war decorations for them.

At times, when we were retreating, some wires had to be abandoned. On other occasions, we were able to pick up German wires. Russian infantry and artillery wires were also on my spools. These were collected here and there on reoccupied battlefields.

The core of the Communications Unit was usually quartered with the regimental staff. The latter consisted of the commander, his adjutant and the senior colonel. The adjutant, Cornet Snejkov, and I lived together whenever possible; when he was away on leave I acted as adjutant. I was also in charge of the packs of explosives in all the squadrons.

Of the incidents with the telephones I particularly remember one. In my command there was a hussar by the name of Niemetz, which in Russian simply means German. Once at the beginning of a big German push our regiment was with an advanced infantry battalion. The telephones connecting the battalion commander with other units of his regiment and with the artillery were in his dugout. Ours connecting him with Groten was also there. Niemetz was the telephone operator at Groten's end. The Germans started to attack in force. One of the companies of our battalion was cut down by bayonets, another retreated after heavy losses. The commander of the battalion lost his head and was talking into one telephone after another asking for help. In the meantime, the news that the battalion was almost surrounded was filtering

THE FIRST WORLD WAR

in. Seizing one receiver after another, the commander got hold of ours and asked: 'Who is speaking?' 'Niemetz,' came the reply. The completely bewildered commander dropped the receiver and exclaimed: 'This is the end!'

Early in December, our regiment was stationed in a German village, Kussen, and functioned as part of a cavalry screen in front of our infantry. Opposite us was a corresponding screen of German cavalry. The latter, by coincidence, was also the 1st Cavalry Division. This section of the front was temporarily quiet, and some sort of mutual *entente* was established between our cooks and the Germans. Many of our forward platoons were stationed at small farms. In order to protect themselves somewhat while feeding the soldiers, our field kitchens had to take roundabout routes; so, after serving one platoon, a squadron kitchen normally returned to the reserve platoon in the rear, went from there to the next platoon, back to the reserve platoon, and so on. The understanding somehow established between the Germans and our cooks allowed them to travel fully exposed, directly from platoon to platoon along the front line. Perhaps this was what led to our meeting German officers.

One morning a German uhlan, holding a lance with a white flag attached to it, crossed no-man's land to one of our advanced posts and delivered a package and a letter. The letter, addressed to the officers of our regiment, consisted of polite greetings. The package contained cigars and brandy. Within an hour one of our hussars, also under a white flag, carried vodka and cigarettes to the German officers. Our letter invited them to meet us that afternoon in no-man's land. Six officers met (three from each side), and were even photographed. The war was never mentioned in the conversation, which was mostly on sporting topics, the European horse shows of the previous summer being especially discussed. Both sides planned to meet again next afternoon; we were to bring hors d'œuvres with us and the Germans were to bring cognac. That evening the new commander of the division found out about the meeting and forbade its repetition. So as to inform the Germans of this order, the next morning all our advanced posts fired in the air. Perhaps if the commander had been Gourko he would have felt differently about it, but a few days earlier Gourko had been promoted and was now commanding an infantry corps.

Shooting at the Germans (although over their heads) that morning made us feel we were behaving in a very ignoble manner. We were embarrassed and wished for an opportunity to explain to them how it had happened. Occasionally during the next few months we operated against the same regiment. We tried once, unsuccessfully, to get in touch with them again. We knew of a path in a woody region which they patrolled periodically, so we wrote them a letter, put it in a large envelope and nailed it to a tree. The letter was picked up, but no answer ever reached us.

At the end of January and in the beginning of February, before and during the German push which threw us out of East Prussia, the regiment suffered substantial losses. Two officers were killed outright and one died of wounds. One of these was Vladimir Sokolov, who had introduced me to Caprilli's method of riding while we were still in Moscow. Seven officers were wounded, Rachmaninov and Shwed among them. Rachmaninov never returned to the regiment; he died of typhus during the Civil War.

The loss of ten officers within ten days, or twenty-five per cent of the total compliment, would have been large in any case, but because of the previous decimation, this number represented an even higher proportion of those actually functioning. Many platoons were now without officers, and yet our losses were negligible in comparison with those suffered by the infantry. It was commonly said that the chances of being killed in the infantry were much higher than those in the cavalry. This statement always annoyed Menschikov, who invariably retorted: 'And if I'm killed, I shan't care what sort of chance I had.'

Constantine Sokolov wrote very humanly about the death of his brother and I would like to quote his account as an example of an unpretentious description of one of many thousands of such unspectacular tragedies.

'Our lines in front of the village of Bladzen were about three hundred yards from the German position. Since we expected to be attacked, no one in our squadron slept during the night. In the morning, some men were allowed to go to the village to rest while others remained in the firing line. The battle began around noon. Our battery opened a well-directed fire; the shells were bursting low, just above the trenches. The Germans jumped out of them and ran. When our infantry rose with a "hurrah", the commander of the squadron, Captain Poliakov (not to be confused with Cornet Poliakov), ordered his men to advance. The hussars moved forward, while those who had been resting in the village rushed out of the huts to join them. Noticing the absence of my brother, I ran to the village and found him fast asleep on a pile of straw; he quickly joined the firing line. In the meantime the Germans reorganised and opened a strong rifle- and machine-gun fire. Our advance was halted. At one point Captain Poliakov stood up and, shouting to me that he was wounded, walked back to the village with the help of a hussar. The German fire increased. The hussars were lying flat, their heads in the snow; the wounded were crawling back. The next in command was my brother; I looked around and could not find him. Seeing that there was no sense in staying on open ground, I ordered the squadron to pull back. The hussars were afraid to move and remained where they were. I ran from one platoon to the other ordering them to retreat. They finally obeyed. When we got back to the village I asked: "Where is Cornet Sokolov Senior?" The hussars were silent. Suspecting bad news, I repeated the question. "He was killed," someone replied. I ran to the edge of the village and saw my brother lying some 150 feet ahead. The hussars wanted to pull his body out, but in order to avoid further losses I forbade it. Nevertheless, while I was busy checking the squadron's dead and wounded, the hussars brought my brother's body back.'

In the latter half of February, the attacking Germans succeeded in isolating the Russian 20th Corps; they then surrounded it with three of their corps. The 20th Corps, fighting heroically against overwhelming odds, was retreating toward the Russian fortress of Grodno. The remnants of these troops perished when they were just a few miles short of the protective range of the Grodno guns; only one brigade broke through.

We were soon to see this battlefield, but in the meantime, for a few days our regiment occupied infantry-built trenches on the river Niemen. While we were there, Cornet Poliakov was killed and the commander of the 6th Squadron severely wounded. Poliakov's death was one of those many unnecessary deaths that happen during wars and accomplish nothing. His squadron had relieved another squadron in the trenches at night. This had to be done in the dark because the trenches, dug in a hurry, were shallow and the German firepower strong. As soon as it was light enough to see, everyone wanted to orient himself and find out what he had to face. While many only cautiously peeped out of the trenches, Poliakov climbed out and stood up, examining the German position. The first bullet to hit him wounded him, the second pierced his heart.

On March 2nd, nine days after the defeat of the 20th Corps, our 10th Army began a counter-attack. Our regiment moved ahead in a blinding snowstorm, which fortunately ended in the afternoon. Then we saw German cavalry retreating along the same road a mile or so ahead. At dusk we entered the region of the Augustov Forest, where the 20th Corps had finally perished. There we came across large piles of something stacked on both sides of the road; they resembled cords of firewood. But the dimensions were not right, and they really did not look like wood. Snejkov rode over to one of these stacks and reported that it was a pile of bodies.

Ever since the battle nine days before, the population of the local villages, which had been mobilised to bury the dead, had been at it from sunrise to sundown but had not had time to finish the job. They had not even completed the task of assembling the bodies into piles. Certain areas of fields and woods were literally carpeted with the dead—both German and Russian. During the last phase of the battle in the woods and in the small fields in between, the German and the Russian formations had obviously succeeded each other like the layers of a cake. At times it must have been impossible to know where the enemy was, and some small units were annihilated from unexpected directions and at short range.

I remember the ghost of a battery, with the guns in firing position, the caissons farther behind, all the men and horses in their proper places, and all dead. I also remember an infantry company that had died in just such an orderly manner—everyone lying on the spot where his place in the formation had been. Judging by the number of bullets in every body, the company had been destroyed by machine-gun fire and had probably been killed almost immediately. On a path in the woods I stumbled over half a dozen stretchers with German soldiers on them. The soldiers, the stretcher-bearers and the two Red Cross men were all dead. There was also the dead wagon transport of a Russian regiment. All the horses and all the men of this small group of wagons had been killed as they travelled on the road. The last in the line was, as usual, the carriage with the priest. He had died as he sat in it. Where the road passed over a stone bridge there was a large heap of German dead. They had probably taken refuge under the bridge and had eventually been shot from the side.

Even on the outskirts of the village where we halted there was a large pile of dead Germans. Someone told me there were 400 of them. They must have been unexpectedly machine-gunned from the nearby woods while standing in a column waiting for orders.

The village houses were full of Russian wounded. These were the severely wounded, whom the Germans had not evacuated as prisoners because it would have been too much trouble. After being placed in the huts they were given some aid and then left to themselves. The German doctors had probably barely had time to take care of their own. There I saw wounds infested with maggots. The soldiers' joy in seeing us was indescribable. The stench in the houses was such that on that night I chose to sleep in the snow. The next morning we evacuated these unfortunate men.

Soon after this, while moving behind our front line, we passed a monastery. It was Lent. The commander of the regiment thought that we should take this opportunity to make confession. As there was no time for individual confessions, it was decided to hold a mass one. The regiment lined up in the large monastery church. Our priest asked aloud: 'Have you killed?' 'Yes, Father,' answered the whole regiment. 'Have you stolen?' 'Yes, Father,' answered almost the whole regiment. Here I got the giggles, and I do not remember how the confession progressed.

The next year we made confession while we were in the trenches on the bank of the river Dvina. Again, we had no time for individual talks with the priest. We confessed by squadrons. The men left the trenches and lined up in the wood behind these. This time the same regimental priest, instead of asking questions, urged us to imagine that we were facing God and in silence to remember our sins and ask forgiveness for them. A German plane was flying overhead, and here and there shots were heard, while the hussars stood in complete silence with bowed heads. This was the only confession of my life that stirred my emotions.

Besides the usual scouting and skirmishing, our division was frequently transferred from one part of the front to another. These marches were often made at night, on top of the normal daily activities. Even we young cornets were frequently exhausted, and it must have been proportionately harder on our twenty-year-older colonels. During these night marches I often rode with Colonel Rot; I still remember his tall figure swaying back and forth in the saddle as he was falling asleep. It was then that he coined a saying that I remember him afterwards repeating without changing a word. He did it whenever he was tired: 'Enough of this. It is high time to go to Kaiser Wilhelm and say to him: "Excuse us, Uncle; we won't do it any more." All the Germans are asleep and we are moving.'

In the middle of April 1915, our 1st Cavalry Division could

hardly be considered in battle condition. Our regiment was now only one-third of its normal size; one squadron had only thirty men (the regular number was 150). Those horses that remained in the ranks could barely walk. But still, orders from the Army Staff far in the rear were pouring in, 'Move there', 'Attack this'. One morning after receiving such an order, the commander of the division reported back that he could not execute it. We were replaced by a fresh cavalry division and were ordered to proceed to the rear. For two days we walked, mostly leading our horses in hand, to the fortress of Grodno. There we boarded trains which took us to the city of Vilna, where we were to rest.

CHAPTER 12

FIGHTING IN THE BALTIC PROVINCES

WHILE resting in Vilna, we received the splendid news that the Emperor wished to see the division that had suffered so much. A few days later we boarded trains and were taken to the vicinity of St. Petersburg, and lodged in the Krasnoe Selo camp.

Nearing St. Petersburg, our train passed several small stations that were familiar to me from my childhood as summer resorts. It was fun to plunge into recollections that didn't have a single burst of shrapnel in them. They made me anxious to see the city where I grew up, where my family lived and where I had many friends. So, as soon as I had a chance, I went there.

By now the capital was no longer called St. Petersburg; it had been renamed Petrograd. This renaming was part of a vogue to change German names into Russian ones; even family names were changed. This was done from a variety of motives, from purely patriotic ones to the simple desire to get rid of an unpopular German-sounding name. Colonel Rot joked that his name was now Krasnov (Rot in German and Krasnov in Russian both mean red). After the Bolshevik Revolution the name of the capital was changed again, this time to Leningrad. I never lived in Leningrad and only a few months in Petrograd, so the city of my childhood and youth has always remained in my memory as St. Petersburg.

It was rather strange to find myself among people who neither shot nor were shot at as a daily routine. Many of them saw war as a series of heroic deeds, and practically no one had enough imagination to realise that most of it consisted in being tired, sleepy, dirty, and often hungry. The army saying that 'in war one is either bored or frightened' had not yet reached St. Petersburg. My plain stories satisfied no one. Most people expected to hear fabulous tales in which the dying 'grey hero' uttered noble sentiments about his devotion to his country. In the safety of the deep rear too many civilians were romantically patriotic and could not understand that the enemy's machine guns interfered with such dreams. What we, the actual fighters, did as a matter of work and duty or bravado they expected us to do emotionally. The tragedy of thousands upon thousands who were killed without ever seeing the enemy had not yet been felt.

For the next six weeks the regiment was quartered in the Krasnoe Selo camp. This brought back memories of the 'Glorious School' and of the innocent foolishnesses we had indulged in.

In the regiment itself the peacetime routine of daily exercises was re-established almost at once. While it was a normal part of our life during real peace, it annoyed us when we had only six weeks to rest from the many strenuous months of fighting. But these drills were necessary, for during this time we received new men and horses to complete our ranks.

Once I had a rendezvous in the city and, wishing to spend the night there, did not expect to return before noon the next day. I told my sergeant, Krasikhin, to take my command to the fields for the whole of the next morning and simply to loaf. 'Dismount, loosen the girths, let the horses graze in hand, and do what you wish yourselves.' To this I added: 'If Groten should be riding around, mount and get out of his sight.' As it happened, Groten was checking exercises that day and saw my men at a distance doing nothing. He rode towards them. They quickly mounted and tried to escape, but Groten caught up with them. The following afternoon Groten and I met on the village street. Without any explanation he simply asked me: 'Which do you prefer—five extra duties or five days under arrest?' As briefly, I replied: 'Five days under arrest,' and we parted without saying another word. I was advised later that I would be put in jail after the Imperial parade.

On this particular occasion we were to pass at a slow canter instead of at a gallop. It was rumoured that the Emperor wanted to have a better chance of looking at us. During a parade the commander of the regiment rides far ahead of the ranks; after passing the reviewing officer he makes a wide half-circle and places himself in front and to the side of him. Thus the commander sees his regiment go by.

My own horse, 'Moscal', had had dressage training, as had all army horses of the time. He and I together could produce a good collected canter. Riding some twenty feet ahead of the first line of my command, I knew I was doing well. 'Moscal' moved softly, with high elegant steps, his neck arched and his head brought in, resembling horses in battle pictures of the past. I was told afterwards that as I was cantering past the Emperor the latter smiled, looked towards Groten and smiled again.

Later in the day Groten and I met again on the village street. As was his habit, he spoke in disconnected words rather than in phrases. 'Very good—your canter—and you—and that nag of yours; you can forget the arrest.'

There was another reason for cancelling my impending arrest. The Germans had begun a push in the Russian Baltic provinces and we were to go to the front in Latvia immediately. We boarded trains with full ranks, fresh horses, and ourselves in good spirits. Our destination was the town of Mitava, and on the way we passed through the city of Riga. Nearing it, our trains were greeted by multitudes of people at the many small stations of the adjoining summer resorts. Everyone carried flowers with which to decorate the trains. Entering Riga, our cars looked like carnival floats. In Riga itself there were waving and shouting people in every window and more of them on every roof. The Germans were only thirty miles away; we and the other troops behind us were the hope of the population. Within an hour after detraining in Mitava, we were in a battle. The still fresh recollections of life in St. Petersburg quickly became memories of a seemingly remote past.

On 24 July, our division was ordered to go to the support of a Siberian infantry regiment. The Siberian troops had an excellent war record, but this particular regiment had been depleted by previous battles and the remaining men were exhausted. They began to move forward at nine o'clock in the morning; by eleven they had succeeded in pushing the Germans back. But then the enemy brought up reserves and counterattacked. The infantry fought until evening without success on either side. I do not remember what part the Dragoons and the Cossacks played but the Uhlans were held in reserve, while some of our squadrons guarded the infantry's flanks. It was almost sunset when we suddenly heard the roar of hundreds of voices: the Germans were charging; our infantry had lost heart and was running away. The Uhlans and Hussars were ordered to get ready for a charge in order to stop the advancing Germans. Our regiment needed a few minutes to bring its squadrons together from the flanks, and so we were to charge behind the Uhlans. The Uhlans' lookouts shot forward at full

gallop; soon there appeared behind them the long lines of their
regiment, still walking. The Hussar's squadrons were assembling at a gallop and opening formation, with my unit on the
left flank. Some 1,600 horses drawn up in four rows with
hundreds of lowered lances formed a beautiful and menacing
sight. The scene was dramatically lighted by the setting sun.
Our battery opened fire to soften the Germans while the
regiments moved ahead. The Germans ran even before our
charge started, while their artillery intensified its fire to cover
their retreat. It seemed to us that the threat of a large cavalry
attack had decided the outcome of the battle.

My name-day, the day of the saint whose name I bear,
came four days later. In Russian life this is a big personal
holiday, more important than a birthday. On that day we
fought dismounted; I do not recollect exactly where it was,
but the regimental staff's position was near a farm from which
emerged a huge flock of geese. This small engagement remained in my memory as 'the battle for the goose farm'.
During a part of it, Groten was standing up just a couple of
hundred feet behind the firing line. Colonel Rot, Snejkov, and
I were obliged to stand also, while everyone else was flat on the
ground. It was rather foolish: first, because a couple of German
artillery pieces had got our range, and second, because there was
a substantial brick barn nearby behind which we could stand
if we had to stand. Snejkov and I discussed it. I particularly
disliked the idea of being killed on my name-day. But we did
not dare approach Groten, so we urged Rot to speak to him.
Rot suggested that we stand behind the barn. 'And why do you
think that the next shell will burst here and not behind the
barn?' asked the fatalistic Groten. And so we continued to
stand in the open.

Of the episodes of this period I remember with particular

vividness a mounted attack of the 1st Squadron, which was now commanded by Captain Petrjkevich who, you may recall, had had a wild household in Moscow. The squadron, supported by artillery, attacked a village defended by a company of cyclists and a squadron of cavalry. Petrjkevich began the charge while he was still a mile and a quarter away from the village. At the beginning of it he had been lightly wounded. As he neared the Germans, he noticed that there was a sizable ravine in front of the village. The ravine was crossed by a bridge, and Petrjkevich directed the attack towards this. For a moment no one could predict who would be the first to lose their nerve—the Germans or the Russians. It was the Germans who gave up and ran.

A hussar named Levitzky was the first to ride over the bridge; there he was severely wounded. Despite a Slavic name, he was Japanese. During the Russo-Japanese War he had, as an orphan, been adopted by a Russian general, Levitzky.

This successful attack impressed Petrjkevich perhaps even more than it did the Germans. He became conceited about his abilities to lead a charge. From then on, whenever he heard of an officer being praised, he said: 'Let him lead a squadron in a charge and I'll sit on a fence and laugh.' He said this, of course, after having a few drinks, but he always had a few drinks in him; he was never without a flask of vodka in his saddle-bags. He had a rule that whenever the regiment halted his orderly would begin to fry potatoes. If the halt was short, the unfinished potatoes were thrown away, but if it was a long one Petrjkevich had his vodka with potato hors d'œuvres.

Once our cavalry division, strung out in a long column, was moving through a large forest; the Cossacks were in the vanguard. Coming out of the woods they were stopped by fire from shallow trenches in front of a village. These were manned by a squadron of German cavalry supported by two field guns.

The Cossacks dismounted and began to attack on foot. As they gradually neared the Germans they tried every so often to charge. At each attempt we in the woods would first hear a 'hurrah' shouted by a few voices, soon joined by more and more, until finally a thunderous 'hurrah' would tell us that the Cossacks were up and charging. But then the German machine guns would start rattling and the Cossacks' 'hurrah' would peter out. One of our squadrons was ordered to dismount to help the Cossacks, while another mounted squadron was moved forward to the edge of the forest. When the Cossacks rose to charge again our mounted squadron charged with them. Both the mounted hussars and the dismounted Cossacks overwhelmed the trenches and the village at the same time. The German artillery escaped, but the men of the German cavalry were either killed or captured. As it turned out, they were guard cuirassiers, who had evidently been selected because they were all big fine-looking men.

A common scene in this captured village that day was Hussars and Cossacks, both clutching German prisoners, squabbling about whose prisoners they were. The controversy over to whom the victory belonged went on for a couple of days. At last we conceded that it belonged to the Cossacks.

The commander of the German squadron had been run through by a lance three feet of which came out of his back. The only way to determine who had killed him was to find out whose lance was missing, because the hussar who had done it was too horrified to admit it. Two other German officers were taken prisoner. One of these, a frightened young lieutenant surrounded by our men, held his wallet in his hands, distributing his money among them.

For the past three weeks we had been constantly fighting or moving and had had little sleep. To sleep and sleep was every-

Plate 23   Scouting party, under command of an officer.

Plate 24   Field telephones in use during action.

Plate 25 A peasant's cottage (*izba*), typical of northern Russia. There were variations in style depending upon area and wealth.

Plate 26 A manor house was occasionally available for officers on the march. Typical of such houses all over Russia, of classical design and frame construction, many of them painted and the finer ones plastered.

one's dream. In the official history of my regimente[1] there is the following entry: 'Cornet Littauer was busy all night laying telephone lines and repairing them. It was only in the morning that, tired out, he had a chance to sleep. As soon as he had fallen asleep, the Germans began a push. Awakened and advised of it, he said in a positive manner, "This is merely a demonstration," turned over on his side and went to sleep again.'

All this time the division fought very efficiently, often repulsing or attacking superior forces. Most of these skirmishes and battles, however, were so monotonously repetitious that it is a bore to recall them today.

In the middle of August the regiment fought a battle that was significant to all of us because in it Colonel Groten was wounded. Only four squadrons were on hand that day; two of these remained in reserve, while the other two dismounted to attempt the capture of a strongly defended village. The German fire kept our lines immobile some 200 yards from the objective. The topography of the ground was such that our hussars were fairly safe where they were, but moving forward a few steps would probably mean the destruction of the two squadrons. Groten knew it; everyone knew it but the people in the rear, and our lines simply marked time by firing. The commander of the brigade, on the other hand, demanded a rapid advance.

The officers of the two reserve squadrons plus Rot, Snejkov and I sat on the ground near the telephone that connected Groten with the commander of the brigade. Every half-hour the general phoned to ask Groten whether or not we were advancing. 'No.' 'Why? Are your losses heavy?' 'No. Our losses are light.' 'Then why aren't you advancing?' 'Because the

---

1. Compiled in 1954 by the officers of the Sumsky Hussars then alive and published in Buenos Aires. It is in Russian.

enemy is too strong for us. We need artillery support, at the very least.' These were the bad days of an ammunition shortage. Our battery fired three shells, two of which did not explode. The Germans answered with several salvos of heavy artillery. Groten pleaded again for substantial artillery support; the brigade commander again inquired about our losses. This sporadic conversation went on for a couple of hours. Finally Groten received an order to move ahead until we had suffered fifty per cent casualties. Enraged, Groten shouted: 'All right, if all they want is losses, I'll produce them,' and addressing Snejkov, inquired: 'Which squadron is the next in line?' A complete silence fell on us officers sitting around the telephone. Snejkov answered: 'The 4th.' The 4th Squadron was commanded by Captain Pankov, the officer who had lined everyone up in the bar in Moscow. Turning to Pankov, Groten ordered: 'Move along this forest to the right for a quarter of a mile, and then come out of it and attack the German trenches.' In silence Pankov saluted, walked to his squadron, and ordered it to mount; in another minute they all disappeared into the woods. In the meantime, Groten was going through an emotional struggle. He could not convince himself that his order was humanly right. Finally he said: 'No, I just can't do it,' and turning to his trumpeter, ordered: 'Gallop across the field and stop the charge. Hurry!' The trumpeter's horse lunged forward, but before he could take a dozen strides we heard 'Hurrah'— the 4th Squadron had begun its hopeless attack.

At that time a heavy shell burst about thirty feet from our group, which was now watching the charge. Surprisingly, none of us was hurt, although a dozen horses standing some 500 feet away were killed or wounded.

The 4th Squadron attacked in dispersed formation on a thousand-foot front. The attack was a failure even before the trumpeter was able to halt it. The left half of the formation soon found itself floundering in a swamp. The horses began to sink and the hussars jumped off them. The right half of the formation halted when it saw this. The impression from the outside was that the squadron was suffering heavy losses. Actually they were negligible. The German machine-gunners had evidently miscalculated the distance.

Groten, very upset by then, murmured: 'I shall give them another kind of casualty.' With these words he walked forward to the firing line and, when he reached it, did not bother to lie down. In a matter of minutes he was wounded. The Red Cross wagon picked him up. While it was crossing an open field bringing him to us, shrapnel burst right above it. The stunned driver instinctively halted the horse. The wagon had a white canvas top on it. When the driver stopped the horse, we saw Groten's fist suddenly appear from under the canvas and start to pound him on the head. The driver came to, whipped the horse, who lunged forward, and they crossed the field at a gallop. We roared with laughter.

When Groten was brought back to our group around the telephone he ordered: 'Tell the brigade commander that the commander of the regiment is wounded.' Half an hour later when Groten had reached the staff the general asked him: 'How are you Colonel?' 'I am all right,' replied Groten, 'but why are you damaging my men over there?' This particular word, 'damaging', was Groten's own, and it sounded as out of place in Russian as it does in English; but he used it all the time.

About three months later, Groten returned to the regiment for a few days. He had been promoted to the rank of general and given a guard regiment—the Horse Grenadiers—to command. His farewell to his officers was very touching. He readily admitted that his appraisal of us in Moscow had been wrong, bowed very low asking our forgiveness and even shed a few tears.

Groten had commanded the Horse Grenadiers for only a few months when he was appointed assistant commandant of the Imperial Palace. His farewell to that regiment, as described to me by one of its officers, was different from his parting with us. Groten had a very dramatic way of coming up to his regiment. He always approached it at full gallop, often with drawn sword (ready to give orders with it), and as he passed the squadrons in formation he would shout: 'Good morning, First, good morning, Second,' and so on. In this manner he approached the Horse Grenadiers on his last day with them. Then he placed himself in front of the centre of the regiment, swung his sword over his head a couple of times, and after the usual formal farewell, added: 'May you all lay down your bones for the glory of your country!' and galloped away.

After the Revolution he was arrested, but was soon released; eventually he emigrated to France. When American troops entered Paris towards the close of the Second World War, Groten was selling National Lottery tickets in the cafeteria of a French ten-cent store. This cafeteria had been requisitioned by the American forces; an amusing and typically 'Groten' incident ensued. The story harked back to his days in the Russian army. There was an unwritten law in our regiment that every officer should speak daily to as many soldiers as he could about personal matters. Because a platoon only had about thirty-five men it was easy for its commander to get to know his men fairly intimately and to carry on such conversations with them. On the other hand, a squadron commander had a much harder time conversing with his 150 men, and it was impossible for the commander of a regiment to talk to all of his. It became even more complicated during the war, when men were frequently replaced. Groten was forced to boil his conversations down to a formula. He would ask: 'Where are you from?' The soldier would reply: 'From Poltava.' With a smile Groten would then ask: 'Is it nice in Poltava?' The beaming hussar would answer: 'Very nice.' During the war Groten would usually add, quite seriously: 'All this nonsense will soon be over and you will go back to Poltava.' When the Americans took over the cafeteria in Paris and Groten found himself again surrounded by men in uniform, he automatically began to behave in his old manner. The fact that he spoke English helped the matter. 'Where are you from?' he asked the first G.I. who bought a lottery ticket from him. 'From Cincinnati,' was the reply. 'Is it nice in Cincinnati?' further queried Groten. 'Sure, very nice,' answered the soldier. 'Well,' said Groten, 'all this nonsense will be over soon and you will go back to Cincinnati.' The next man was from Philadelphia, and the next from Chicago; according to them these cities were very nice. Groten cheered them all up by assuring them that 'This nonsense would be over soon'. In a few hours he was evicted from the cafeteria as a suspicious character who was trying to undermine the *morale* of the army.

He died a couple of years ago at the age of ninety-three, in a home for old people near Paris. He never lost the warm feelings he had acquired for the regiment during the war, and he continued to correspond with some of us.

When Groten was wounded, Rot, as senior colonel, automatically became the commander of the regiment. His first order was 'Call Petrjkevich'; he was certain that the latter would have vodka with him. Because, in his former post, he had had few responsibilities, but now was abruptly saddled with all the concerns of a regimental commander, he wanted some 'Dutch courage'.

Rot commanded the regiment for over three months, until the arrival of the new regular commander. The first half of this period was particularly hard for us. Battles were fought almost daily, and when not fighting we were moving from one section of the front to another. The men were so tired that they fell asleep in the firing line. At times it was hard to tell who was dead and who was asleep. Just the same, lighter incidents occurred here and there.

One day the regiment fought on the outskirts of an estate. The firing lines were in the orchard and the park. In the meantime, lunch was being served on the veranda of the main house to the officers of the two reserve squadrons. Good wine from the estate's cellar was in abundance and Colonel Rot, sitting at the head of the table, was telling stories apropos. Shrapnel was bursting all around as more bottles were emptied and more stories told. By the time the Germans brought up more troops and began to surround us Rot was quite tipsy. Bad news was beginning to pour in, and Snejkov, who was receiving it, soon began to look worried. He finally approached Rot and read the scout's very unpleasant report to him. We obviously had to get away from the place in a hurry. Rot looked at him, smiled sweetly, and said: 'Nicholas, read it once more; we all love your melodious voice.'

People find occasion to laugh even in the most tragic circumstances, and so did we during this exhausting and bloody summer.

In one village where we stopped overnight we found a man who claimed to be 115 years old and that, as a little boy, he had witnessed the invasion of Napoleon's army in 1812. He described the French uniforms and equipment with surprising accuracy. We were fascinated by his tales. Then someone asked: 'Did you see Napoleon himself?' 'Of course—a big fellow with a long beard,' answered the old man, lowering his hands to his belt in a dramatic gesture to indicate the length of the beard!

It is hard to forget another incident of this period because it is so typical of military bureaucracy. When we stayed in one place for a few days we received forage from the army's depots. When on the move within Russia we fed our horses by purchasing hay and oats from the local population. When we were in Germany we simply stole it. Occasionally, even when in transit, oats would be sent to us on the road. The oats were delivered in bags which were supposed eventually to be returned. Naturally, this was done in Moscow, but during the war no one was interested in such small items and the bags were thrown away. It went on this way for a year, until the regiment unexpectedly received a bill for the missing sacks. The commander of the regiment divided the bill among commanders of the six squadrons and of the Communications Unit. My share amounted to several hundred roubles. At a meeting we decided to cancel our debt gradually by reporting that the bags had been lost in action, because they had been filled with sand and used as protection. From then on, the reports of losses in every little skirmish included so many dozens of lost bags. Within three or four months all the missing bags were accounted for. This was all that the army's bureaucrats required.

It was during this period of the war that both the Russians and the Germans made changes in their manner of carrying their rifles and swords. At the beginning of the war both the rifle and the sword in the Russian cavalry had been carried by the soldier; in the German army both weapons were attached to the saddle. Eventually, we found that a sword carried on a strap over the shoulder interfered with movement during dismounted action. So we attached it to the saddle. On the other hand, the Germans discovered that if both weapons were attached to the saddle, then a man who had lost his horse was totally disarmed. So the Germans began to carry their rifles Russian style—across their backs. Another change in the equipment of our regiment was the abolition of curb bits. The experiences of war proved them to be not only unnecessary but even a handicap in cross-country riding, and they were sent to our wagon transport. From then on we rode on snaffles.

At the very end of August the 1st and the 2nd Cavalry Divisions were ordered to halt a German local advance until the arrival of Russian infantry. The Germans succeeded in pushing our dismounted regiment from the forest's edge into the depths of the forest itself. In its darkness both sides spent an uneasy night. There were moments when there was no firing at all. Then a nervous soldier would begin to shoot, another would join him and, in a minute, bullets would be flying like a swarm of bees. Some of our men fired so rapidly and for so long that the thin wooden sheaths covering their rifle barrels were carbonized in parts.

The infantry, which was supposed to arrive in two hours, did not show up until the evening of the next day. The first sign that they were coming was the appearance of one of their field kitchens, which had somehow got ahead of everything else. Next, unfortunately, one of their batteries appeared and, mistaking us for German cavalry, fired at us. Artillery fire from the rear could easily have caused a panic, but it did not, and our galloping messenger quickly made them stop shooting. During this battle, Captain Govorov, two other officers, and Wilenkin were wounded.

When the infantry at last replaced us that night, we moved

to the rear. The swampy forest road, full of roots and pot-holes, kept us down to a walk. Here and there we crossed narrow bridges over small streams. A rotten bridge collapsed while one of our kitchens was crossing it. The kitchen was pulled by a heavy draft horse, 'Mishka', who had originally belonged to a brewery and been conscripted for the war. For the next few minutes a part of our column had to stop while the hussars, waist-deep in water, were pulling 'Mishka' and the kitchen out of the boggy stream.

On 15 September, the Russian army began a withdrawal to the Dvina river. Our regiment was ordered to cover the retreat of an infantry division. We were told to 'hold at all costs'. All day the regiment held the attacking Germans back. Towards evening their lines were so close to ours that we could hear the German artillery observer with the infantry giving telephone orders to his battery: '*Feuer, feuer*'. When they were this near to our lines the Germans could no longer move forward; our fire kept them down. At one point a German lieutenant commanding a platoon rose up and quietly walked from one of his men to another. He hit every man with his stick and gave the order: '*Vorwärts*'. Each man in turn jumped a few feet forward. Our hussars stopped shooting and cheered the lieutenant. Some time later Sheinoga, a platoon sergeant, of our 1st Squadron, did the same, with the same results—the Germans cheered him!

When we finally pulled back during the night, contact with our infantry had been lost. In the meantime, it had safely crossed the Dvina river over a wooden bridge and had already started to set fire to it. When we approached the river, barrels of kerosene were flaming under the bridge which was beginning to burn just as our horses stepped on it.

The following appraisal of our behaviour can be found in a

German book, *Die Deutsche Kavallerie in Litauen und Kurland*, by von Pozek, describing this summer campaign in Latvia: 'The Russian cavalry was a worthy enemy. Its personnel was excellent. It particularly distinguished itself in scouting. Its lookouts appeared everywhere and knew how to make use of the terrain. The Russian cavalry knew well how to hide itself and how to disengage itself imperceptibly, as well as how to mask its retreat. The Russian cavalry never declined a mounted or a dismounted action. The Russians often charged our machine guns and artillery, even when such an attack was doomed to failure; they disregarded both the strength of our fire and losses they suffered.'

CHAPTER 13

TRENCH WARFARE

AS a boy I was very fond of the caramels labelled Skirno, which were sold in one or two shops in St. Petersburg. They were named, I believe, after the estate of Skirno, south of Dvinsk on the Dvina river. In September 1915 our regiment held the trenches near this estate; the officers' mess was quartered in the main house. It was a comfortable squire's manor house and, when all was quiet in the trenches, our life in it resembled the normal life on a typical Russian estate in peacetime: the officers played cards and guests came for meals.

A forest lay between Skirno and the trenches. It hid the manor house from the Germans; but they knew it was there, and from time to time they threw a few shells in its direction. A shell burst in the courtyard only once. It killed our luncheon guest, an artillery officer. He was hit as he was dismounting from his horse.

Our regiment was the only one in our division, and one of the few in the cavalry in general, that preserved the regimental mess throughout the war. In the great majority of cases each squadron's officers ate in a group by themselves. During fast-moving field warfare the mess obviously could not function every day. But from now on, during the many months spent sitting in trenches, besides furnishing meals, the mess played an important role in the life of the regiment. By now the officers' corps had changed its face considerably. Since the beginning of the war seven of our officers had been killed and twenty-eight wounded. Many of the latter never returned to the regiment. A large percentage of these casualties were the original officers who had served with the regiment in Moscow. Some old-timers were transferred to desk jobs. All these were replaced by graduates of special accelerated wartime courses. These new-comers had to be turned into Sumsky Hussars in a hurry, and daily conversations with them in the mess enabled the remaining original officers to indoctrinate them in the spirit and the traditions of the regiment.

Nothing of any particular interest occurred in the life of the regiment during our stay in the vicinity of Skirno. Later, we were put in reserve nearby. These days though uneventful for us were not so for the infantry. In October and again in December it tried hard to push the Germans back. In the course of these attacks it suffered greatly. Once a quartermaster came to the village occupied by the 3rd Squadron to ask for shelter for his infantry regiment. The village was small, consisting of a dozen houses. Our squadron commander, knowing that an infantry regiment normally numbered more than 4,000 men, asked: 'How can we give you shelter? We haven't enough room for ourselves.' 'Give us one large barn,' answered the quartermaster. 'It will do. We have only ninety men.'

During the December attempt to turn the Germans back we were placed behind an infantry corps which was expected to break a hole in the German lines. We were to go through this opening into the German rear to produce as much damage as we could. For this occasion we had received canned emergency rations. Though our infantry failed to break through, our hussars ate the rations anyway, and we returned to reserve.

One night, while we were still in reserve, I attended a party given by one of our squadrons stationed in a neighbouring village, and I got drunk. My batman, Kourovski, was advised about it and came for me with a peasant cart. The road was full of pot-holes and the cart did not have any springs, so I, lying on its floor, was jolted considerably. When I angrily asked: 'What is this damned vehicle?' the disgusted Kourovski replied sarcastically: 'An automobile.' A special familiarity always existed between an officer and his batman.

While doing nothing in reserve other people got drunk, too. Once, for instance, I witnessed the following scene from a bridge over a small river. Two boats, with a few soldiers in each, were going downstream. The first boat also carried an officer, a peasant woman, and a collection of bottles. The soldiers sang the old Russian ballad about the river pirate, Stenka Razin. The words of the song begin by describing the return of Stenka Razin's boats from the plunder of a Persian town. The chief pirate sits in the first boat with a captured Persian princess. Pleased with his prize, he talks of marriage. But then he hears discontented murmurs among his men, who object to his paying so much attention to a woman. They fear that it will make him woman-like. Stenka Razin rises and, 'to stop discord among free men', casts the princess into the river.

The drunken officer in the boat was playing Stenka Razin. When the words of the song reached the point where the princess was tossed into the river, the officer rose and threw the peasant woman overboard. The second boat fished her out, she was then transferred back to the first boat, the drinking was resumed and the soldiers began the song all over again. The woman had clearly been hired to perform the role of the princess. By the time I watched the performance no one was laughing any more as she hit the water; she must have already been thrown in many times.

Later in December our division was moved to the woods on the western shore of the Dvina river. There the situation was quite unusual. Our sector was a large swampy forest, crossed and re-crossed by long narrow fire breaks. We stood on one side of the forest, the Germans on the other. The average distance between us was about four miles. Warfare on both sides consisted in sending dismounted platoons and squadrons into the woods to ambush each other. Once, our 3rd Squadron fell into one of the German traps. In wild hand-to-hand fighting the squadron broke through, but a wounded cornet was left behind and taken prisoner. Neither one side nor the other was particularly successful in these exploits.

My Communications Unit did not take part in these skirmishes, so I had plenty of free time on my hands. I used it to teach the two or three men in each squadron who were in charge of the explosives how to deal with them. The TNT bricks were not dangerous to handle. You could drop them, and we were even told you could burn them. They exploded only in response to a prior explosion of a specific wave length. This was provided by a nitro-glycerine capsule inserted into a hole in the brick. A Bickford cord with a heavily insulated powder core was inserted in the capsule. It burned at a constant rate, and you cut it to whatever length would give you enough time to get away.

In the course of the war much of our Bickford cord dried out and, because it was carried in rolls, the powder stream inside the insulation separated in some places. In such cases the course of the flame was stopped and there was no explosion. If this happened during a lesson, according to regulations, the officer alone approached the charge and disconnected it. A certain number of minutes was supposed to elapse before it was considered safe to approach the charge. This failure to explode occurred with me on several occasions but, although I felt reasonably certain that no danger was involved, I always approached the charge thinking that perhaps the flame was still smouldering and that my handling of the cord would connect it with the next stretch of powder. Once, when walking towards a charge attached to a tree I heard someone running behind me. It was a young soldier, who explained: 'I'm an orphan and unmarried; I've neither brothers nor sisters nor anything to lose in this world; I'll keep you company.' Although I appreciated his sentiments, what he said was not what I wished to hear at that moment.

On the whole, our stay in this sector of the front was quiet and boring. The 1st Squadron, the Machine Gun Command, and my Communications Unit were quartered together in the little village of Arglan. About a dozen officers shared a small schoolhouse, where we were like herrings in a barrel.

To amuse ourselves, six or seven of us wrote a musical satire, making fun of the regiment. The entire musical score was made up from popular tunes of the time. We wrote verses to go with these. Probably as many as three-quarters of the lyrics were written by Wilenkin, but the rest of us worked on them with equal enthusiasm.

First of all, those officers who had changed their fighting posts for the safety of desk jobs in the rear were sarcastically ridiculed. Then, friendly fun was made of those who had stuck to the regiment through all its bloody and strenuous experiences. Everyone's weak points were exposed, and jokes were even made about some courageous deeds. In its absence of glorification of any kind the show was very human. We could not invite officers of other units; there was too much in the life of our regiment that we did not wish others to know. So there were only about twenty-five spectators in the converted class-room when we performed our masterpiece. Each of us played several roles. We sang our lines to the accompaniment of a guitar. Even before the curtain went up our audience knew what to expect: we had strung barbed wire between it and the stage.

The play began by one of us reciting a rhymed prologue. Here is a free translation of the first three stanzas:

> Amidst the toils of war,
> Amidst the army's boredom,
> Not always reigns
> The roar of battle.
>
> Sometimes the fighters'
> Hands are idle,
> Sometimes their brains
> Are apt to dwell on jokes.
>
> We shall now present
> For your approval
> A review
> Of regimental life.

The first act lasted much longer than was expected. It was a scene in a Moscow restaurant, where those who had deserted us were sitting around two or three tables. We enjoyed playing these roles, while Wilenkin acted the part of a waiter. Real wine was served, and it happened to be good. Petrjkevich, who was one of the actors, became enthusiastic about it and repeatedly called: 'Waiter, bring another bottle.' The worried Wilenkin, bringing more wine, was whispering: 'Theodore, don't drink so much. You will ruin the show.' To keep the audience cheerful while the actors held an unscheduled party on stage, wine was served to everyone.

One of my roles was that of a 'madame' who procured girls in St. Petersburg. It was the result of our stay there early the previous summer. My song in this role began with the words 'Sumsky Hussars tenderly call me *ma tante* . . .' My batman, Kourovski, was very much upset by my playing this role, and blushed as he helped me turn myself into a fat woman with too much rouge on her cheeks. With the liberty of a batman he said to me: 'You should be ashamed to look like this; you will be a captain soon.' And such I soon was—promotions came fast during the war.

No one left the show with hurt feelings and later, during supper, we had to repeat many of our songs. Only poor Wilenkin was stepped on. After having many drinks and feeling gay and happy he carelessly called the musical his 'child'. A colonel rose and said: 'Are you certain that the woman who bore you this child has never deceived you? I drink for Snejkov, Littauer . . .' and he mentioned all of us who had made individual contributions to the review.

The regiment remained in Arglan until the middle of April, then, after another uninteresting assignment, it was placed in the army reserve in Dvinsk.

A provincial repertory troupe arrived in the city at the same time. On many nights for the next two months, almost the entire first row of the small theatre was occupied by Sumsky officers: after the show the actors often had supper in our mess. Nearly all the actresses had elegant stage names; the one whom I particularly liked called herself Murat. A divisional horse show was organised in Dvinsk and, hoping to please our lady friends, some of us changed the names of our mounts. This was not a success; 'The mare Murat' or 'The mare Bernard' listed in the programme did not please anyone. It was only because my 'Moscal' was a gelding that I did not get into trouble. After the show I was a few points ahead with 'Madame Murat'. These two months were fun, and later, when we were in the trenches, we often recalled these feeble actresses but charming girls.

While we were in Dvinsk there was a parade. I remember it as a big affair, so the reviewing general was probably the commander of the 5th Army, to which we were now attached. The night before the parade we held a gay party in our mess. We were to start for the parade ground at six o'clock in the morning; it would be quite silly to go to bed for just two or three hours. So everyone stayed up all night, and at a quarter to six was ready to ride. The exception was Colonel Rot, who then commanded the regiment; he was very happy where he was. It was a few minutes past six when our head waiter finally roused him. He respectfully reported that the hors d'œuvres, vodka and wine had already been transferred to the mess wagon and that the latter was about to start for the parade ground. 'In that case,' said Rot, 'nothing keeps us here.' Sometimes we spent as much as an hour waiting about on the reviewing ground while other troops took up their respective positions. During this hour the mess wagon sold food and vodka.

In peacetime this two-wheeled cart followed officers on manœuvres and during other country activities. It always played an important role in Rot's life. One day Rot was in charge of shooting exercises on the Hodinka field outside Moscow. On that morning one of the cart's wheels broke and the wagon never started on its usual trip. Rot could not know this, and at the time that the mess cart was due to arrive he began to look anxiously in the direction from which it would appear. Half an hour later two hussars trotted up from that part of the field. Rot asked them how far back they had passed the wagon. 'We didn't pass it at all, Your Honour,' replied the hussars. 'What fools you are,' said Rot, 'you ride and don't even see what you pass.' When later Rot found out what had happened he grumbled, 'I've always said that our repair unit is no good; those idiots can't even fix the mess cart so that its wheels stay together.'

In June we were again in a situation that was strange to us. At that time we held trenches forming part of a bridge-head on the river Dvina. A bridge-head is a fortified zone on the enemy's side of the river. It is held in the hope of a future counter-attack in which the bridge may be useful. It must be strongly fortified and amply garrisoned. So it was in this case.

The regiment occupied the very right flank trenches, which ran down to the river. Our sector was less than a quarter of a mile long, and our hussars were jammed in the trenches as they had never been before. These had been constructed by the infantry; they were deep, some of the large dugouts having roofs nine logs thick, and there were numerous communicating trenches. Special anti-attack artillery guns were placed in the trenches, while the regular artillery was stationed on the other side of the river, as were our horses. Immediately behind our sector stood thirty-two field guns, with the heavy artillery farther back. The thirty-two guns would open up whenever our commander telephoned the artillery command-post for support; they would start firing within a few seconds. If this was not enough, the big guns would join them. We had never had any support like this.

All this impressed and excited us, and the night we arrived in these trenches none of us could sleep. In all our moves we were shy and careful. When nothing drastic happened to us we began to feel more at ease, and in a couple of days the squadron commanders and the sergeant-majors were sufficiently relaxed to notice the good grass that grew all around us. We decided to cut it during the next two nights. This we did; in a couple of days we had hay ready to be loaded and taken to our horses. We planned to do this the following night. But the news that we were about to be relieved changed the plan and, in order not to lose the fruits of our labour, we decided to load the hay during the day. Many parts of the field were hidden from the Germans by woods. If careful, we could avoid exposing ourselves. In this spirit the work progressed all morning, while cockiness grew with success. Finally, early in the afternoon, I watched an attempt to load a wagon in full view of the Germans. It began with the driver moving carefully, the soldiers picking up the hay and halting before they exposed themselves. An optimistic sergeant walked ahead into the open and, since he was not shot at, beckoned to the driver to follow him. The Germans opened shrapnel fire; our wagon crossed a ditch at a gallop, but miraculously it did not turn over.

Later in the year we were ordered into trenches on the eastern shores of the Dvina river, some sixty miles north of Dvinsk. When it was not frozen this wide river was sure protection against any kind of surprise. But if there was ice, it was relatively easy to cross it despite a few mines, and on winter nights we did not sleep. This part of the front in general was very quiet while we were there. It was obviously expected to be quiet, for our sparse occupation of the very extended trenches was only a token one. At the time, a dismounted squadron had about eighty men and these were distributed along a mile of trench. One platoon in each squadron was kept in reserve; the remaining three platoons were posted in the trenches at three fortified points, with nothing between them. In some places these points were farther apart than the distance to the German trenches on the other side of the river. Walking the length of our trenches during a winter night checking my telephone service, I could expect to encounter Germans as readily as our own hussars.

Snejkov and I lived together in a hut behind the trenches. The hut had two rooms: one for us and the other for our batmen and the telephone operator. Except for a table and a long bench, there was no furniture but our two cots. The walls were decorated with our weapons and clothing, which hung on nails. We both frequently received parcels from our families and friends. These parcels contained food that kept well: canned fish, salami, pressed caviar, chocolate and, of course, wine. When we had more than we could consume ourselves we would invite guests. To make it festive we would have trumpeters or singers. Either of the choruses completely filled the room, so the number of our guests had to be limited to two or three. Sometimes we had music or singing just for the two of us. Sitting on our cots or on the wooden bench we drank good champagne and ate caviar, while the singers or trumpeters entertained us. Every condition of life has its own luxury.

Our soldiers built a log cabin near our hut to serve as a Russian bath for the regiment; this gave us another great pleasure. The Russian peasant was very skilful with an axe, and often carried one stuck in his belt. With it he was able to build a house or carve a shepherd's flute with equal ease.

Once we experienced an unusual form of Russian bath. One of the several bath-trains that had been donated to the army stopped nearby. The whole regiment visited it by squadrons. The process, if I remember correctly, was as follows: we entered at one end of the train and undressed in the first car.

We were steamed in the second car, washed ourselves in the third, cooled off in the fourth, and our clothes were returned to us in the fifth. These had been deloused in the meantime. In the last car we were treated to tea and rolls. Such trains travelled constantly along the front. The organisation that donated them was founded by Purishkevich, the leader of the ultra-conservative party (who was also one of the future assassins of Rasputin), and the trains bore his name.

On the German side, opposite the sector of the 1st Squadron, there was a large farm (or small village) called Dubena. Whenever Petrjkevich had had a drink too many he would begin, on his own initiative, to plan the capture of Dubena. To the objection that this was occupied by forces stronger than his squadron, Petrjkevich always replied, 'I don't need a squadron; all I need is seven men.' Another drink, and Petrjkevich would put on his overcoat to go out to find the seven volunteers. In the meantime the batmen of the squadron were telephoning a warning to all the posts. As Petrjkevich staggered the length of his squadron's trenches, entering the dugouts on the way, he could not find a soul; everyone was in hiding. The empty trenches did not disturb his drunken mind beyond making him swear, but his attack on Dubena had to be cancelled again.

Since the introduction of Prohibition at the beginning of the war, it had become progressively harder to purchase vodka. But through our doctor or our veterinarian we could always obtain prescriptions for pure alcohol for medicinal uses. With this we could make quite decent vodka by diluting the alcohol with water and adding one or two drops of glycerine per quart. Flavouring it with lemon was in vogue at the time. The proportion of alcohol and water depended on the individual's taste, but the brew tended to be stronger and stronger as the war progressed. Wine continued to be available to us on the front, but its sale was either prohibited or restricted in some cities.

During the period when we were in reserve in Dvinsk ten-day leaves became regular for us officers. This continued while we were in the trenches on the Dvina river; that year I went to St. Petersburg at least twice. The only person who did not like to see me in the capital was my uncle Bachmetov who, as you may remember, was a devotee of the Russian bath. With his ultra-patriotic attitude, he always greeted me by asking: 'What are you doing here? Your duty is fighting.'

During one of these furloughs I took part in the unsuccessful elopement of a childhood friend, Olya, with the young composer Prokofief. Olya, her sister and I had grown up together; our fathers had been friends since their student days. The mother and both daughters were very much interested in music, and Prokofief, from the time he was eighteen, was a frequent guest in the house. One of my early recollections of him was during a party given on Olya's birthday. He presented her with a musical score, sat down at the piano, and played the piece. I was still in the 'gymnasium' and was very much impressed by this performance. Later, Olya wrote the words for Prokofief's famous composition, *The Ugly Duckling*. This might easily have been the beginning of the romance. By the winter of 1915–16 they wanted to get married, but because Olya's parents opposed the match they decided to elope. My part in the plot consisted in hiring a fast *troika* and waiting for Olya a block away from her house. I was to take her to a church some fifteen miles outside the city, where Prokofief would be waiting for her. A winter night, a sleigh, a hussar, all these were the classic attributes of Russian elopements. I sat waiting for half an hour until, instead of Olya, a chambermaid appeared. She announced that the plot had been discovered.

Olya was sent off to the provinces to cool off, I was given hell by her mother, and the marriage never took place. Later I found out that it was the chambermaid herself who had given the whole thing away.

On any day of the year St. Petersburg was full of officers on leave as well as of recuperating officers recently discharged from the city's numerous hospitals. All of the former and many of the latter were to face bullets soon again, and a spirit of making the most of the moment prevailed. So life was gay, and the girls who cared to take part in it had a lively time. The centre of our activity was the Hotel Astoria. An old general, probably dug up from the reserve, was there to keep an eye on us. In the Astoria one was allowed only one bottle of wine for dinner. By ordering two dinners one could have two bottles, but the table also had to be set for two. The general checked whether there were plates before the empty chairs. The girls who frequented the Astoria and who were concerned with the happiness of the officers were helpful in this respect. They sat at one's table, ate the second dinner, and drank practically nothing.

Quite a few private hospitals in St. Petersburg were run by wealthy society women—run both expensively and well. But as often happens where there is an abundance of energy, some of it was misdirected. One of our soldiers who had stayed in one of these aristocratic hospitals had dreadful recollections: the ladies, taking turns, had read Russian classics aloud to him for hours on end.

In February 1917 (one month before the Revolution), two squadrons of each cavalry regiment (excepting the Cossacks) were dismounted and became the core of a new infantry regiment in every cavalry division. Recruits were added to this core, making each regiment 3,000 strong. This reduction in the number of horsemen was the result of trench warfare and of the growing belief that mounted cavalry actions would be more restricted from then on. One very sad day the commanders of our squadrons pulled chances out of a hat to determine their fortunes. The 2nd and 5th squadrons had bad luck and lost their horses. Govorov was appointed to command the Hussars' part of the infantry regiment and my old friend Yazvin, with whom I lived in Moscow, to command one of the squadrons. Yazvin was, by the way, wounded three times, but so lightly each time that he was never evacuated. It became almost a standing joke whenever Yazvin was wounded: it was assumed that the injury must be slight. When he was wounded for the third time and a hussar entered our mess to report it, the only response from one of the officers was: 'Ask the captain to join us; tell him we have good wine.' Yazvin was wounded once more during the Civil War, but he survived this, too, and succeeded in escaping from the Bolsheviks. He died about five years ago in Indonesia, where he had lived for a long time.

Before Christmas 1916, our new commander, Colonel Jukov arrived in the regiment to replace Colonel Leontiev who had gone sick. It would be difficult to choose a man more unsuitable to command us. Very provincial, both in his point of view and in his manners, he was afraid of his superiors. When during a discussion someone once remarked: 'The trouble with our army is that we are more afraid of our generals than we are of the Germans,' Jukov sincerely replied: 'But that is the way it should be.' He had received a high decoration while still the senior colonel of his original regiment. We were told by an officer of that regiment that one day Jukov, who was commanding two squadrons, did not dare to charge when the moment was ripe. A cornet who noticed this and who feared the precious opportunity would be lost, shouted: 'The commander of the division is coming!' This was a lie, but before he had time to close his mouth the squadrons were galloping with drawn swords. The attack was a success, hence the decoration. Even if this story was an exaggeration, it well describes Jukov.

Before Jukov's arrival many rumours concerning him were current in the regiment. One was that he did not drink. Rot was very upset by this: 'It may not make any difference to you at the other end of the table, but what shall I do sitting next to him?' At the hour of Jukov's expected arrival all the officers assembled in a schoolhouse. When a hussar posted outside reported that the commander's car was approaching, Rot went out to greet him. A moment later, a tall slender man with a red nose entered the room. Behind him Rot was beaming. He assumed that such a nose was bound to bring good news. Surprisingly, it did not.

Possibly Jukov's sobriety had something to do with his fear of his superiors. In any case he was always apprehensive lest a general might see some of his officers enjoying good wine. In those days I drank quite a bit and did it boisterously. On New Year's Eve we were lucky enough to be in reserve. So we decided to have a party in the schoolhouse. We expected the commander of our cavalry corps to attend it. Jukov was frightened to death of his coming. He was afraid that Kalachev would play the guitar and that everyone would start singing and that some of us might over-indulge. I was one of the suspects. Early that afternoon Jukov begged me: 'Please don't drink much tonight. Promise me you won't. Let's go to the kitchen and you may choose any bottles you wish me to save you for tomorrow. Tomorrow you can do what you like.' Kalachev promised not to play the guitar, and I promised not to drink. After the deal was concluded, Jukov and I visited the kitchen. I chose the bottles, and Jukov ordered one of our waiters to take them to his hut.

The Commander of the Corps liked gaiety, songs and wine, and although trumpeters and singers constantly took turns performing, the General wanted something more intimate. 'Don't you have someone who plays the guitar?' he asked. 'Kalachev, where is Kalachev?' Jukov asked, as he ran around looking for Kalachev. This was also a green light for me. As Kalachev played his guitar and sang gypsy songs, the General became sentimental and made several speeches all on one theme —'women and cornets'. He departed early in the morning and we had barely reached our beds when he returned and ordered a practice alarm. Somehow the regiment got together in record time.

Jukov commanded the regiment for less than three months —until the Revolution—and in this short time succeeded in doing several foolish things. I shall never forget one. On many winter nights parties were sent out on to the ice-covered river to set up large wooden trestles strung with barbed wire. These trestles were made behind our trenches during the day by a special work battalion of elderly bearded men, who set them up on the ice during the night. A small group of our hussars protected them and kept them in order. If the Germans heard a noise on the ice they would light the section with rockets and then open fire. The bearded men would run. After this had happened several nights in a row, Jukov lined them up and appealed to their patriotism. The men's expressions did not change; they continued to stare at him with glassy eyes. Jukov understood that his speech was a failure and he suddenly added: 'If you run away again, I'll shoot every tenth man of you; do you understand? Every tenth man of you. I'll count—one, two, three . . . ten—shoot!' The men still stood motionless with their stomachs stuck forward. 'I'll shoot all of you, every one of you!' shouted Jukov in despair. Again he met glassy eyes. 'I'll machine gun you!' proceeded Jukov. This threat produced no effect either. The men were quite certain that they would die on the ice anyway. 'Bring the machine guns,' ordered Jukov. Two machine guns were brought up and placed facing the workers' formation. 'Do you see these machine guns?' screamed Jukov, 'I'll shoot you with these machine guns.' Not a twitch could be seen on anyone's face. Jukov's failure was complete. The machine guns were taken away, and everyone dispersed.

All that winter, life in the trenches was for the most part quiet. Hours might pass without a single shot being fired. The officer at the observation post, who was supposed to write down every movement observed on the German side, had a hard time finding four lines to write in twelve hours. The exception was a cornet of German ancestry, who had no trouble filling pages with nothing. He was from one of the Russian Baltic provinces and had recently arrived in the regiment. He spoke Russian slowly and with a German accent. He was extraordinarily literal-minded and I had fun teasing him. The fun consisted in repeatedly asking him the same stupid questions. He never caught on. About once a week, I would ask him: 'How many cups of coffee do you have every morning?' To this he would answer, as if repeating a lesson in Russian grammar, 'Every morning I have two cups of coffee.' 'Why don't you have three cups of coffee?' 'I do not drink three cups of coffee every morning because three cups of coffee are too much for me.' 'Then what about having just one?' 'One cup of coffee every morning is not enough for me.' Such a pastime illustrates better than anything else how dull life in the trenches could be.

Almost the only military activity on our side was a periodic crossing of the river by our scouts, who attempted to capture prisoners in order to identify the German regiments stationed against us.

We were still occupying these trenches when the Revolution broke out in March 1917.

The Revolution

CHAPTER 14

THE FIRST DAYS OF THE REVOLUTION

L ATE in the evening of March 15, 1917, while we were still in the trenches on the east bank of the Dvina river, we received an unexpected order to proceed with speed to the town of Rejitza to suppress a riot of its garrison. At the same time we heard rumours that there had been trouble in St. Petersburg—either a general strike or a hunger riot, no one knew for certain which. In actuality a revolution there was in full swing.

Rejitza was fifty miles away from our trenches, but our orders were to ride there without halting. We were relieved the same night and started at dawn of the 16th. Travelling was difficult; the road was under deep snow and the bitter cold and a strong wind added to our hardship. We stopped only twice for a short time on the way, to feed our horses and to warm ourselves in huts. On the road we met an officer of our regiment who was returning from St. Petersburg. He told us that the capital was in the grip of a revolution and that the Emperor was expected to abdicate. This all sounded so preposterous that we could not believe it. In fact, the Provisional Government was already in power; the Emperor had abdicated shortly before midnight of the 15th, as we were leaving the trenches. But we, struggling through the snow, were not to know this until the next morning.

Just as the sun began to rise on March 17th, the regiment, icicle-encrusted and frozen to the bone, entered Rejitza. A few blocks inside the town we met a group of soldiers wearing red ribbons. They were drunk and gay, and they failed to salute us. The commander halted his horse and inquired about this omission. 'Don't you know what's happened in Russia?' asked one of the soldiers; he added cheerfully: 'We're all equals now.' The commander ordered these men to be taken 'between the stirrups', that is, between the horses. This was a sort of arrest on the move. As we proceeded towards the centre of town, we met more and more such groups, and more and more soldiers wearing red bows were taken 'between the stirrups'. The small, four-squadron regiment had no more than 500 men, and by the time we reached the square we probably had as many as 100 men walking inside our ranks. Our frozen, hungry and annoyed hussars were kicking them, and by now most of our prisoners were begging for forgiveness.

As we reached the town square a cornet who was in charge of the forward lookouts rode to the commander, pointed to a large building, and reported: 'A meeting of a "Soviet (Council) of Soldiers' and Workers' Deputies" is being held in there. I don't know what it means, but that's what I was told.' None of us riding at the head of the column knew what it meant either. Petrjkevich, who was in front of the 1st Squadron, addressed the commander of the regiment, saying: 'May I have your permission to go there and see what it is?' The commander agreed to this.

Petrjkevich dismounted at the building and disappeared into it. We stood waiting. A few minutes later crowds of dishevelled soldiers, and civilians, obviously in panic, began to pour out through the door. Behind the last men to emerge from the house came Petrjkevich, wildly hitting anyone in reach with his riding stick. By himself he had dispersed the local revolutionary group in power.

In the course of the next four hours we arrested and imprisoned 300 people. We occupied the two railway stations, the post office and other government buildings and began to patrol the town. Rejitza became calm and orderly; there was no more rioting, and only small incidents occurred here and there.

The regiment was partly quartered in an empty barracks and partly billeted in private houses; we officers were lodged in a small hotel. It was probably eleven o'clock by the time order was more or less restored, and I stopped in a cafeteria near the hotel to have breakfast. I was alone in the dining room when two soldiers, one armed with a pistol and the other with a sword, rushed in and ran towards me shouting insults. I jumped up and ran towards them with equal speed. They turned and fled, and when I tried to seize the man with the sword he dropped it. None of the revolutionaries was sure of his ground yet. In a short while some other officers of the regiment joined me, and around noon the newsboy came in. From the large headlines we learned of the abdication of the Emperor and of the progress of the Revolution. We had been two days too late in suppressing it in Rejitza. But if we had been able to do it, then why had no one in St. Petersburg done it? Rejitza's garrison was 10,000 strong and it had artillery. It was not strength, but will, that won the day for us. Why didn't enough people in St. Petersburg have it? Besides these questions there were others in our minds. What were we to do from now on? How were we to behave? What was our position while our world was being rocked? To all these and similar questions none of us had answers at the moment.

It was a big mistake to stay in a hotel apart from our soldiers. We did not immediately grasp all the dangers of the peculiar situation in which we found ourselves, so we behaved in a normal manner. In our absence our soldiers were propagandised. When Petrjkevich entered the school where his 1st Squadron was billeted he found a revolutionary there addressing the hussars. Petrjkevich beat him up with his riding stick and threw him out. But if we caught one we missed dozens of others by being quartered apart. We soon realised, however, that the propaganda was reaching the hearts of our soldiers, and the commander of the regiment, Jukov, repeatedly telephoned the staff of our 5th Army to ask for permission to return to the trenches. These requests were not granted; the staff insisted that we remain in Rejitza as a police force. For three days we successfully maintained order, but we knew that we could not do it much longer. The Army's Staff was to be blamed for what followed.

Late in the afternoon of 21 March our soldiers marched in formation to our hotel and asked us to join them in a parade through the town as a sign of acceptance of the new regime. Only four or five of us were in the hotel at that moment; the others had gone down town. We felt that under the circumstances our first duty was to be with the regiment, so we came out. As we stood on the entrance steps a few shots were fired from the very large crowd that surrounded the regiment. The regiment looked small inside this sea of people. As more shots were fired someone shouted: 'Hussars, your officers are shooting at us.' A colonel, recently attached to the regiment, ran back into the hotel and tried to escape through the courtyard and gate that led to another street. There he was killed. In the meantime the enormous crowd had panicked in all directions and split our regiment in many parts. Some of our soldiers lost their heads and sought the protection of doorways and shops. Sporadic shooting continued. At that moment, as stated in the history of our regiment, 'Littauer ran forward and in a loud voice ordered, "Hussars, to me, obey my command." Littauer's presence of mind immediately restored order.' Actually it took longer than that. I had to run from one separate group to another saying: 'Do you know me? I am now commanding the regiment. Take your places in the ranks.' Finally the regiment was back in formation; almost instinctively I felt that the next thing to do was to move—no matter where, but to move. I don't know why we marched towards the railway station. In the course of this march, I called the four sergeant-majors forward and asked their advice about what to do next. The unanimous answer was: 'Let's return to the trenches immediately.' Unfortunately we could not do this, as we could not get permission from the Army Staff. Little by little, other officers joined the regiment and I relinquished my command to my superiors.

Jukov, learning what had happened, left for the Army Staff in Dvinsk. Govorov, commander of the hussars' battalion of our infantry regiment, came to Rejitza and temporarily took command. In the meantime the regiment had joined the new regime; a soldiers' committee was established for the purpose of limiting the power of the officers. Fortunately, its first chairman was Wilenkin. Only because of the diplomatic skill of both Govorov and Wilenkin was some sort of order re-established. By now our soldiers no longer wished to return to the fighting line, but to stay in Rejitza and 'defend the Revolution'. It took three days to get the soldiers to move, but finally we started the march back to the trenches. All the soldiers wore red ribbons and Govorov's mare, 'Nora', was decorated from mane to tail. It was much too distasteful to Govorov to mount such a symbol of the Revolution and he whispered to Wilenkin: 'Please do something about it.' Wilenkin immediately said to

Govorov's orderly: 'What's the matter with you? You've put the sacred emblem of the Revolution on a horse. Tomorrow, you may decorate a pig the same way.' The ribbons were removed. As we neared the trenches, Govorov ordered everything that did not belong to our uniform to be taken off. All the red ribbons disappeared.

An ideological revolutionary movement had begun in Russia in the nineteenth century, and the illiterate bulk of the population, held in servitude for centuries, was always apt to riot. The abortive Revolution of 1905 had been a warning to the Imperial Government. Some concessions made by the latter, such as the establishment of the Duma (parliament), were not made in good faith. Twice, Dumas that had opposed the government were simply dissolved and a new Duma elected. At first the war had united everyone for the defence of the country. But it had lasted too long and it had been too bloody.

The March Revolution of 1917 had been foreseen, but was not expected at that time. Peculiarly, it had no outstanding leaders. It had not been organised by a revolutionary committee, but was entirely spontaneous and non-ideological. There had been agitators, however, causing strikes and urging the people to go into the streets to protest against the bad conditions of the time. The trouble started in St. Petersburg, with strikes provoked by the deteriorating economy, and was extended by the hunger riots. When the army units that had been sent to break up the demonstrators joined them, the government found itself powerless. Thousands of reservists in St. Petersburg joined the rioters simply because they did not want to go to war; after two and a half years of fighting everyone was sick and tired of it. The pattern was the same in other cities, and the Imperial Government fell with little bloodshed. In the absence of leaders the Duma took over; from its ranks came the first Provisional Government. Most of the Russian intellectuals welcomed the Revolution as well as the Provisional Government, which was largely composed of well-educated people. The general tone of the Revolution was conservative. But soon leaders of various political beliefs appeared, and a struggle between them began. It culminated with the Bolshevik Revolution in November (October according to the Russian calendar). This was well organised, well led, ideological, but cynical in its execution.

Jukov, Petrjkevich and Snejkov left the regiment in Rejitza. They joined the officers' army pool, where they received fresh assignments. Some felt it would be easier to serve the new regime if they were in new circumstances. During the terror after the Bolshevik Revolution, Petrjkevich was executed. Snejkov was arrested and shot on the way to prison. He was left for dead on the street of a little town, but he was only badly wounded. Some kindly townspeople picked him up and nursed him back to health. He survived, and a year ago I dined with him in Marseilles, where he now lives. Rot was on leave during the Rejitza episode, and he never returned to the regiment. None of us knows his ultimate fate. Replacing Petrjkevich, I became commander of the 1st Squadron and returned in a new role to those trenches with which I was so familiar from the days when I was in charge of the Communications Unit.

CHAPTER 15

THE END OF THE REGIMENT

THE disorganisation produced by the Revolution continued to increase, in both the army and in the country in general. The Sumsky Hussars were among the comparatively few regiments that retained a semblance of order for the next few months. Just the same, in the course of the summer of 1917 the regiment was slowly falling apart.

In May we were put in the army's reserve. Soon a new commander of the regiment arrived. He was Colonel Neyelov, a clever, tactful, cultivated man. The big problem that confronted him was how to preserve the regiment amid the general chaos in the army. During a conference between the squadron commanders and Neyelov it was agreed that something should be done to make our soldiers feel that they were of the *élite*, that they had little in common with the infantry. The first move in this direction was to have the red breeches sent to us that we had left in Moscow at the beginning of the war. This was a success; the men felt that they were once more hussars and, as such, were different from the khaki mass of the army. The red breeches obviously had a peculiar appeal. Our veterinarian even asked permission to wear them. Now, after the Revolution, the fact that he was not a hussar but only a military clerk did not matter any more, and a pair was issued to him.

The Provisional Government wished to continue the war. In order to do so, it had to restore discipline as well as the fighting spirit of the army. For this purpose a number of bright young men were sent to the front to address the soldiers in the name of the government. One of these came to our regiment and, in a brilliant half-hour speech, succeeded in arousing so much enthusiasm among our hussars that they not only agreed to keep on fighting but took off all their silver war decorations to donate them to the war fund. Two sergeants and a corporal were elected to go to St. Petersburg to present the bag of silver to the president of the Provisional Government. They were to take the train that evening.

During lunch, we officers discussed the three soldiers' trip to the capital and concluded that they would be apt to make fools of themselves if left alone on their mission. The ways of a big city were bound to be strange to our country lads, and in spite of the present universal equality, they were certainly not equal to the many situations that they would encounter there. Someone proposed to give them a chaperon, but to do it in such a way that they would not suspect it. I was chosen for the job and, pretending that I was taking a few days' leave, I 'ran into' our delegates on the station platform. Chatting about various things, I casually asked where they intended to stay in St. Petersburg. This matter was obviously worrying them and they were ready to accept any suggestion. Sensing this, I said: 'My father has a large apartment. Why don't you come and stay with me?' They gladly agreed, and I thus placed them where I could keep my eye on them.

Next day we went to the Duma, where the Provisional Government had its offices, to make an appointment to see the president. While there, we found that hundreds of delegates from the front were assembled in the main chamber. They were being addressed by leaders of various political parties. We stopped in this immense hall to see what it was all about, became interested and sat down. Neatly dressed and in red breeches, we were a discordant note in the otherwise dishevelled crowd which looked as if it had just emerged from the trenches. The Sumsky non-coms could not possibly approve of it and, as they critically glanced around, other soldiers looked as critically at us. Then and there my men began to be annoyed. We heard two or three good speeches which they could not fully understand; their annoyance increased. Then Trotzky appeared on the podium. His speech was very well delivered but it was not fully comprehensible; this further irritated the non-coms. A platoon sergeant of my squadron, Sheinoga, sat on my right, next to the aisle. Suddenly, during Trotzky's speech, he rose, and in a commanding voice loudly ordered: 'Down with the *kike*!' Pandemonium broke loose at once. Everyone was shouting, and the words 'Kill them, hang them' prevailed disturbingly. Trotzky was not on the platform any more. Instead, various soldiers appeared on it for a few seconds each, suggesting different methods of murdering us. For a while I was quite certain that my last hour had come. Then, inexplicably, another word crept into the shouting; it was 'Apologise'. The moment I heard it, I whispered to Sheinoga: 'Apologise.' 'I shall not,' he replied in a positive tone, 'now we all have the freedom to speak.' In the meantime the cry 'He must apologise', 'Make him apologise' became dominant. After telling Sheinoga again and again to apologise, I finally said: 'Even if we have had a revolution, I'm still your squadron commander and I order you to apologise.' Sheinoga got up, stepped into the aisle and, making a gesture of disgust with one arm, reluctantly said: 'All right, I apologise.' After this the speeches were resumed.

Very soon after the Revolution the sergeant of the Communications Unit, Krasikhin, became one of the important figures in the regimental Soldiers' Committee. Once, walking in a village, I saw Krasikhin cross the street towards me. An incident of the past leapt to my mind and I thought I was in trouble. It had occurred more than a year before, when we were stationed in Arglan. Krasikhin once asked me for an unusual favour; he wanted to go for a couple of days' rest to a town in the rear. I granted his request but I did not see him leave. I did see his return, however. Dressed as a small provincial merchant, the drunk Krasikhin sat in a borrowed sleigh pulled by a *troika* of the Unit horses. The coachman was one of my hussars. Wearing mufti alone was a case for court martial; using government horses for private business and without permission was another. Of course, I would not have dreamt of ruining his life by being so dogmatic. Instead I halted the *troika*, seized Krasikhin by his fur collar, dragged him out of the sleigh and beat him up. Next day we met as though nothing had happened; the incident was never mentioned again. But this time, when I saw Krasikhin in the glory of his new power deliberately walking towards me, I thought the past was catching up with me. To my delight, Krasikhin said: 'Now that I have the right to talk to you on equal terms, I wish to thank you for beating me up instead of court-martialling me. I realise what a fool I was, and even at the time I took your beating as fatherly punishment.'

Corporal punishment had long been officially abolished in the Russian army, but unofficial use of hands still persisted. In my regiment every corporal and every sergeant, including Krasikhin, struck their soldiers (who had no right to retaliate) now and then. Some officers did the same. I used my fist in a few instances, when the misdemeanour was too serious for me to make it official. I am certain that most of my victims appreciated the fact that I did not bring them before the law.

Throughout the summer the struggle between the various political parties continued. It was becoming clearer and clearer that the intellectuals were losing and that few people could appreciate the theories of a perfect Republican regime. The cynically destructive propaganda of the Bolsheviks, which appealed to the lower instincts, was getting the upper hand. Such of their slogans as 'Stop the war', 'Kill the officers', 'Burn the estates', 'Rob the rich' and in general destroy all those 'who have drunk our blood' easily penetrated the hearts of an illiterate population. This was when we really felt the lack of a large middle class.

During the time we were kept in reserve I was sent with my squadron by train to the large town of Narva to quell a riot. The mutinous garrison was several thousand strong and to send less than 150 men to set it in order was absurd; but this was typical of the prevailing chaos. The railway station in Narva was still held by perhaps 200 soldiers from various units under the city commandant. The latter, a colonel, was in a state of panic and ecstatically greeted me, exclaiming: 'Thank God you've come! Please take command of all my troops.' Although only twenty-five years old, I was fairly mature in practical matters and, quickly summing up the situation, I declined the honour of commanding over a colonel. Leaving the town commandant and his men at the station, I ordered my squadron to mount, and we proceeded to walk up and down the streets of the town, with my singers leading the column. Life here was orderly on the surface, and many people and soldiers cheered us. To the occasional question of why I was in Narva I answered: 'I have no idea why I was sent here.' In the general disorder this did not sound strange. In about three hours I stopped at the telegraph office and wired my regiment that I was patrolling the town. I did not mention, however, that I was doing it with songs. By then it was time to feed my horses, but I hesitated to order my men to dismount in the city and thus expose them to prolonged conversations with the population. Instead I rode out of town and gave the men and horses a rest in a village some three miles away. Later in the afternoon I returned to Narva and again sent a wire that I was patrolling the city. I may have been doing so technically, but the manner in which I did it prevented the touchy rebels from feeling they were being thwarted. For safety's sake I spent the night in the village; the next day I was recalled.

During the same period my squadron was also sent by train on another short and uneventful police mission, and it is only the end of it that stands out in my memory. As my soldiers were reloading at the railroad station I was approached by the superintendent of the estate where we had been billeted; he demanded cash for the hay and oats consumed by my horses. Earlier in the morning I had given him an official receipt for these and had told him that I had no money with me. Now, at the station, he kept insisting on being paid in cash. The argument got hot; suddenly he pulled out a revolver and pointed it at me. I punched him in the nose; his hat flew off, he dropped the revolver and ran away. A train conductor who had seen this picked up the hat, examined it, and asked my permission to keep it. He took the hat and I took the revolver which, it turned out, was not loaded.

Desertion from the front, which had started soon after the Revolution, increased throughout the spring and summer. In July the individual squadrons of the Sumsky regiment were placed at four different stations to arrest deserters. My squadron guarded the important railway junction of Dno, and we were billeted on a nearby estate. Normally all I had to do was to keep a score of men with an officer at the station. This number was enough to take care of individual deserters. When, on occasion, I was advised that a whole company of infantry, fully armed, had boarded a passenger train which was due at my station at such and such an hour, I went there with all my officers and about 100 men. We developed a special technique for dealing with these mass desertions. The main platform of the Dno station was between two sets of tracks. We prepared an empty cattle train of half a dozen cars on the opposite side of the platform to that on which the deserters' train was supposed to arrive. Some of my men with raised rifles were placed on both sides of the track on which we expected the train. As the latter pulled in, our men loudly and continually repeated: 'Don't lean out; don't lean out!' Now and again they fired into the air. I myself or one of my officers accompanied by a few men would enter the first car and shout: 'Get out of here, you sons of bitches, before we shoot you. And leave your arms behind.' As they jumped out of the car in single file they found themselves in a corridor of our soldiers. This corridor led to a cattle truck on the other side of the platform. Once the deserters were packed into it, its wide gate was closed and fastened from the outside. This done, my soldiers moved to form a new corridor between the next passenger car and another cattle truck, and the performance was repeated. We could do such a job in twenty minutes and the train of cattle trucks would head back to the front. While this was going on half a dozen of my men would be collecting the weapons left in the passenger cars.

Once an unusual incident occurred. I was advised by telephone from St. Petersburg that the secret police had information that a Bolshevik agitator was going to the front by a train which was to stop at Dno around midnight. The police did not know the man and could not give me his description. The only thing that they knew was that he might be wearing an officer's uniform. I had to find him and arrest him. That night I took enough officers and men with me to the station so as to be able to search all the cars of the train simultaneously. Mine was a sleeping car, but it was so crowded that no one could lie down; there were six or eight people to a compartment. I asked to see the identification documents of the men only. In one compartment they all presented them immediately except for one officer who had a hard time finding his. He searched for them in all his pockets and even in his suitcase. His trench coat did not bear the insignia of his regiment, but at that time there was nothing unusual about this. His manners were excellent and while he was searching he continually apologised for the delay he was causing. I became convinced that he was genuine and had simply lost his papers. In order to prevent unnecessary delay I said: 'Don't bother to look for the papers—just tell me what your regiment is.' He nearly knocked me over by answering: 'I am a Sumsky Hussar.' 'If so,' I said, 'you will have to follow me.' Later I found out that he was the man the police were looking for. It was a case of extraordinarily bad luck for him. Of the hundreds of regiments in the Russian army he had chosen the wrong one for the occasion. Perhaps as a civilian from Moscow, the name of our regiment was the most familiar to him.

In September the regiment passed a few nights in a wooded district of the province of Pskov. This district was known for its wolves. Now that there had been no wolf-hunting for three years, with the male population away at the war, the animals had multiplied considerably. We were quartered in four villages that were quite a distance apart. The villagers travelling in their carts were prepared to protect themselves and their horses from the wolves. One of their defence measures was to carry balls made of twisted straw with them. If attacked, they set fire to a ball attached to a long rope and threw it out behind. The flaming ball trailing in the rear of the cart kept the wolves away. When it was burnt up another ball was thrown out. We, in our innocence about such things, found ourselves in trouble from the very first hour. A pair of our hussars riding unarmed from one village to another were attacked by wolves. They galloped into a small lake by the roadside and stood there in the water watched by the wolves, until someone saw them and brought help.

My squadron was billeted in a village of about fifty houses. Each house probably had at least one dog. These were large mongrel shepherds with, I suspect, wolf blood in them. One moonlit night a pack of wolves approached the village, placed themselves on a nearby ridge, and howled. All done, as you see, in classic fashion. Intrigued, I went outside; there I saw the village dogs assembling in the street. As a group of them trotted in the direction of the howling wolves, more and more dogs joined them. At least one dog came from almost every courtyard. This column of about fifty dogs moved out of the village towards the ridge overlooking it. Soon the noise of a fight could be heard. Next morning I walked to the battlefield. The remains of one or two dead dogs and a couple of dead wolves lay on the ground. I had probably simply witnessed one incident of a centuries-old warfare.

Chaos in the army increased throughout the summer, as more and more soldiers joined the Bolsheviks. The great majority of them refused to fight. Our own infantry regiment went on strike when it was ordered to move against the Germans. A story was told that when one infantry regiment had

244

The Times History of the War

Plate 27 St. Petersburg after the Revolution.
Checking identification papers.

The Times History of the War

Plate 28 Revolution, March 1917. A military mob in St. Petersburg.

Plate 29   The meeting of the soldiers' delegates in the Duma in the spring of 1917.

refused to go forward, its officers had attacked alone and had been buried the next day by the Germans with military honours in no-man's-land. Here and there one heard of officers being killed by their own soldiers. Desertion in the army assumed mass proportions, and the number of armed men in the rear ready to support the Bolsheviks increased correspondingly. When the second (Bolshevik) revolution came, what few troops were left to defend the Provisional Government faded away almost at once.

Immediately after the Bolshevik Revolution, the regiment began to disintegrate rapidly. Several unpleasant incidents marked these grim days. The rate of deterioration increased noticeably after our Polish soldiers left us. Poland had declared its independence and, according to the agreement between it and the new Russian government, all the Poles serving in the Russian army were to be released and returned to Poland with their weapons. At that time our Poles, having no particular interest in the achievements of the Russian Revolution, constituted the conservative element in the regiment. One day they all mounted with full equipment and, in an orderly fashion, rode off to their native country. My batman Kourovski was among them. The night before, their delegates had come to see me to persuade me to go with them. 'Nothing good will happen to you here after we are gone,' was their argument. And they were right. Kourovski asked me to join them with tears in his eyes.

Soon afterwards we almost had an assassination in the regiment. The intended victim was a squadron commander, Captain Ivanov, whose brilliant reconnaissance a couple of years earlier I have described. The plan of the assassins was to call him to a meeting, start an argument and, in the heat of it, kill him. Ivanov was informed of the plot, and when a couple of soldiers came to his hut they found him sitting at a table reading. They politely invited him to the meeting and he refused to go. A few minutes later several armed men came into Ivanov's room and, throwing all pretences away, intended to take him to the meeting by force. Ivanov was still sitting at the table reading, but now two revolvers lay on the table. Ivanov was not holding them, he did not even look at the soldiers. His eyes were still fixed on his book when he simply said: 'I am not going, but you can try to take me there.' Every one of his soldiers respected him for his bravery. They all knew that a couple of them would be killed in the struggle and probably each feared that it would be he. They did not touch Ivanov, and in a few hours he left the regiment at the insistence of the other officers. He was killed later, fighting in the Civil War.

In my squadron the biggest trouble maker of the period was my platoon sergeant, Sheinoga, who had been insolent to Trotzky in the Duma. He was an excellent sergeant and had become one in the first place because he was very ambitious. Now the only road open for his ambition was to join the Bolsheviks and to become a leader among them. Up to that time we had both appreciated each other and been on very good terms. Suddenly he became my worst enemy in the squadron. With my usual optimism I still hoped that I could hold the squadron together as a military unit, and one day I sent for Sheinoga. He entered my room with his hands in his pockets and a smirk on his face. I told my batman to get out of the hut, and asked Sheinoga to close the door behind him. The moment he did this and was sure that no one was watching us he stood at attention as in the old days. Slowly and deliberately I approached him and struck him in the face. He did not strike back, although he could now do so with impunity, but continued to stand at attention. Then as slowly and deliberately I said to him: 'Desert tonight. If I find you around tomorrow I'll kill you.' He had disappeared by morning. But this did not help me, as a few days later the Soldiers' Committee took my squadron away from me. After privately saying 'goodbye' to some of the men with whom I had served since my days in Moscow as a cornet, I left the regiment. The hardest parting perhaps was from my 'Moscal' whom I had to leave behind; my future was too unpredictable to take a horse with me. I gave him to my orderly Kaurkhin.

I went to St. Petersburg and stayed with my father. While in the capital, to legalise my desertion, I presented myself to a medical committee that examined crippled officers to determine their serviceability. I frankly told these half a dozen doctors that I felt it was no longer possible for me to be an officer in the army and that I would appreciate their finding something wrong with me. 'Is there anything wrong with you?' asked one of the doctors. 'Now think hard of your former illnesses and accidents.' The injury to my knee in the 'School' came to my mind. The doctors examined my leg and in a few minutes I was holding a discharge certificate. It did not, however, terminate my military service. The Civil War was still ahead.

Soon after the Bolshevik Revolution the regiment was moved to quarters in the deep rear, on the river Volga. There, by February 1918, only four officers remained—the commander, Ncyclov, Govorov, Shwed and Gukovski. They suggested that the regiment simply disperse. The Soldiers' Committee approved the plan, and one day the men mounted and rode away in different directions to their respective homes. By then the old army did not exist any more anyway, and the Red Army was being formed.

Colonel Neyelov brought our standard to Moscow. The big question was where to keep it. Nearly all our officers and friends were members of anti-revolutionary organisations and at any time could be arrested or at least have their homes searched. A safe place was finally found, and there are good reasons to believe that it is still there intact. One day some of our officers assembled at Wilenkin's apartment to bid farewell to the standard of the Sumsky Hussars. It was put in an ordinary wooden box and in complete silence everyone in his turn hammered a nail in the cover. Suddenly Wilenkin burst into tears: 'I can't bear this hammering any longer. You are burying the glory of the regiment.' The staff of the standard was cut into small pieces and one of these was sent to me in St. Petersburg.

CHAPTER 16

ST. PETERSBURG AFTER THE REVOLUTION

M Y father and sister (my mother had died at the beginning
of the war) lived in an apartment in St. Petersburg. It was
in a large private house built at the beginning of the nineteenth
century, which had been divided into four apartments of varying sizes, from one of three rooms to ours of fifteen rooms.
The staff consisted of a housekeeper, a cook, two maids and a
laundress.

The housekeeper, Anna Stepanovna, had been the household
seamstress prior to my mother's death; she began working for
our family when I was a small boy. She saved my life twice in
the course of the year 1918.

The house stood on a short street (Millionnaia) which ran
from the Winter Palace to the Champ de Mars, by then an
awkwardly conspicuous location for anyone belonging to the
old regime. The apartment, decorated in the prevailing
Edwardian style, was cosy and comfortable. Only one thing
was lacking there when I arrived from the army: food.

Instead of improving, the food situation had deteriorated
subsequent to the Revolution. People had to stand in queues
for hours to buy their food, and what little food was available
was very poor. Bread was at times impossible to get and I

remember our waitress bursting into tears when forced to serve potato cakes in its place.

Prior to my return home my family had not been under too much pressure from the new regime. But, just the same, my father had been arrested once. A commissar and two armed soldiers came for him. They did not take their hats off when they walked into the apartment, but they removed them when my father ordered them to. Nevertheless, they arrested him. He was imprisoned for no other reason than that of being an important industrialist. There was nothing specific against him, and he was released in a few days.

One of the first things I did when I got to St. Petersburg was to order civilian clothes. In spite of the fact that they were made by a very good tailor, they did not look right on me. I had never worn anything but a uniform; even in the gymnasium we wore them. The well-bred nonchalance in movements and manners that make a civilian elegant is quite different from the special sort of stiffness that is required to carry a uniform well. Ruefully I passed the house where my former military tailor, Brunst, was located. He kept a smart establishment and in this differed from my bootmaker, Shmelov, who had a dingy shop up two flights of stairs. But he was considered the best boot-maker in the city. Because he did not wish to expand, he kept his clientele to a limited number. I put my name on his waiting list as soon as I became a younker. But I had to wait for a year and a half before, due to someone's death or retirement, he took me on. His prices were more than double, but his boots were more than twice as good as those made by others.

Soon after my return home, a soldier of the Red Army brought me an invitation to come to its recruiting office. There I was met by a colonel of the former Imperial Army who had switched his allegiance. Rising to greet me at the door as I entered the room, he very cordially invited me to join the new army with the rank of colonel, a high salary, and various privileges. I asked him only one question: 'Is this an order or an invitation?' Upon learning that it was only an invitation I declined it. The colonel was still pleasantly polite as he said 'goodbye' to me.

Many officers joined the Red Army. Some eventually made careers in it. One of these, Tuhachevski, formerly of a foot-guard regiment, became a marshal of the Red Army. He was executed during the big Stalinist purge of the thirties. Another, Shaposhnikov, fared better and was Stalin's private military adviser during the Second World War. Thus, during the Civil War, officers of the former Imperial Army fought on both sides; but the bulk of them were with the 'Whites'. A few wartime officers of my regiment joined the Bolsheviks.

The optimistic feeling that one would be able to live and work with the new regime, and that the latter was bound to change for the better, persisted with many people both military and civilian. While these optimists were correct in believing that the chaos could not last, they failed to foresee that the new system might be organised along a pattern different from the one the conservative liberals hoped for. My father was so optimistic that soon after the March Revolution he refused to sell a piece of property in St. Petersburg. Eventually, it was taken over by the state; the plan and the deed of our apartment house are all I now have.

But while most people were passively waiting for a change, some worked towards the destruction of the Bolshevik rule. In January 1918, Russia was full of various counter-revolutionary organisations, some headed by civilian political leaders, but mostly by military. At least a dozen former officers of my regiment living in Moscow belonged to such secret organisations. In these the conspirators were divided into groups of ten, whose members were not known to each other but only to the commander of the group. Five groups constituted a detachment. Only the commanders of the groups knew the commander of the detachment. Six detachments formed a fighting unit. Despite all this theoretical secrecy, most such organisations were quite amateurish; there were also spies within their ranks. One of these was discovered and killed in the organisation to which some Sumsky Hussars belonged. Constantine Sokolov, who was involved in the apprehension of this spy, remarked a few minutes before the assassination: 'This is not life, this is a novel!' And he was correct. Since none of the officers were professional conspirators, the whole movement of secret organisations had a strongly romantic flavour. They could survive only as long as the Bolshevik secret service remained inefficient. When the Bolshevik Government established the 'Extraordinary Commission to Fight the Counter-Revolution' (the C.H.E.K.A.) the search for counter-revolutionaries became well organised. Most of those arrested were executed; among them were Petrjkevich, Wilenkin and seven other officers of the Sumsky Hussars.

Prior to this débâcle, one of the Moscow secret organisations made an unsuccessful attempt to liberate the Emperor and his family. At the time they were being kept under arrest in Siberia, in the town of Tobolsk. There were nine Sumsky Hussars involved in the plot, and among the three 'scouts' who were the first to go to Tobolsk was Sokolov. As far as I know, this was the only attempt of the kind.

The failure of the secret organisations and fear of the C.H.E.K.A. drove officers into forming the 'White' armies. For this activity they were well suited by their upbringing and education. As a result, the Civil War lasted over two years, and at times the 'Whites' seemed to have the upper hand.

In February our family had its first serious trouble with the new regime. It was started by our cook's son. Then a young man of twenty and a soldier in the Red Army, he had been living with us for several years. He had been a good boy until he succumbed to the Bolshevik propaganda; it completely changed his outlook on life, and he became insolent towards us. Finally, he brought us to the Peoples' Court. He accused both my father and me. Unfortunately, the charges he made against me were true. He claimed that once, when a Red Army regiment was marching down the street, I looked out of the window and exclaimed: 'What a bunch of bandits!' He was correct: I had said this. His second accusation was that I kept firearms, a practice then prohibited. This was also true. Besides several German rifles, I had my service revolver, the little Browning that I always carried in my pocket, and the revolver left by the estate superintendent on the platform of the railroad station. Since the last two were not of the regulation army type, he became particularly suspicious that I was collecting weapons for an uprising. Luckily, the accusation against my father was false, and because of this we won the day in court. My father owned a large apartment house in the city as an investment; the cook's son accused him of hoarding provisions in its cellar. Because there was a food shortage at this time, hoarding was a capital offence.

The Peoples' Court of the district sat in a requisitioned private house; the court room was the former ballroom without its furniture. There were three judges: a sailor, a soldier, and a worker. The day opened with my father's case. It began by the cook's son making his charges. He had no one to support him; even his mother was against him. So the next to speak was a witness for us, the superintendent of my father's apartment house. He was a clever peasant, with a well-kept black beard that gave him an air of respectability. He was also a good actor, as we were soon to find out. As he entered the long ballroom from the opposite end to where the judges sat, he halted and looked towards the corner where the icon usually hung. Although he did not find any, he ceremoniously crossed himself and, with the unconcerned presence that only children and primitive people possess, slowly walked the length of the room and approached the judges' table. He took his time and with great dignity bowed deeply to each judge in turn. Then he folded his arms and calmly stood like a monolith. The chairman briefly repeated the accusation and then asked him: 'Is what this comrade says true?' The superintendent looked intently at the soldier, then turned to the judges and said simply: 'May God forgive him!' All this was so impressive that the case was won then and there; what was said afterwards did not matter. The soldier was clearly a liar, and my case was dismissed so as to not waste time.

Later in the spring the terror began; at first it was directed primarily against former officers. Although I did not belong to any secret counter-revolutionary organisations, the fact that I had been an officer made me suspect. In those days being arrested on suspicion was as good as being shot. Officers were killed by the thousands. When the secret police came the first time to arrest me I was no longer living with my father. Expecting trouble, I had moved from his apartment a few days earlier. From then on, for some time, I spent the nights with various friends. This was very unpleasant, for while I used their hospitality I was turning them into accomplices. It amazes me today to think how many were ready to take this chance.

Being safe at night was not enough; men's identification papers were unexpectedly examined in theatres, restaurants, trolley cars, and even in the streets. It was essential that I obtain papers that did not state that I was a former hussar. For this purpose my father arranged a job for me as clerk in the Salamander Insurance Company. I still have the certificate identifying me as an employee of this firm. Only the director knew who I was; to the rest I was simply a civilian, impoverished by the Revolution, who was beginning a working life.

During my ten days as clerk, an incident happened that could have had grave consequences. A client once spoke very rudely to a girl clerk whose desk stood near mine. I lost my temper, walked up to him, told him to behave, and warned him that unpleasant things would occur unless he did so. He changed his tone and fortunately did not complain; there was no investigation and my identity was not discovered. During my few remaining days in the office I was much admired by all the typists.

In the meantime, at least twice a week, always at night, the secret police searched for me in my father's apartment. Finally they came during the day, and I was almost caught. This time the two uniformed agents remained in the street and only one, in plain clothes, entered the building. He asked the doorman where he could find me, saying he had an important message to convey to me. The porter was fooled and told him that he would find me at the Salamander offices. As the man left, the doorman looked out the window and saw him joining the two soldiers; he instantly ran upstairs and told Anna Stepanovna what had happened. The insurance company was no more than fifteen minutes from our house by foot and the police agents walked, but Anna Stepanovna took a cab and got there four minutes ahead of them. I rushed out of the office, and as I was going out of the building through one side of the revolving door, the men who came to arrest me entered it from the other. They did not know me by sight, and so I made my escape. This was the end of my job as a clerk. The certificate, however, continued to serve me well on several occasions.

In July the extermination of officers reached such proportions that remaining in St. Petersburg was suicidal. I decided to flee to the south of Russia, to the Ukraine, which, since the Revolution, had proclaimed itself an independent state. At that time it was temporarily occupied by German troops.

The border station on the shortest route from St. Petersburg to the Ukraine was the town of Orsha. Through it ran the demarcation line between Russian territory controlled by the Bolsheviks and that occupied by the Germans. The Ukraine itself began still further south, but was within the same German-occupied area. So, to cross the border into the German zone at Orsha with a Ukranian visa was actually admission to the Ukraine. In normal times Orsha was less than fifteen hours away from St. Petersburg by train. To go to the Ukraine I had to have a certificate that I was not a counter-revolutionary, a permit to leave Russia, a paper proving that the Red Army had no claim on me, a medical certificate of some sort, and a *visa* to my passport, of course. These were not the only papers needed to cross the border; there were others, and altogether they formed a substantial volume. Because I had no passport I could not obtain any of these certificates. False passports were available at a price; they were sufficient to fool ignorant soldiers searching for officers in the street, but it was much too risky to present them in government offices. Without a passport I could only buy a railway ticket.

My plan of travelling to Orsha was based on the mistaken assumption that the trains were searched during stops at stations. I decided that I would jump off the train when it slowed down approaching a station, take a walk, and pick the train up again as it began to roll off. This was possible because the steps of the Russian cars of the time always remained open like the steps of commuters' trains in the United States. The matter of how I was to get across the border itself I left alone until I should get there; I simply hoped for luck.

All good Russian trains had one *Wagon-Lit International*. I bought a sleeping berth in it. This car was made up exclusively of compartments, but the corridor that ran the length of it had collapsible seats and people were usually standing or sitting there. As we were leaving St. Petersburg I stood in this corridor and by chance overheard a conversation between two men. Guessing what time they would arrive at their destination, one man observed that we would not be delayed at stations by searches for illegal travellers because these were now being conducted on the train. For this purpose a detachment of security police was travelling with us. Thus during the first five minutes I found out that my plan was impractical. I decided to leave the train at the next station and return to St. Petersburg to think the matter over. Then something changed my mind. When the two men moved away I was able to see a woman, sitting on a flop-seat looking out of the window. She was pretty and well dressed; her face was very familiar, but it took me a while to place her. Finally I came to the conclusion that I had never met her, but had only seen her many times on the stage. Another minute or two and I was quite certain that she was a famous tango dancer—Lydia Johnson. She was pure Russian, and the 'Johnson' part was assumed simply because it sounded exotic in Russia. Looking at her, which was easy to do, I had an idea. During those days of mob rule the old Roman principle 'bread and circuses' prevailed, and entertainers were held in particular respect and admiration. Perhaps she could help me. I went up to her and asked her whether she was Lydia Johnson. She replied that she was, and I most awkwardly said something that delighted her for a long time afterwards. This something was: 'Please don't think that I'm flirting with you.' After this stupid introduction, I told her my story. She was a courageous woman and when she heard it she simply said: 'I am also going to the Ukraine and I shall try to get you to the border and across it. Here is my compartment; move your luggage into it; for the duration of this trip you're my dancing partner.'

Since the railways were as disorganised as everything else in Russia at the time, the trip to Orsha lasted a day and a half. During it, the train was searched several times by different detachments of police agents. Some people were arrested. In our compartment the same routine was repeated every time a knock on the door announced a search. I sat near the window and Lydia Johnson sat near the door. As she presented her numerous documents she flirted gracefully with the police, who in no time were all smiles twirling their moustaches. The smiles and moustache twirling invariably increased when Lydia Johnson began to distribute passes to her forthcoming show. When she felt that she had the full attention of everyone and that no one was any longer interested in documents, she would point casually to me and add: 'And this is my partner.' No one cared who I was by then, but they all greeted me saying: 'How are you, *tovarisch*,' and shook my hand. Not one of these search parties asked for my documents. Smiling, joking and wishing our show success, they would reluctantly part from Lydia Johnson. When all was over and the compartment door was closed again, she would nearly collapse from the nervous strain.

Lydia Johnson's real partner and six other actors were

travelling on the same train. They all knew each other. In the course of the trip she interested them in my case. Together they planned how to smuggle me across the border. They had an exciting time inventing and discarding one scheme after another. Their final plan was very simple and it was based mainly on their ability to act.

At Orsha, at this time, the railway was cut in two. The passengers detrained on the Russian side and had to walk perhaps a quarter of a mile to the station on the German side. First, one passed the Russian inspection post and then, after crossing a stretch of neutral territory, came to the German post. The baggage was transferred from one station to the other on carts, passengers walking alongside so as to keep an eye on their belongings. There was always a crowd at the gate and a score or so of people in the neutral zone who had just crossed the Russian border and were putting their inspected suitcases in order before proceeding further.

My actors believed that in a situation where eight people had all the necessary documents, the ninth could pass unnoticed, that is, if the eight knew how to act. To accomplish this they decided to present themselves as a troupe of actors of which I was a member and Lydia Johnson the manager. Because of this she carried all their documents and walked some distance ahead of us. By the time our intentionally slow-moving group reached the Russian border, all the guards were in love with Lydia Johnson.

I had previously been instructed that when, after examining our papers, the border guards opened the gate to let us through, I was to go first. I was told that I could be certain that none of the guards would look at me at that moment— the actors were to occupy them in conversation. I was to walk straight ahead towards the people who were rearranging their belongings, sit in the roadside ditch, turn my face away from the border, and nonchalantly eat the sandwich that had been given me.

Upon reaching the border gate the actors joined in the conversation with the guards. There was a lot of banter, the guards roared with laughter, Lydia Johnson kept on distributing passes for her show, and only a couple of sets of documents were glanced at. But they were counted; all the guards knew there were eight sets. Lydia Johnson still held all of them and we were to pass, not as individuals, but as a troupe of eight. A friendly atmosphere prevailed and finally, in the clamour of farewells, the gate was opened and I boldly marched through first. With long steps I walked some three hundred feet and sat down in the roadside ditch.

I was told later that as I went through the gate the next four actors passed quickly to form a group (of which I supposedly was a part) on the other side of the gate. The rest, to give me time to get away, although pressed by the crowd behind, engaged each of the guards in separate conversation and crossed the border with various delays. But the guards continued counting and when the word 'nine' was heard there was a moment of excitement: 'You are nine; all back!' In a matter of seconds all the actors were back on the Russian side of the border. By then I was choking on my sandwich.

They were counted again; jokes were made about Russian grammar schools, and again with laughter and good wishes they were let through. Their baggage had not been inspected and they did not have to stop to rearrange it. They walked past me without noticing me and a couple of minutes later, when other people passing through the gate obscured me from the guards, I rose and hurried to catch up with my actors. I found them as boisterously happy as children. This was the

Plate 30   General Baron Peter Wrangel. The last leader
of the White Army in the uniform of a Cossack of the
Kuban. The inscription reads, 'To the glorious Sumsky
Hussars. General Wrangel'.

Plate 31   The author with his father and sister in
Japan, after their escape from Siberia.

greatest show of their lives. They wanted to repeat it at the German border. This was not necessary, since both the Ukrainians and the Germans would welcome me as a former officer of the old army. The actors knew it, but they wanted an encore.

So, again Lydia Johnson went ahead holding all the documents, while our group walked slowly behind. When we reached this check point, its commander, a German captain, was more than intrigued by Lydia Johnson. With very gallant manners he was quite ready to do anything for her, and was only disturbed by the fact that she held all our documents. The methodical German wanted each of us to present his documents personally. All the actors tried hard to make the captain relax to the point where he would forget the strict rules of his job. He relaxed considerably and was most obliging in every way but this—he still insisted that everyone carry his individual papers. From this point neither Lydia Johnson's flirting, nor the other actors' jokes and stories, either in German or Russian, could budge him. Reluctantly, the actors conceded defeat. I stepped forward and admitted who I was. An interpreter, a former officer of the Russian Imperial Army, asked me a few identifying questions, shook my hand and welcomed me. The next morning we arrived in Kiev, the Ukrainian capital.

CHAPTER 17

IN THE WHITE ARMY

W HEN I arrived in Kiev, the Ukraine was ruled by a dictator who bore the ancient title of Cossack chiefs, *Hetman*. A general of the old Russian Army, Skoropadski had been set up as *Hetman* by the Germans and the Austro-Hungarians, who needed the Ukraine as a source of grain. Kiev was occupied by German troops, besides which the *Hetman* had his own Ukrainian regiments. The Russian White counter-revolutionary force in the city was represented by a small detachment which favoured the *Hetman*. The political situation was stable only on the surface; a nationalistic republican movement with a strong infusion of Communists, and headed by a certain Petlura, was growing in the country.

In Kiev itself one enjoyed security, which was a real pleasure after the underground life in St. Petersburg. Because I was glad to have some respite from such an existence, I did not rush to join the White Army. But I was obliged to work as I had little money; by then most private funds had been confiscated. My father had given me a letter of introduction to the Under-Secretary of Commerce of the Ukraine, Boradaevski. He knew my father well and received me most cordially. After a ten-minute talk he offered me the post of Secretary Extraordinary to him. I held this position for about two months, and if I was of any use it was only in soothing

Boradaevski into good humour. He was a very nervous man and was perpetually worried about the stability of the regime. 'Do you suppose we will last another week?' was a question he repeatedly asked me. I invariably replied: 'Don't worry, everything will be all right.' As the situation deteriorated my answer became a sort of opium to him; he had to hear it over and over again.

Two of my old Sumsky Hussar friends soon joined me in Kiev. They were Captain Count Borch and Captain Berg.

Borch had joined the regiment the same year I had. He was probably the smartest-looking officer among us and undoubtedly the most flirtatious. It was said of him that he would make love to a broom if he were certain that it was of the feminine gender. He summed up his own attitude thus: 'Obviously, one can't have all women, but one can at least aim at it.' During the first year in the regiment Borch acquired an unfortunate notoriety. Once, entering a restaurant in Moscow, he had met a drunken civilian in the door. The man said something Borch did not consider proper and Borch took his bamboo cane away from him and struck him with it. This incident was described with awkward humour in a leftist newspaper: 'Boom! Boom! Boom! You may think these are church bells ringing. But, these are not church bells. It is only a society bandit with slicked hair beating up a peaceful citizen.' When Borch read this, he went to the newspaper office and beat up the editor. He was an efficient and brave officer, gay, and a good friend.

The other Sumsky Hussar, Berg, was a charming fellow with unlimited imagination. It constantly made a liar of him. When he was telling his tall stories he knew no one believed him, but this did not matter to him. He did not tell them to deceive anyone, he simply enjoyed inventing impossible exploits. He told his tales so well that one did not really care whether they were true or not; it was like listening to a novel read aloud. But the Revolution produced a shattering effect on him and he became a drunkard.

Soon after his arrival in Kiev, Borch started a love affair with a married woman. Her husband (a civilian) found out about it and challenged Borch to a duel. Borch asked Berg and me to be his seconds. Instead of meeting the other gentleman's seconds, we were to talk over such matters as the choice of weapons directly with the husband. Why it was done in such an unorthodox manner I don't remember—probably the general disorder around had something to do with it. I made an appointment, and used all my best arguments to keep Berg sober in the meantime. But they were of no avail, and by the time we drove to the husband's hotel Berg was plastered. On the way, Berg gave me a lecture on how to behave (neither of us knew anything about the duelling code). He particularly stressed two points: we must be very correct and stiff, and we must not take our gloves off. As we entered the room and the gentleman rose to meet us, Berg recognised an old acquaintance from Moscow. The latter's quite ordinary name had precluded an earlier identification. Berg, forgetting both the stiff correctness and the gloves, rushed to the man with a joyful 'So glad to see you again! How have you been? How did you escape?!' In another five minutes he was telling the hurt husband that it would be foolish to attempt to kill Borch for such trifles, which were a daily occurrence in the latter's life. The duel never took place.

On 3 November 1918, a revolution broke out in Germany. Soon afterwards the German troops began their evacuation of the Ukraine. At the same time, Petlura's Ukrainian Republican troops became more active, and the *Hetman's* soldiers less dependable. Obviously, the regime was coming to its end. Then Borch, Berg and I joined the Whites. We enlisted in a partly mounted squadron composed entirely of officers, in which even colonels served as privates. We three were quickly promoted. Within two weeks I was commanding a platoon, while Borch was my sergeant and Berg a corporal.

Only once, during the few weeks that we served in this squadron, did we take part in a small engagement outside the city against Petlura's troops; the rest of the time we guarded the headquarters of our forces. One evening I was called to the staff commander's office. When he closed the door he said to me: 'Promise that you will never repeat what I am about to tell you.' I promised and he proceeded: 'At this very moment our commander and another very influential general are having a conference. The relationship is strained, and the meeting may take such a turn that it will be necessary to arrest the other general. Would you arrest him if I gave the order?' I answered simply: 'I shall arrest anyone you wish me to.' After this conversation I was told to bring my platoon to the headquarters' courtyard and wait for developments. We stayed in this courtyard for three hours, until an adjutant came out of the building to tell me that our services would no longer be required that night. I was never told whom I was to arrest, but I then suspected that it was the *Hetman* himself. I could not see why a whole platoon would be needed to arrest a less important person.

My father, sister, and Anna Stepanovna now also arrived in Kiev. With the help of invitations from the Ukrainian government which I was able to procure for them, they travelled legally. This does not mean that they were treated particularly well *en route*. Once a search party took the flat silver that they were carrying away from them. Anna Stepanovna, however, followed the police agents and made such a racket that they returned the silver and told her to go to hell with it. My sister, on the other hand, was so panic-stricken that when asked who her father was, she answered: 'I don't know.'

One December day, Petlura's troops stormed and captured Kiev. On this last day of the *Hetman's* regime my platoon erected a barricade around our headquarters. A losing battle outside the city had been going on for a week or more, and on this cold winter morning we were quite depressed. Borch assembled all of the belongings of the three of us and took them to the house of his latest sweetheart. From this visit he returned to the barricade with a bottle of cognac, which gave us extra courage. By afternoon, Petlura's troops were entering the city from all directions. The situation was hopeless, and a staff officer came to us and declared: 'Our commander has given up; you are free to do whatever you please.' In complete bewilderment our officers, intent upon dispersing, leaned their guns against the barricade. Some, I suppose, were terrified, remembering the several thousand officers who had been executed in a Kiev park a few months previously. Here the cognac played its helpful role. Raising our rifles, the three of us ordered the officers to form ranks so we could try to break through. They lined up and we marched towards one end of the main street, where we hoped to pick up more men from our squadron. As we went along we met many armed officers from already dispersed units. The usual question was 'Where are you going?' Hearing that we were planning to attempt to break out of the city, most of them asked: 'Can we join you?' 'Of course,' was our reply. By the time we reached the head of the main street we were about two hundred strong. The question arose as to who should command us. General Keller, who was in the city, was a very popular figure, and three

270

officers went to him to extend the invitation. Within half an hour he was with us. While waiting for Keller, I telephoned my father; he and my sister came to say farewell to me. They arrived just as we began to move down the street. I ran out of the formation to kiss them, and after this they insisted on walking alongside our detachment. Soon the noise of people greeting Petlura's victorious troops could be heard at the other end of the street. Before we had marched many blocks, bullets began to fly. My father and sister ran into a restaurant, and when the shooting was over and they came to their senses they found themselves lying under a table.

Petlura's large column did not have much trouble in brushing us aside; we soon gave way and split. I had the good luck to escape into a small deserted street. I leaned my gun against a building and, in the darkness of a courtyard passageway, cut my epaulets off with a penknife. I was wearing the uniform of a common soldier, and without my epaulets I was not noticed in the streets. Borch and Berg also escaped; but some officers, General Keller among them, were captured and shot on the spot.

An hour later, I was back in civilian clothes and underground. This time I was hiding from the Ukrainian nationalists against whom our unit had fought. It was hard for me to find places to sleep in Kiev, for I had no more than two or three civilian friends there. So the burden of hiding me fell particularly upon my best girl of the time. A couple of weeks afterwards, I had a document to the effect that I had never fought against Petlura's Republican Army. I do not remember how I obtained it, but I still have it. But even with this I did not dare stay in my father's apartment, for Ukrainian soldiers had searched for me there soon after the capture of the town; evidently a neighbour had reported me.

I optimistically believed that New Year's Eve would be a safe night to spend with my family. I felt sure that everyone would be merry-making. At eleven o'clock in the evening I entered the hall of the apartment house where my father and sister lived. After I was inside I noticed two armed soldiers standing there. It was too late to retreat; they would let me in but not out. Calm on the surface, I began to climb the stairs to the fourth floor. Another soldier stood on one of the landings, but I still hoped that the search was not for me. When I reached my floor and saw the door of our apartment standing open optimism left me. There was nothing to do but to walk in. At that moment three soldiers were searching the apartment but were fortunately in the back rooms. By chance Anna Stepanovna passed through the hall of the apartment the very second I entered it. Without saying a word she seized me by the hand, dragged me to the kitchen and, still in silence, pushed me out on to the servants' stairway. There was no one there; in no time I was down in the snow-covered courtyard. Instinctively I rushed towards the solid wooden gate. Through the six-inch gap between its closed portals and the ground below I suddenly saw four feet; so this route of escape was blocked. Our apartment house was situated on a rather steep hill. At the back of its yard there was a vertical stone-faced 20-foot drop into the yard of a house facing on to a street lower down the hill. I jumped down and fortunately landed in deep snow; although I was almost buried, I was not hurt. I scrambled out of the snow and walked through the strange gates into another street.

Obviously, it was time to get out of Kiev. The nearest city outside of Petlura's control was Odessa on the Black Sea. It was occupied by French and Greek troops, who also held a small zone around it. These troops were there because at that time

the Western Powers were supporting the counter-revolutionary movement. They had previously helped a small detachment of the White Army to capture the city. We decided to
go to Odessa.

My father, through his various mining activities, was in
close contact with the Commercial Bank of Siberia. When a
group of its directors decided to flee Kiev, we were invited to
join them in a *de luxe* escape. They bribed everyone in sight at
the railway station and thus procured a special car and four
policemen to protect us from search parties *en route*. To obtain
a private car at a time when there was a shortage of cars, and
people were forced to travel on the roofs of trains, was a
magician's trick. I was nominally enrolled in the Kiev branch of
the bank, and was given a certificate that I was being transferred to the Odessa branch. Both Borch and Berg were also
invited to travel with us.

As we entered the one unlocked door of our car and our
special policeman saluted us, the railway station looked like an
oriental bazaar: the number of people expecting to get on that
train and into our car was prodigious. The crowd succeeded in
beating up two of our policemen, and the other two fled. The
only guard left on the steps of our car was the bank's porter.
This smart fellow quickly restored order by claiming that the
car was reserved for a foreign mission. The crowd stopped
rushing forward, but someone asked: 'What kind of a mission?'
English was the first nationality to come to the porter's mind,
and so he said: 'English.' The news spread quickly through the
train and from then on we were left alone but had to play the
role. The penalty for playing it badly would probably have
been death at the hands of those who had been hoodwinked.

Only my sister and one gentleman in our group spoke
English. The sole document in a foreign language that we

273

possessed belonged to my father; it was in Swedish. This imposing paper, with stamps and seals, certified that my father was one of the directors of a Swedish engineering concern in Russia. It had to stand for the official document of our English 'delegation' and, because none of the police agents whom we met on the road could tell the difference between the two languages, it served the purpose well. Borch and I had fun playing Englishmen in the presence of the police. We simply spoke gibberish. Thus rather gaily, but with occasional scares, we reached Odessa.

In overcrowded Odessa my father, my sister, Anna Stepanovna and I lived in one room. At night, a sheet was strung across the room to divide the ladies' from the gentlemen's compartment.

One day, Borch, Berg and I were walking down the street. A very well-dressed man stopped us and asked: 'Are you the three officers whom I saw a few weeks ago preventing a detachment from dispersing when Petlura's troops entered Kiev?' When we admitted that we were, he asked: 'Won't you have lunch with me?' The invitation was particularly welcome, since we had not eaten too well for some time. In a quarter of an hour, we were sitting in one of the best restaurants in the city. This man desired to establish himself as a political figure, and to this end had to overthrow someone, somewhere. We never reached the stage of learning who the intended victim was or where the action was to take place. What primarily interested our host was how cheaply it could be done. We understood that he was betting on our recklessness, and we played the game. When asked how many men we would need to capture an objective defended by a hundred men we answered: 'About a dozen.' This was precisely what our acquaintance desired to hear from us, and another bottle of wine was opened. We were to meet for lunch again the next day; in the evening, however, we three talked things over and decided that we could not become mercenaries. So in the morning, we stopped at the man's hotel to excuse ourselves.

Lieutenant-Colonel Shwed was in Odessa too. He had arrived early in December with the White detachment that had chased Petlura's troops out of the city. Since then Shwed had been forming 'a squadron of Sumsky Hussars'. At first there were only two platoons in it, composed of officers from different regiments, younkers, and civilians in their teens. This unit became a part of a 'Combined Cavalry Regiment' and fought the Bolsheviks up to the very end of the Civil War. During this time the two platoons grew to a full squadron and, for a while, even to two squadrons. Borch and Berg joined this squadron, but I left for Siberia.

Siberia at that time was occupied by a White army commanded by Admiral Kolchak. My father wanted to go there on his mining business, and we all thought that we should stay together from then on. Kolchak in the east had a shortage of officers, but there was such an abundance of them in southern Russia that, as I have mentioned before, many were serving as privates. Therefore a number of career officers of the old army were sent out to Kolchak in Siberia. It was easy for me to get an official transfer to his army and a permit to travel independently. As to my father—I still have a paper signed by the British consul-general in Odessa certifying that my father was a director of two English-owned mining companies in Siberia and that he was travelling there in the interests of the English shareholders. This is where the money for the journey came from.

The territory lying between that occupied by the White armies of southern Russia and that held by the Siberian White

Army was in the hands of the Red Army; there was no way of reaching Siberia by land. We had to go almost half-way round the world by sea. We travelled via Constantinople, Port Said, Ceylon, Shanghai, and Japan to Vladivostok, on the Russian shores of the Sea of Japan.

About forty miles north of Vladivostok was a former Imperial Army military post, now occupied by White troops. It was near the railway station of Razdolnoe. The barracks were strung along both sides of a country road and continued for more than a mile; they lodged infantry, artillery, and one cavalry regiment—the Primorsky Dragoons. The officers of the latter, in their attempt to re-establish the regiment as a unit of the White Army, had assembled three partly mounted squadrons. When I arrived in Vladivostok I was assigned to these Primorsky Dragoons and served (as a Sumsky Hussar attached to the regiment) for the next five months, or until 15 January 1920.

The garrison in Razdolnoe included a detachment of United States infantry and a Japanese company. These foreign troops were part of larger forces officially in Russia to help us fight the Bolsheviks, but they undoubtedly were there also for less disinterested reasons—particularly the Japanese who had, I believe, 70,000 men in this easternmost province of Siberia. The advance units of Kolchak's White Army were fighting hundreds of miles to the west, and the purpose of having troops in the far rear was to deal with the guerrillas in the area. Thousands of these lurked in the wooded hills of the region and occasionally came out of hiding to attack railway and military posts.

Besides Whites and Reds there were also 'Greens', who fought both sides. To complicate matters, there were strong bands of individual adventurers in Siberia, as there were in the south of Russia. At least two of these fought on our side in eastern Siberia; one of them was led by a Cossack officer named Semenov. Semenov, who had been a captain of the old army, now assumed the title of *Ataman*, or chief of a Cossack district. He travelled in a four-car armoured train. A different word was painted in large letters on the sides of each car. The cars were arranged permanently in such order as to read: *Mighty-Avenger-Ataman-Semenov*. On many occasions I read this menacing legend as his train passed our barracks. Once I was at the Razdolnoe station when it stopped there. Even before the train came to a complete halt, the obvious brigands who manned it jumped out of the cars and surrounded the train. Each one carried enough cartridges to win a battle, and hand-grenades hung in profusion from every belt.

The Japanese made a strong effort to win our sympathy. Periodically they gave dinner parties for our soldiers. At these each dragoon had a Japanese host and received a gift, a package containing such things as tobacco and tea. On the wrapper was a coloured print of a Japanese and a Russian soldier shaking hands beneath the crossed flags of the two nations. We officers received gifts of money from the Japanese Emperor—each one equal to our monthly salary. Not only were our rifles Japanese, but so was a part of our clothing. One night during a confused skirmish against the partisans, my detachment bumped into a Japanese platoon from another garrison and the officer asked me in very broken Russian what kind of a Russian I was. I felt that the friendliest way out of the predicament was to say: A Japanese Russian'. The officer saw the humour of this reply, laughed, and shook my hand for a long time.

The Japanese officers stationed in Razdolnoe were the daily guests of our club: they all spoke Russian. Our relations with the Americans were much more formal, but we occasionally invited them also. One evening, when both Americans and Japanese were dining with us, an unpleasant incident occurred. An American officer who did not speak Russian rose to make a speech. Smilingly and with good will towards all, he raised a fist, opened a finger, and said: 'Russia'; then he opened another finger and said: 'Japan'; upon opening the third finger and saying, 'the United States', he united the three fingers with the other hand, and added, 'One.' A Japanese officer, who had evidently had more wine than he could handle, jumped up and shouted: 'Russia and Japan one; United States—*pfui*,' and spat on the floor.

At the same party, during which too much wine was consumed by many, I overheard a conversation between two officers sitting next to each other across the table from me. Very calmly and with good manners, they were planning to fight a duel. When I began to listen, the question of weapons was already settled. These were the revolvers they had with them. The next matter to decide was the shooting distance. One of them proposed in a mild voice: 'As we are sitting.' The other agreed, and by the time I ran round the long table to them they were already pulling their guns out.

Our fighting consisted of an occasional sortie into the hills and an occasional repulse of the attacking partisans. Once, our spies advised us of an imminent attack on our post. At that particular time we did not feel that we could depend on the loyalty of our soldiers. There were reasons to suspect that if the partisans should invade our grounds some of our dragoons would join them. To us officers the big question was what we would do if the partisans were successful. Each of us solved this problem individually. Three or four of us decided to try to escape to Manchuria. The nearest point on its border was less than seventy-five miles from Razdolnoe, with practically no human habitation on the way; consequently this route was comparatively safe. For this escape I assembled a large bag full of canned foods, cartridges and hand-grenades. The latter were not distributed to the soldiers and were exclusively in the hands of the officers. Thus we had a powerful short-range weapon that our unreliable men did not possess. My father once stayed with me overnight; as he was going to bed I put two hand-grenades on his night table. A typical civilian, he did not appreciate this part of my hospitality.

The partisans attacked on the night we expected, but they were easily repulsed. One episode produced much laughter the following day. A group of partisans had a special mission to capture our infantry musicians with their instruments. Life in the hills was lonely, and entertainment was needed. The musicians were the last ones who would have cared to go to the bush, and they scattered in all directions. The partisans who were trying to catch them became disorganised, and we killed or captured many of them.

Some ten miles from our post was a glass factory, which at that time had a White Army order. The factory's manager asked for protection against the partisans, and I was sent there with eighty dismounted men. The factory was in a narrow valley surrounded by wooded hills. The trees came all the way down to the small oval plain on which the factory stood. The partisans could approach it unnoticed from any direction. There was a small railroad station a couple of miles away under the control of American troops, who also patrolled the region of the factory.

In a conversation with the director of the factory I found out that several thousand Red guerrillas were in the hills a few miles away and that the majority of the factory workers were sympathetic to the Communists. When I added these facts to the topographical situation I became worried. Standing with my sergeants on the road which ran through the workers' settlement, I was trying to figure out what to do. Suddenly I saw an American patrol approaching. It was a platoon moving on the alert, that is, in single lines on both sides of the road, the men some fifteen feet apart. The officer and I exchanged salutes and the men passed us in silence. As the last men were marching by, I remarked that these particular Americans looked very much like Russians. I later remembered that as I was saying this the American soldier who was walking past me looked at me and smiled. Within ten minutes I telephoned the American post to report that their platoon had passed through my post. I was told that no American platoon could have been near the factory at that hour and that this detachment was unquestionably a guerrilla one disguised in American uniforms.

I then also learned that a few weeks previously the guerrillas had wrecked a train delivering American equipment and that they had enough American uniforms to outfit at least a company. When I heard this, it took me only a minute to make my decision. Obviously, it was not a question of how to protect the factory, but rather of how to protect my men and myself. With this aim in mind I made a tour of the factory grounds.

I was particularly attracted by the situation of the school. The building stood in the centre of a very large playground, and the whole was surrounded by an eight-foot-high, solid board fence. Along this fence hung big lanterns on very tall poles. They were not electric, and to be refuelled they had to be lowered on cables. Therefore, they were not firmly fixed to the poles and moved a little in a strong wind. I decided to lodge my men and myself in the school.

Nothing happened for the next two days, but neither I nor

many of my men were able to sleep: our nerves were on edge. During the third night, a sentinel ran into the schoolhouse to report that guerrillas were jumping the fence. Seconds later I was out of the house and saw silhouettes of men methodically dropping over the fence. In no time my men were also outside and in a firing line. In order to keep the nervous men disciplined, I decided to fire by volleys. So, I gave the command: 'Half-squadron, fire.' The first volley had no effect; the dark bodies kept on coming over the fence with the same regularity. Another volley, and then another, with no results; there was no return fire. It was like shooting at ghosts. The blood began to freeze in my veins. There was nothing to do but to advance. I gave the order to move forward. We had gone no more than 200 feet when we stopped and looked at each other sheepishly. Greater proximity and a change of angle revealed that what we had taken for jumping men were only the shadows of a gently swinging lantern. We discussed it at length later and I found out that not a single man had realised that we were shooting at shadows. The other lanterns, at which we looked from different angles, did not produce the same effect.

The next morning the infantry relieved us. A couple of days afterwards the guerrillas finally attacked the factory. The soldiers joined them and the officers were killed.

During the autumn of 1919 the army of Admiral Kolchak continued to disintegrate, and on 4 January 1920 he resigned. There was no room left for wishful thinking: it was obvious that we had lost the Civil War in Siberia. Now the big question was how to get out of Russia while it was still possible. The Polish consul in Vladivostok was married to a friend of my family's and he came to our rescue; he issued us Polish passports. In mine I was listed as a captain of the Polish Army, and consequently was released from the White Army. On 7

February, the very day Kolchak was executed, our passports were stamped with a permit to leave Russia. A few days later, we were in Japan.

The struggle continued in southern Russia. When General Denikin felt further fighting to be hopeless, he resigned. On 4 April 1920, General Baron Wrangel took over command of the remnants of the White Army. He fought the Bolsheviks until the middle of November. Then the great evacuation took place. Some 130,000 refugees, two-thirds of them still armed, manned every boat available and, helped by naval forces of the Western Powers, reached Constantinople.

Some of the rear-guard troops that covered this evacuation perished. Among them was the squadron of Sumsky Hussars commanded by Borch. At one point the retreating squadron was surrounded; Borch was killed fighting. Berg had died earlier. Altogether, six of our officers were killed in the battles of the Civil War. Several others were wounded, among them Constantine Sokolov who lost a leg.

After my escape from Siberia, I would still have had time to join General Wrangel's army. But outside Russia the hopelessness of the situation was even more apparent than in Razdolnoe. And so, instead of going to the south of Russia, I went to Canada with my family.

Leaving Russia, perhaps for good, it seemed best to us that the very Russian Anna Stepanovna, whose life was in no danger, should remain in her country. So we parted from her in Vladivostok. But she took the next boat and caught up with us in Japan; she felt her life to be inseparable from ours. From then on until her death in New York, she shared all the vicissitudes of refugee existence with us. By that time she was not a housekeeper any longer, but a member of the family.

On the Canadian boat, the *Empress of Russia*, that took us

across the Pacific, Anna Stepanovna had a chance to observe people of other nationalities. She had seen them before, of course, but had never been curious about them. Now, facing a new life, she became interested in foreigners. A cabin near ours was occupied by a stunning-looking American woman, who was well dressed, had good manners, and produced the impression of being a lady. But she used rather too much rouge and this made Anna Stepanovna suspicious that she was not one. To Anna Stepanovna, in her attempt to orient herself in a new world, the question of whether this American woman was or was not a lady became of primary importance. One afternoon Anna Stepanovna, in great excitement, found us on the deck to tell us: 'At last I know: she is not a lady. The door of her cabin was partly open and I could see her washing her stockings!'

We were sailing into a different world, and not only Anna Stepanovna but every one of us would have to make many adjustments in our ways of living and thinking.

N

St. Petersburg

BALTIC SEA

Trenches · Dno
Riga
· Rejitza
2 · Dvina
Dvinsk

Moscow

Nieman

Danzig EAST
PRUSSIA
Grodno

GERMANY

Warsaw

RUSSIA

BORDER

AUSTRIA-HUNGARY

RUMANIA

BLACK SEA

0   100   200   300
                    MILES
        SCALE

MAP NO. I

284

Area 1   Where the 1st Cavalry Division was in action from the autumn of
1914 to the spring of 1915.

Area 2   Where our division was in action from July 1915 to June 1916.
   We occupied trenches in this sector on the right bank of the Dvina
river from July 1916 to June 1917.

Rejitza. Where the Sumsky Hussars were sent to combat the Revolution in
1917.

Dno. Where in July 1917 my squadron was assigned to guard the railway
station, and to arrest the deserters from the front.

*Place names are spelt as the author knew them in Imperial Russia. Some
are now Polish or Latvian and the spelling has been changed. In a few cases
the name has been changed.*

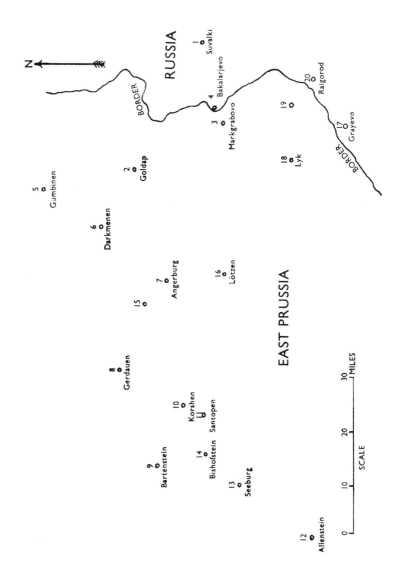

N

RUSSIA

BORDER

1 Suvalki

4 Bakalarjevo

20 Raigorod

19

17 Grayevo

3 Markgrabovo

BORDER

2 Goldap

18 Lyk

5 Gumbinen

6 Darkmenen

7 Angerburg

16 Lötzen

15

EAST PRUSSIA

8 Gerdauen

10 Korshen

11 Santopen

9 Bartenstein

14 Bishofstein

13 Seeburg

30

20

SCALE

10

MILES

12 Allenstein

0

MAP NO. 2

286

LEGEND FOR MAP No. 2

CHAPTERS 8, 9 AND 10

(These sites and the incidents connected with them are
listed in the order of their appearance in the text.)

1. Suvalki	Here we detrained for the front at the beginning of the war.	
2. Goldap	Three squadron commanders were dismissed for dis-	
3. Markgrabovo	obeying Gourko's orders while scouting in the region of these towns.	
4. Bakalarjevo	It was here that I crossed the border for the first time with a scouting party.	
3. Markgrabovo	The site of our division's first battle.	
2. Goldap	When we re-entered East Prussia after the Markgrabovo raid we crossed the border in the direction of Goldap.	
5. Gumbinen	It was south of this town that I acted as liaison officer with our infantry when it defeated a large German force.	
6. Darkmenen	Near this little town our 1st and 6th Squadrons made the unsuccessful mounted charge during which I picked up a wounded sergeant.	
7. Angerburg	It was here that Colonel Rachmaninov interfered with the looting of a shop.	
8. Gerdauen	In the region of this town I took part (under Rachmaninov's command) in blowing up a railway track.	
9. Bartenstein	Once my scouting party penetrated as far west as this town.	
10. Korshen	It was here that we blew up the railway station and found wine in its cellars.	
11. Santopen	Here I charged and panicked.	
12. Allenstein	The objective of the raid of the three regiments of the 1st Cavalry Division.	

287

13. Seeburg	It was here, during the withdrawal from Allenstein, that we had to carry our artillery by hand over ditches and ravines.
14. Bishofstein	In the vicinity of this village (during the return from Allenstein) our regiment was saved by a blinding downpour.
15.	It was approximately here that during the same withdrawal we at last joined our infantry and Cornet Snejkov gave three roubles to a Russian infantryman.
7. Angerburg	After a short rest, the division was moved to a point
2. Goldap	between these towns and ordered to scout south in the direction of Lötzen (16) and beyond.
17. Grayevo	A few days later, the division was ordered to proceed to Grayevo, just across the Russian border, to join the new 10th Army.
16. Lötzen	While moving towards the Russian border, we stopped
18. Lyk	twice in the region of these towns to help our infantry.
19.	It was approximately here that I earned but missed getting my first war decoration.
20. Raigorod	Our regiment crossed the border near this town.

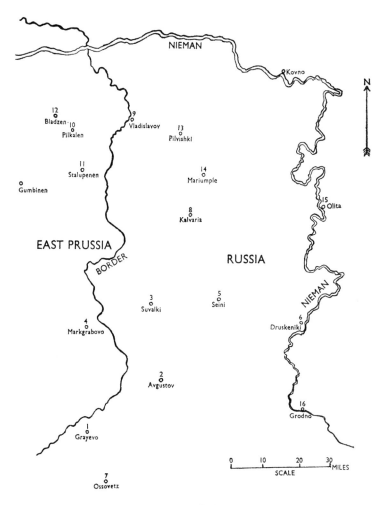

NIEMAN

o Kovno

N

12
o
Bladzen · 10
        o
        Pilkalen

9
o
Vladislavov

13
o
Pilvishki

11
o
Stalupenen

14
o
Mariumple

o
Gumbinen

15
o Olita

8
o
Kalvaria

EAST PRUSSIA

BORDER

RUSSIA

NIEMAN

3
o
Suvalki

5
o
Seini

4
o
Markgrabovo

6
o
Druskeniki

2
o
Avgustov

16
o
Grodno

1
o
Grayevo

0   10   20   30
|_____|_____|_____|_____| MILES
              SCALE

7
o
Ossovetz

MAP NO. 3

289

CHAPTER II

(These sites and the incidents connected with them are
listed in the order of their appearance in the text)

1. Grayevo	From Grayevo (lower left-hand corner of the map),
2. Avgustov	where we joined the 10th Army, we moved north to
3. Suvalki	the region of Avgustov, Suvalki and Markgrabovo; we
4. Markgrabovo	were continuously engaged in this sector, and were eventually pushed north.
5. Seini	The scouting party of Cornet Ivanov working towards Seini from the north discovered two large German columns moving towards Druskeniki (6).
6. Druskeniki	The scouting party of Cornet Poliakov discovered a German retreat from this crossing point on the river Nieman.
2. Avgustov	Shortly after the German retreat from the Nieman, the Russian troops (Sumsky Hussars among them) re-occupied Avgustov.
7. Ossovetz	To this fortress I delivered the new code.
4. Markgrabovo	Around October 8th, as a result of a local advance, the 1st Cavalry Division was again facing Markgrabovo.
8. Kalvaria	In the latter part of October our division was moved north to the region of Kalvaria. We were back in the 1st Army.
9. Vladislavov	About 1 November, we were ordered further north to Vladislavov.
10. Pilkalen	From Vladislavov the division fought its way across the
11. Stalupenen	border to Stalupenen and Pilkalen. It was early in January, in the vicinity of Pilkalen, that a meeting of German officers with officers of our regiment took place.

290

12.	Bladzen	Where Cornet Sokolov the First was killed.
13.	Pilvishki	At the beginning of February 1915 the Russian infantry
14.	Mariumple	was pushed back and the Sumsky Hussars retreated to
15.	Olita	Pilvishki, Mariumple, and Olita.
16.	Grodno	From Olita we were moved to Grodno and then north to the region of Druskeniki (6) where Cornet Poliakov was killed.
6.	Druskeniki	On 2 March the Russian 10th Army (to which we were again attached) began a counter-attack. The Sumsky Hussars crossed the river Nieman at Druskeniki and advanced in a south-westward direction.
2.	Avgustov	Nearing Avgustov we stumbled upon thousands of dead soldiers. Here, between Avgustov and Grodno, the Russian 20th Corps had perished.
2.	Avgustov	In this region we worked until the middle of April. By
16.	Grodno	then our ranks were so depleted that we were ordered to the rear for a rest.
16.	Grodno	We boarded trains in Grodno and were taken (after a two weeks' stop at Vilna) to the vicinity of St. Petersburg.

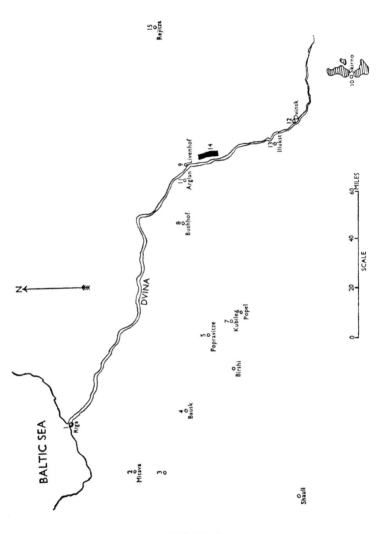

BALTIC SEA

DVINA

N

1 Riga
2 Mitava
3
4 Bausk
5 Popravitze
6 Birzhi
7 Kubile
Popel
8 Bushhof
9 Livenhof
11 Argian
14
13 Illukst
12 Dvinsk
10 Kirno
15 Rejitza
Shaull

SCALE

0   20   40   60
MILES

MAP NO. 4

292

FROM THE MIDDLE OF JULY 1915 TO JUNE 1917

CHAPTERS 12, 13 AND 14

(These sites and the incidents connected with them are
listed in the order of their appearance in the text)

1.	Riga	(upper left-hand corner of the map). Here crowds with flowers greeted the trains bringing us as reinforcements to the front.
2.	Mitava	Where we disembarked.
3.		Where our impending mounted charge caused German infantry to retreat.
4.	Bausk	South of this town the Sumsky Hussars were fighting on my name day.
5.	Popravitze	The 1st Squadron, under command of Petrjkevich, charged here.
6.	Popel	Where I had a hard time staying awake.
7.	Kubile	Here Colonel Groten was wounded.
8.	Bushhof	The battle in the woods took place in this region.
9.	Livenhof	In the vicinity of this town we crossed the river as the bridge was burning.
10.	Skirno	(lower right-hand corner of the map). The estate near the trenches that we occupied.
11.	Arglan	Where we produced the musical review.
12.	Dvinsk	Where we stood in reserve.
13.	Illukst	Near Illukst the regiment occupied a small section of the *tête de pont* trenches.
14.		To these trenches on the east bank of the Dvina river, the regiment was moved in the middle of June 1916. We occupied them until June 1917.
15.	Rejitza	Where the Sumsky Hussars were sent to suppress the Revolutionary forces.

293

APPENDIX

Infantry

Cavalry

A REGIMENT = 4 battalions, each comprised 4 companies. The wartime strength of a company was about 250 men, of a battalion 1,000, and of the regiment (with various auxiliary units) over 4,500.

= 6 squadrons, each of about 150 men, and the regiment (with various auxiliary units) over 1,000 men. This number remained the same in peace or wartime.

A BRIGADE = 2 regiments.

= 2 regiments.

A DIVISION = 2 brigades. With its artillery and various auxiliary units the division totalled approximately 20,000 men.

= 2 brigades. With its artillery it totalled approximately 5,000 men. A division had 2 batteries, each consisting of six (3″) guns.

A CORPS = 2 divisions. An infantry corps totalled about 40,000 men.

= Only in some instances 2 or 3 cavalry divisions were assembled into a corps. Ordinarily a single cavalry division was attached to an infantry corps. Unattached cavalry corps or divisions were under direct command of the staff of the army.

AN ARMY. Several infantry corps, with several cavalry divisions and corresponding artillery and auxiliary troops, formed an army. At the beginning of the war the strength of the 1st Army (to which the 1st Cavalry Division then belonged) was upward of 300,000 men.

A MILITARY DISTRICT. In peacetime 'armies' did not exist and the armed forces were divided into military districts. Before the war the Sumsky Hussars belonged to the Moscow Military District. During the war, at different periods, it was a part of the 1st, 10th, and 5th Armies.

295

APPENDIX

STRUCTURE OF THE CAVALRY

The Russian cavalry was composed of 4 categories of regiments: guard regiments, line regiments, Cossack regiments and irregular cavalry.

GUARDS. The horse guards consisted of:

2 divisions	8	regiments
1 separate brigade	2	,,
1 Cossack brigade	3	,,
Cossack bodyguard of the Emperor	1	,,

LINE CAVALRY. The line cavalry consisted of:

15 numbered divisions	60	,,
1 dragoon division	4	,,
3 separate brigades	6	,,
3 separate regiments	3	,,

COSSACK REGIMENTS. Besides the 15 Cossack regiments that were included among the 15 numbered divisions, there were other mounted Cossack regiments that were assembled into special Cossack units. These totalled (in peacetime): 38 ,,

IRREGULAR CAVALRY. In peacetime it consisted of one regiment (Dagestansky) and two pairs of squadrons (Osetinsky and Turmensky): about 2 ,,

Total 127 ,,

WARTIME STRENGTH OF THE CAVALRY

1. The Cossacks almost quadrupled their ranks, having 160 mounted regiments and 176 separate 'sotnias' (squadrons); the latter equalled almost 30 regiments. A total of about 190 regiments.

2. To the irregular cavalry were added 5 native Caucasian regiments.

3. The cadre of the Officers' Cavalry School was expanded to form a new regiment.

4. The regular Border Guards, who were not normally a part of the army,

formed during the war, mounted regiments—at least ten, to my knowledge. During the war the Russian cavalry strength rose to the equivalent of about 270 regiments.

THE MOUNTED COSSACK TROOPS DURING THE WAR

Cossack District	Regiments of the Line	Separate Sotnias	The Guards
1. Don	58	100	2 regiments
2. Kuban	33	30	2 sotnias
3. Terek	12	16	2 ,,
4. Orenburg	18	18	1 ,,
5. Ural	9	8	1 ,,
6. Astrakhan	3	—	1 platoon
7. Siberia	9	—	2 ,,
8. Trans Baikal	12	—	2 ,,
9. Seven Rivers (Semirehie)	3	—	1 ,,
10. Amur	2	—	1 ,,
11. Usuri	1	—	1 ,,
	Total 160	172	20 sotnias assembled into 4 regiments

Besides the above mounted troops the Cossacks supplied 52 batteries of horse artillery. They also had some infantry.

THE STRUCTURE OF A CAVALRY REGIMENT

A REGIMENT. 6 squadrons plus several additional units totalling upwards of 1,000 men.

A SQUADRON. 150 men, including the sergeant-major and the trumpeter. In official language the strength of a squadron was 150 swords—that is, not counting the 5 swords of the officers. The 5 batmen and the 2 cooks were not included in this number, although also armed.

A PLATOON. 36 men plus the platoon sergeant.

MACHINE-GUN UNIT. At the beginning of the war, a machine-gun unit of the division (8 guns) served the 4 regiments. In the latter part of the war each regiment had its own unit of 4 heavy Maxim guns.

COMMUNICATIONS UNIT. The Communications Unit was enlarged during the war to about 60 men. It was trained to operate heliograph, telegraph, telephones and searchlights. During the war only the telephones proved to be practical and their number was greatly increased.

TRUMPETERS. The regiment had 16 trumpeters.

TRANSPORT. There were 2 Transport Trains. That of the 1st order consisted of about 40 officers' pack horses, 7 kitchens, an ammunition cart and one Red Cross Cart. The heavier wagons comprised the Train of the 2nd order. During field warfare the Transport Train of the 1st order usually tried to follow the regiment closely and to join it whenever possible, During trench warfare it always was with the regiment. The Train of the 2nd order always kept some 10 to 20 miles in the rear.

OFFICE CLERKS. About 6.

WARTIME CHANGES IN THE STRUCTURE OF THE REGIMENT. Late in 1916, when trench warfare predominated, all the line cavalry regiments (I believe), except the Cossacks, were reduced to four squadrons. The two squadrons that were dismounted formed the cadres for an infantry battalion of 1,000 men. In this manner the three battalion infantry regiments attached to cavalry divisions were formed.

THE OFFICERS OF A CAVALRY REGIMENT

The Commander of the regiment.
The Adjutant.
The Senior Colonel.
The Senior Lt.-Colonel.
The Junior Lt.-Colonel.
6 Squadron Commanders.
The Commander of the Communications Unit.
24 Platoon Commanders.
2 Officers of the Machine-Gun Unit.
The Commander of the Transport Train of the 1st order.
The Commander of the Transport Train of the 2nd order.
The Treasurer.

APPENDIX

THE OFFICERS' RANKS

The infantry and the cavalry and the Cossack troops used different titles for certain corresponding ranks. All these, although they had Russian names, corresponded to the ranks in western armies. For instance, a 'Cornet' (in the cavalry) corresponded to a second lieutenant, a 'Polkovnik' to a colonel; the rank of a captain in Russian Cavalry was 'Stabs Rotmistr'. 'Stabs' stood for the *staff* and 'Rotmistr' was a corruption of the German *Rittmeister*—a master of riding.

Doctors, veterinarians, masters of arms and bookkeepers did not belong to the officer corps. They wore a special uniform, identical for the whole army, and had civil service ranks.

THE EDUCATION OF A CAVALRY OFFICER

CADET SCHOOLS. An officer's education usually began in one of the military Cadet Schools, although some officers had their basic schooling in civilian gymnasiums (a school which provided the equivalent of a secondary school education and about two years of university in this country). One entered the Cadet School at the age of 10 or 11 and graduated at 17 or 18 There were 30 Cadet Schools located all over Russia.

MILITARY (YOUNKER) SCHOOLS. Upon graduating from Cadet School, the future officer entered a Military (Younker) School. These were specialised schools; 11 for the infantry, 2 for the artillery, 1 for the engineers (sappers), 1 (a small one) for topographers, 2 exclusively for Cossacks (besides the Cossack section of the Nicholas Cavalry School), and 3 for the cavalry. The latter were the Nicholas Cavalry School in St. Petersburg, the School of Elizavetgrad in southern Russia, and the School of Tver, situated between St. Petersburg and Moscow.

THE CORPS DES PAGES. This school was an exception; it combined both the Cadet and the Younker Grades and prepared officers for all branches of the service. Most of its graduates served in the Guards.

OFFICER CANDIDATES. A gymnasium graduate who had served for one year as a private in a regiment had the right to take an examination for officer's rank. Upon passing the examination he was given a special rank, 'Prapor-schik', which rated below that of second lieutenant. There was an army saying about this rank—'chicken is not a bird, Praporschik is not an officer'.

299

SCHOOLS FOR OFFICERS. A cavalry officer, after serving in the regiment for three years, could enter either the Officers' Cavalry School, the Staff Academy, or the Academy of Military Law. Although graduation from the first accelerated promotion in the cavalry, graduation from the last two eventually terminated one's service in the cavalry ranks proper. Other branches of the service had their own advanced schools corresponding to the Officers' Cavalry School.

This is not an exhaustive summary, but consists of additional information prepared by the author for the benefit of the interested reader.

INDEX

301